Defence Administration

Then and Now

Defence Administration

Then and Now

Col. (Retd.) S. C. Narang

Prashant Publishing House
DELHI - 110094 (INDIA)

PRASHANT PUBLISHING HOUSE
C-34, 28 Foota Road, Gali No. 3
West Karawal Nagar, Delhi-110094
Phone : 9810396373, 22963970

Defence Administration : Then and Now

First Published : 2010

ISBN : 978-93-80565-04-0

PRINTED IN INDIA

Published by Mr. R. K. Jha M/s. Prashant Publishing House, Delhi and Printed at H.S. Offset Press, Delhi.

Preface

In India defence has been uniquely managed since the dawn of civilization. War weapons, transport, war tactics and strategies, fortification, soldiery, officials and reward and remuneration etc. were the distinct features, which were given special attention in defence administration.

Defence Administration is a system, weapon, or technology involved in the detection, tracking, interception and destruction of attacking missiles. Originally conceived as a defence against nuclear-armed Intercontinental ballistic missiles, its application has broadened to include shorter-ranged non-nuclear tactical and theatre missiles. The interception technology used has varied over time. In the 1960s, missile defence against ICBMs emphasized nuclear warheads. In recent decades non-nuclear kinetic warheads have been used. Directed-energy weapons such as lasers have been investigated and deployed on a limited basis. For example, India's DRDO is developing a laser-based weapon system as part of its ballistic missile defence program to intercept and destroy missiles soon after they are launched towards the country. The United States, United Kingdom, Russia, France, Israel, China, and India have all developed such air defence systems. In the United States, missile defence was originally the responsibility of the Army, but in recent years the Navy and Air Force have developed their own systems.

The present compilation portrays a panoramic yet in-depth picture of defence administration in India. It describes defence administration in ancient India i.e. since Aryan or Vedic period. With the invention of firearms and weapons during medieval time war strategies and defence organisation etc. changed somewhat.

—Author

Contents

Preface

1. Indian Armed Forces 1
2. Indian Navy 26
3. Indian Air Force 49
4. Indian Security Guards and Forces 71
5. Royal Engineers and Tank Regiment 101
6. Indian Rifles and Regiments 121
7. Naval aviation 153
8. Commando 177
9. Wing (Military Aviation Unit) 197
10. India Defence Consultants 208
11. Defence Administration: Its Planning and Program 225
12. The Department of Defence 253
13. Indian Army and Frontier Warfare 1914-1939 260
14. National Defence: Scientific Formula 285

Bibliography 295

Index 296

1

Indian Armed Forces

The Indian Armed Forces is the overall unified military of the Republic of India encompassing the Indian Army, the Indian Navy, the Indian Air Force and various other inter-service institutions.

With an estimated total active force of 1,325,000 personnel, India maintains the world's second largest armed forces. Auxiliary services include the Indian Coast Guard, the Central Paramilitary Forces (CPF) and the Strategic Forces Command. India's official defence budget stands at $32.35 billion but the actual spending on the armed forces is estimated to be much higher than that. Undergoing rapid expansion and modernization, the Indian Armed Forces plans to have an active military space program and is currently developing a potent missile defence shield and nuclear triad capability.

India is moving to build a $2 billion or Rs 9,970.16 crore dedicated, highly secure and state-of-the-art optical fibre cable (OFC) network for the Army, Navy and Air Force. This will be one of the world's largest, closed user group (CUG) networks for exclusive

MILITARY HISTORY OF INDIA

India has a long military history dating back several millennia. The first reference of armies is found in the Vedas as well as the epics Ramayana and Mahabaratha. There were many powerful dynasties in India such as the Maha Janapadas, Shishunaga Empire, Gangaridai Empire, Nanda Empire, Maurya Empire, Sunga Empire, Kharavela Empire, Kuninda Kingdom, Chola Empire,

Chera Empire, Pandyan Empire, Satavahana Empire, Western Satrap Empire, Kushan Empire, Vakataka Empire, Kalabhras Kingdom, Gupta Empire, Pallava Empire, Kadamba Empire, Western Ganga Kingdom, Vishnukundina Empire, Chalukya Empire, Harsha Empire, Shahi Kingdom, Eastern Chalukya Kingdom, Pratihara Empire, Pala Empire, Rashtrakuta Empire, Paramara Kingdom, Yadava Empire, Solanki Kingdom, Western Chalukya Empire, Hoysala Empire, Sena Empire, Eastern Ganga Empire, Kakatiya Kingdom, Kalachuri Empire, Delhi Sultanate, Deccan Sultanates, Ahom Kingdom, Vijayanagar Empire, Mysore Kingdom, Mughal Empire, Sikh Empire, Maratha Empire, etc. Classical Indian texts on archery in particular, and martial arts in general are known as Dhanurveda.

India has a maritime history dating back to 5,000 years. The first tidal dock is believed to have been built at Lothal around 2300 BCE during the Indus Valley Civilization, near the present day Mangrol harbour on the Gujarat coast. The Rig Veda written around 1500 BCE, credits Varuna with knowledge of the ocean routes and describes naval expeditions. There is reference to the side wings of a vessel called Plava, which give stability to the ship under storm conditions. A compass, Matsya yantra was used for navigation in the fourth and fifth century AD.

The earliest known reference to an organization devoted to ships in ancient India is to the Mauryan Empire from the 4th century BCE. Emperor Chandragupta Maurya's Prime Minister Kautilya's Arthashastra devotes a full chapter on the state department of waterways under *navadhyaksha* (Sanskrit for Superintendent of ships). The term, *nava dvipantaragamanam* (Sanskrit for sailing to other lands by ships, i.e. Exploration) appears in this book in addition to appearing in the Buddhist text, *Baudhayana Dharmasastra* as the interpretation of the term, *Samudrasamyanam*.

Sea lanes between India and neighboring lands were the usual form of trade for many centuries, and are responsible for the widespread influence of Indian Culture on other societies. Powerful navies included those of the Maurya, Satavahana, Chola, Vijayanagara, Kalinga, Maratha and Mughal empires. The Cholas excelled in foreign trade and maritime activity, extending their influence overseas to China and Southeast Asia. During the 17th and 18th centuries, the Maratha and Kerala fleets were expanded, and became the most powerful Naval Forces in the subcontinent, even defeating European Navies at various times. The fleet review of the Maratha navy took place at the Ratnagiri fort in which the ships Pal and Qalbat participated. The Maratha Kanhoji Angre and Kunjali Marakkar, the Naval chief of Saamoothiri were two notable naval chiefs of the period.

Colonial Era

The British Indian Navy was established by the British while India was a colony. The first Indian to be granted a commission was Sub Lieutenant D.N Mukherji who joined the Royal Indian Marine as an engineer officer in 1928. Indian sailors started a rebellion also known as the The Royal Indian Navy mutiny, in 1946 on board ships and shore establishments which spread all over India. A total of 78 ships, 20 shore establishments and 20,000 sailors were involved in the rebellion. When India became a republic on 26 January 1950, it became known as the Indian Navy, and its vessels as Indian Naval Ships (INS). On 22 April 1958 Vice Admiral R. D. Katari assumed office as the first Indian Chief of the Naval Staff.

Structure

The headquarters of the Indian Armed Forces is in New Delhi, the capital city of India. The President of India serves as the *de jure* commander-in-chief of the armed forces while the *de facto* executive power is held by the Union Government headed by the Prime Minister of India. The Ministry of Defence (MoD) is the ministry charged with the responsibilities of countering insurgency and ensuring external security of India.

Command organisation

Gen Deepak Kapoor is new head of Armed Forces Chiefs panel. The Indian armed force are split into different groups based on their region of operation. The Indian Army is administratively divided into 7 tactical commands, each under the control of different Lieutenant Generals.The Indian Air Force is divided into five operational and two functional commands. Each Command is headed by an Air Officer Commanding-in-Chief with the rank of Air Marshal. The Indian Navy operates four Commands. Each Command is headed by a Flag Officer Commanding-in-Chief in the rank of Vice Admiral.

Doctrine

The Armed Forces have five main tasks:

1. To assert the territorial integrity of India.
2. To defend the country if attacked by a foreign nation.
3. To send own amphibious warfare equipment to take the battle to enemy shores.
4. To support the civil community in case of disasters (e.g. flooding).
5. To deploy forces to international peace support operations.

SERVICE BRANCHES

Indian Army

The Indian Army is the world's second largest army in terms of military personnel, and the largest in terms of active manpower. It is a completely voluntary service, the military draft having never been imposed in India. The army has rich combat experience in diverse terrains, due to India's diverse geography, and also has a distinguished history of serving in United Nations peacekeeping operations. Initially, the army's main objective was to defend the nation's frontiers. However, over the years, the army has also taken up the responsibility of providing internal security, especially in insurgent-hit Kashmir and northeast. The force is headed by the Chief of Army Staff of the Indian Army, currently Deepak Kapoor. The highest rank in the Indian Army is Field Marshal, but it is a largely ceremonial rank and appointments are made by the President of India, on the advice of the Union Cabinet of Ministers, only in exceptional circumstances. Late General S.H.F.J. Manekshaw and the late General K.M. Cariappa are the only two officers who have attained this rank.

The Indian Army has seen military action during the First Kashmir War, Operation Polo, the Sino-Indian War, the Second Kashmir War, the Indo-Pakistani War of 1971, the Sri Lankan

Civil War and the Kargil War. Currently, the Indian army has dedicated one brigade of troops to the UN's standby arrangements. Through its large, sustained troop commitments India has come in for much praise for taking part in difficult operations for prolonged periods.

The Indian Army has participated in several UN peacekeeping operations, including the ones in Cyprus, Lebanon, Congo, Angola, Cambodia, Vietnam, Namibia, El Salvador, Liberia, Mozambique and Somalia. The army also provided a paramedical unit to facilitate the withdrawal of the sick and wounded in Korea. The 1965 war resulted in a ceasefire mandated by the United Nations on Indian request. However, it lost much territory in the Sino-Indian War which till date it has not managed to gain. The Indian Army has also started modernization program from 2012 to 2020 under Futuristic Infantry Soldier As a System (F-INSAS).

Indian Navy

The Indian Navy is the naval branch of the armed forces of India. With 55,000 men and women, including 5,000 naval aviation personnel and 2,000 Marine Commandos (MARCOS), it is the world's fifth largest navy. The Indian Navy currently operates more than 155 vessels, including the aircraft carrier INS Viraat. In recent years, India has started many ambitious projects to bolster its maritime capabilities including efforts to acquire ships from foreign countries. In recent years, the Indian Navy has undergone extensive modernization and expansion with an intention to increase its capabilities as a recognized blue-water navy. It is fairly advanced in terms of technology and is in control of one of two Asian aircraft carriers. Two more aircraft carriers are currently being produced. The ships of the Indian Navy are of Indian and foreign origin. In addition, three ballistic missile submarine are to enter service by 2010 end. It is also only one of the six navies in the world that has nuclear capabilities. Others include US, Russia, China, France and the UK. In addition it is in command of the BrahMos which is the fastest cruise missile in the world with speeds of 2.8 Mach.

In its maritime doctrine, the Indian Navy establishes its role in providing support to maritime neighbors during natural disasters. This was demonstrated during the Asian tsunami crisis during which the Indian Navy sent 35 ships to support relief efforts in neighbouring countries. The Indian navy has taken part in UN missions in the coast of Somalia and has provided security to an African Union summit held in Mozambique. The Indian Navy is increasing its capabilities as a true blue-water navy; the Indian Navy's doctrine states that this is for the collective good of nations.

Indian Navy is expected to spend about US$40 billion on military modernization from 2008 to 2013. The modernization program includes INS Vikramaditya, Vikrant class aircraft carrier, P-8 Poseidon, Arihant class nuclear-powered submarines, Shivalik class frigate, Kolkata class destroyer, Scorpène class submarine, Improved Talwar class frigate and eight P-8 Poseidon..

Indian Air Force

With a strength of approximately 170,000 personnel, 1,130 combat and 1,700 non-combat aircraft in active service, the Indian Air Force is the fourth largest air force in the world. In recent years, the IAF has undertaken an ambitious expansion and modernization program and is increasingly used for India's power projection beyond South Asia.

In its history, the IAF has generally relied on Soviet, British, Israeli and French military craft and technology to support its growth.

In recent times, however, India has successfully made its own original aircraft, including the HAL Tejas, a 4.5th generation fighter, and the HAL Dhruv, a multi-role helicopter, which has been exported to many countries, including Israel, Burma, Nepal and Ecuador. India also maintains UAV squadrons which can be used to carry out ground attacks and aerial surveillance.

India is testing its own long range BVR air to air missile named Astra and also building a Medium Altitude Long Endurance Unmanned Aerial Vehicle (UAV) called Rustom. India and Russia are building number of next generation aircraft like 5th generation stealth aircraft called Fifth Generation Fighter Aircraft and medium-lift military transport aircraft called Multirole Transport Aircraft.

Indian Coast Guard

The Indian Coast Guard is the maritime Para Military Force (PMF)created to guard Republic of India's vast coastline. It was created on 18 August 1978 as an independent entity as per the Coast Guard Act. its primary objective is to guard India's vast coastline and operates under the effective control of the Ministry of Defence. The coast guard works closely with the Indian Navy and the Indian Customs Department, and is usually headed by a naval officer of the rank of Vice-Admiral. India's coast guard has a large number of fast craft including hovercrafts and hydrofoils. They patrol the seas and river mouths. The coast guard has performed a number of commendable tasks of rescuing distressed personnel. It has also apprehended pirates on high seas and cleaned up oil spills. Heavy patrolling of sensitive areas such as Karnataka, Gujarat, West Bengal and Mumbai have resulted in the nabbing of a large number of smugglers and illegal immigrants.

Border Security Force

The Border Security Force (BSF) is a border patrol agency of the Government of India. Established on December 1, 1965, it is a component of the paramilitary forces of India (PMF) and its primary role is to guard India's international borders during peacetime and also prevent transnational crime. Like most paramilitary units of India, the BSF is under the administrative control of the Ministry of Home Affairs. It is one of the many law enforcement agencies of India.

Indo-Tibetan Border Police

The Indo-Tibetan Border Police (ITBP) is an Indian paramilitary force conceived on October 24, 1962 for security along the India's border with the Tibet Autonomous Region of China, border covering 2115 kilometers. The border posts manned by ITBP are exposed to high velocity storms, snow blizzards, avalanches, and landslides, besides the hazards of high altitude and extreme cold, where temperature dips up to minus 40 degree Celsius. ITBP conducts Long Range and Short Range patrols to keep an effective vigil on inaccessible and unmanned areas on the border.

STRUCTURE OF THE INDIAN ARMY

Initially, the army's main objective was to defend the nation's frontiers. However, over the years, the army has also taken up the responsibility of providing internal security, especially in insurgent-hit Kashmir and northeast. The army has a strength of about a million troops and fields 34 divisions. Its headquarters is located in the Indian capital New Delhi and it is under the overall command of the Chief of Army Staff (COAS), currently General Deepak Kapoor, PVSM, AVSM, SM, VSM, ADC.

COMMANDS

The army operates 6 tactical commands. Each command is headed by General Officer Commanding-in-Chief with the rank of Lieutenant General. Each command is directly affiliated to the Army HQ in New Delhi. These commands are given below in their correct order of raising, location (city) and their commanders. There is also one training command known as ARTRAC. The staff in each Command HQ is headed by Chief Of Staff (COS) who is also an officer of Lieutenant General rank.

REGIMENTAL ORGANISATION

In addition to this (not to be confused with the Field Corps mentioned above) are the Regiments or Corps or departments of the Indian Army. The corps mentioned below are the functional divisions entrusted with specific pan-Army tasks.

ARMS

1. Indian Infantry Regiments
2. Armoured Corps Regiments-The Armoured Corps School and Centre is at Ahmednagar.
3. Regiment of Artillery-The School of Artillery is at Devlali near Nasik.
4. Corps of Signals
5. Corps of Engineers-The College of Military Engineering is at Dapodi, Pune. The Centers are located as follows-Madras Engineer Group at Bangalore, Bengal Engineer Group at Roorkee and Bombay Engineer Group at Khadki, Pune.

6. Corps of Army Air Defence-Center at Gopalpur in Orissa State.
7. Mechanised Infantry-Regimental Center at Ahmednagar.
8. Army Aviation Corps(India)

SERVICES

1. Army Dental Corps
2. Army Education Corps-Center at Pachmarhi.
3. Army Medical Corps-Center at Lucknow.
4. Army Ordnance Corps-Centers at Jabalpur and Secunderabad (HQ).
5. Army Postal Service Corps-Centre at Kamptee near Nagpur.
6. Army Service Corps-Center at Bangalore
7. Corps of Electronics and Mechanical Engineers-Centers at Bhopal and Secunderabad.
8. Corps of Military Police-Center at Bangalore
9. Intelligence Corps-Center at Pune.
10. Judge Advocate General's Deptt.-Institute of Military Law kamptee,Nagpur.
11. Military Farms Service
12. Military Nursing Service
13. Remount and Veterinary Corps
14. Pioneer Corps

OTHER FIELD FORMATIONS

A section of the Indian Army takes charge during a military exercise.

Division: An Army Division is an intermediate between a Corps and a Brigade. It is the largest striking force in the army. Each Division is headed by General Officer Commanding] (GOC) in the rank of Major General. It usually consists of 15,000 combat troops and 8,000 support elements. Currently, the Indian Army has 34 Divisions including 4 RAPID (Re-organised Army Plains Infantry Divisions) Action Divisions, 18 Infantry Divisions, 10 Mountain Divisions, 3 Armoured Divisions and 2 Artillery Divisions. Each Division composes of several Brigades.

Brigade: A Brigade generally consists of around 3,000 combat troops with supporting elements. An Infantry Brigade usually has 3 Infantry Battalions along with various Support Arms & Services. It is headed by a Brigadier, equivalent to a Brigadier General in some armies.

In addition to the Brigades in various Army Divisions, the Indian Army also has 5 Independent Armoured Brigades, 15 Independent Artillery Brigades, 7 Independent Infantry Brigades, 1 Independent Parachute Brigade, Independent Air Defence Brigades, 2 Independent Air Defence Groups and 4 Independent Engineer Brigades. These Independent Brigades operate directly under the Corps Commander (GOC Corps).

Battalion: A Battalion is commanded by a Colonel and is the Infantry's main fighting unit. It consists of more than 900 combat personnel.

Company: Headed by the Major, a Company comprises 120 soldiers.

Platoon: An intermediate between a Company and Section, a Platoon is headed by a Lieutenant or depending on the availability of Commissioned Officers, a Junior Commissioned Officer, with the rank of Subedar or Naib-Subedar. It has a total strength of about 32 troops.

Section: Smallest military outfit with a strength of 10 personnel. Commanded by a Non-commissioned officer of the rank of Havildar Major or Sergeant Major.

REGIMENTS

Infantry Regiments

There are several battalions or units associated together in an infantry regiment. The infantry regiment in the Indian Army is a military organisation and not a field formation. All the battalions of a regiment do not fight together as one formation, but are dispersed over various formations, viz. brigades, divisions and corps. An infantry battalions serves for a period of time under a formation and then moves to another, usually in another sector or terrain when its tenure is over. Occasionally, battalions of the same regiment may serve together for a tenure.

Most of the infantry regiments of the Indian Army originate from the old British Indian Army and recruit troops from a region or of specific ethnicities.

The list of infantry regiments of the Indian Army are:

- Brigade of the Guards
- The Parachute Regiment
- Mechanised Infantry Regiment
- Punjab Regiment
- Madras Regiment
- The Grenadiers
- Maratha Light Infantry
- Rajputana Rifles
- Rajput Regiment
- Jat Regiment
- Sikh Regiment
- Sikh Light Infantry
- Dogra Regiment
- Garhwal Rifles
- Kumaon Regiment
- Assam Regiment
- Bihar Regiment
- Mahar Regiment
- Jammu & Kashmir Rifles
- Jammu & Kashmir Light Infantry
- Naga Regiment
- 1 Gorkha Rifles (The Malaun Regiment)
- 3 Gorkha Rifles
- 4 Gorkha Rifles
- 5 Gorkha Rifles (Frontier Force)
- 8 Gorkha Rifles
- 9 Gorkha Rifles
- 11 Gorkha Rifles
- Ladakh Scouts.

Artillery Regiments

The Regiment of Artillery constitutes a formidable operational arm of Indian Army. Historically it takes its lineage from Moghul Emperor Babur who is popularly credited with introduction of Artillery in India, in the Battle of Panipat in 1526. However evidence of earlier use of gun by Bahmani Kings in the Battle of Adoni in 1368 and King Mohammed Shah of Gujrat in fifteenth century have been recorded.

Armoured Regiments

There are 97 armoured regiments in the Indian Army.

Indian Army Staff and Equipment.

Strength

Soldiers from the 4th Rajput Infantry Battalion of the Indian Army handling INSAS rifles during a training mission.

- 4 RAPID (Reorganised Army Plains Infantry Divisions)
- 18 Infantry Divisions
- 10 Mountain Divisions
- 3 Armoured Divisions
- 2 Artillery Divisions
- 3 Air Defence Brigades + 2 Surface-to-Air Missile Groups
- 5 Independent Armoured Brigades
- 15 Independent Artillery Brigades
- 7 Independent Infantry Brigades
- 2 Parachute Brigade
- 4 Engineer Brigades
- 41 Army Aviation Helicopter Units.

Sub-Units

- 93 Tank Regiments
- 50 Airborne Battalions
- 50 Artillery Regiments
- 41 Infantry Battalions + 32 Para (SF) Battalions
- 32 Mechanised Infantry Battalions

- 23 Combat Helicopter Units
- 50 Air Defence Regiments.

Rank Structure

The various rank of the Indian Army are listed below in descending order:

Commissioned Officers

- Field Marshal
- General (the rank held by Chief of Army Staff)
- Lieutenant-General
- Major-General
- Brigadier
- Colonel
- Lieutenant-Colonel
- Major
- Captain
- Lieutenant.

Junior Commissioned Officers (JCOs)

- Subedar Major/Honorary Captain
- Subedar/Honorary Lieutenant
- Subedar Major
- Subedar
- Naib Subedar.

Non Commissioned Officers (NCOs)

- Regimental Havildar Major
- Regimental Quarter Master Havildar
- Company Havildar Major
- Company Quarter Master Havildar
- Havildar
- Naik
- Lance Naik.

The Indian Army (IA), now sometimes called the British Indian

Army to distinguish it from the modern army of the Republic of India, was the principal army of the British Raj in India during the last half-century before the partition of India in 1947.

The Indian Army served both in India and, particularly during the World Wars, in foreign regions. Further, in India, it was constituted for the defence of the regions of direct British governance (the Provinces of India, or, collectively, British India) as well as of those under British suzerainty (the Princely States).

The first army officially called the "Indian Army" was raised by the government of India in 1895, existing alongside the three long-established presidency armies (the Bengal Army, the Madras Army and the Bombay Army) of the Presidencies of British India. However, in 1903 the Indian Army absorbed these three armies. The term "Indian Army" was also sometimes used informally as a collective description of the former Presidency armies, particularly after the Indian Mutiny.

The Indian Army should not be confused with the Army of India. Between 1903 and 1947 this consisted of two separate entities: the Indian Army itself (made up of Indian regiments originating in India), plus the British Army in India, which consisted of units of the British Army (with their origins in the United Kingdom) which were on a tour of duty in India.

Organisation

The Indian Army has its origins in the years after the Indian Rebellion of 1857, when in 1858 the Crown took over direct rule of British India from the East India Company. Before 1858, the precursor units of the Indian Army were units controlled by the Company and were paid for by their profits. These operated alongside units of the British Army, funded by the British government in London.

The armies of the East India Company were recruited primarily from Muslims in the Bengal Presidency, which consisted of Bengal, Bihar and Uttar Pradesh, and high caste Hindus recruited primarily from the rural plains of Oudh. Many of these troops took part in the Indian Mutiny, with the aim of reinstating the Mughal Emperor Bahadur Shah II at Delhi, partly as a result of insensitive treatment by their British officers. After the Mutiny, recruitment switched to what the British called the "martial races," particularly Rajputs, Sikhs, Gurkhas, Pashtuns, Garhwalis, Mohyals, Dogras, Jats and Balochis. The "Indian Army" is the name for the Indian Armed forces of India, and the meaning has changed over time:

1858–1894: The Indian Army was an informal collective term for the armies of the three presidencies; the Bengal Army, Madras Army and Bombay Army.

1895–1902: The Indian Army had a formal existence and was the "army of the government of India", including British and Indian (sepoy) units.

1903–1947: Lord Kitchener was Commander-in-Chief, India, between 1902 and 1909. He instituted large-scale reforms, the greatest of which was the merger of the three armies of the Presidencies into a unified force. He formed higher level formations, eight army divisions, and brigaded Indian and British units. Following Kitchener's reforms:

- The Indian Army was "the force recruited locally and permanently based in India, together with its expatriate British officers."
- The British Army in India consisted of British Army units posted to India for a tour of duty, and which would then be posted to other parts of the Empire or back to the UK.
- The Army of India consisted of both the Indian Army and the British Army in India.

Command

The officer commanding the Army of India was the Commander-in-Chief in India who reported to the civilian Governor-General of India. His command was known as India Command and his staff were based at GHQ India. Indian Army postings were less prestigious than British Army positions, but the pay was significantly greater so that officers could live on their pay instead of having to have a private income. British officers in the Indian Army were expected to learn to speak the Indian languages of their men, who tended to be recruited from primarily Hindi speaking areas. Prominent British Indian army officers included:

- Claude Auchinleck
- William Birdwood, 1st Baron Birdwood
- Frederick Roberts, 1st Earl Roberts
- William Slim, 1st Viscount Slim.

After World War I the British started the process of Indianisation by which Indians were promoted into higher officer ranks. Indian cadets were sent to study at the Royal Military Academy Sandhurst and were given full commissions as King's Commissioned Indian Officers. The KCIOs were equivalent in every way to British commissioned officers and had full authority over British troops (unlike VCOs). Some KCIOs were attached to British Army units for a part of their careers.

I CORPS (BRITISH INDIA)

The I Indian Corps was an army corps of the British Indian Army in World War I. It was formed at the outbreak of war under the title Indian Corps from troops sent to the Western Front. The British Indian Army did not have a pre-war corps structure, and it held this title until further corps were created. It was withdrawn from the Western Front in December 1915 and reconstituted as I Indian Corps in Mesopotamia until the end of the war.

Western Front

In 1914 Indian Expeditionary Force A was sent to reinforce the British Expeditionary Force (BEF) fighting in France. In France it formed the Indian Cavalry Corps and Indian Corps composed of 3rd (Lahore) and 7th (Meerut) Divisions. (In France, these formations were simply known as 'Lahore' and 'Meerut' Divisions, to distinguish them from the 3rd and 7th British divisions.) Despatch from India was delayed by the activities of the German raiders *Emden* and *Konigsberg* operating in the Indian Ocean, and by the slow speed of the transport vessels. Lahore Division began landing at Marseilles on 26 September 1914, but there were further delays while the troops were re-armed with the latest pattern rifle, and the supply train could be improvised, using tradesmen's vans procured locally. The corps finally got into action at the Battles of La Bassee, 1st Messines and Armentieres in October-November 1914.

Order of Battle October-December 1914

General Officer Commanding: Lieut-Gen Sir J. Willcocks, KCB, KCSI, KCMG, DSO

Brig-Gen, General Staff: Brig-Gen H. Hudson, CB, CIE

Brig-Gen, Royal Artillery: Brig-Gen H.F. Mercer, CB, ADC

Colonel, Royal Engineers: Col H.C. Nanton

- Lahore Division
- Meerut Division
- Divisional Troops (attached from 12 October, left to join Indian Cavalry Corps 23 December 1914)
    - o Secunderabad Cavalry Brigade
    - o Signal Troop
    - o N Battery Royal Horse Artillery
    - o H Section Ammunition Column
    - o 1st Indian Field Troop, 1st King George's Own Sappers & Miners
    - o Jodhpur Lancers (Imperial Service Troops)
    - o Jodhpur Cavalry Field Ambulance.

Operations

- The Battles of La Bassee, 1st Messines and Armentieres
- Winter operations 1914-15
- The Battle of Neuve Chapelle
- The Battles of Aubers Ridge and Festubert. At this period the corps was reinforced by 51st (Highland) Division of the Territorial Force in addition to 3rd (Lahore) and 7th (Meerut) divisions.
- The Battle of Loos.

Mesopotamia

On 13 August 1915, General Sir John Nixon, commanding Indian Expeditionary Force D in Mesopotamia, requested one of the Indian infantry divisions in France as reinforcements for his advance on Baghdad. Coincidentally, on the same day, the Secretary of State for India, Austen Chamberlain, told the Viceroy of India that he was anxious for the Indian infantry to be withdrawn from France before they had to endure another winter. The system for supplying drafts had broken down and the Indian battalions were becoming very weak after the heavy casualties they had suffered. Although the Secretary of State for War, Lord Kitchener, objected to their withdrawal from the Western Front, orders were issued on 31 October for the two divisions of Indian Corps (3rd (Lahore) and 7th (Meerut) Division) to embark at Marseilles for Mesopotamia. Indian Corps was relieved in the front line on 6 November by XI Corps and the two divisions were due at Basra in December, but their departure from Marseilles was delayed because of fear of submarine attack. 3rd (Lahore) Division finally arrived in Mesopotamia in April 1916 and joined Tigris Corps, too late to relieve 6th (Poona) Division at Kut-al-Amara

MOUNTAIN GUN

Due to their ability to be broken down into smaller "packages", they are sometimes called pack guns or pack howitzers. The first designs of modern breechloading mountain guns with recoil control and able to be easily broken down and reassembled into highly efficient units were made by two Greek army engineers, P. Lykoudis and Panagiotis Danglis (after whom the Schneider-Danglis gun was named) in the 1890s. Royal Artillery The Royal Artillery (RA) is the common name for the Royal Regiment of Artillery, an arm of the British Army. Despite its name, it comprises a number of regiments.

History

Before the 18th century, artillery 'traynes' were raised by royal warrant for specific campaigns and disbanded again when they were over. On 26 May 1716, however, by royal warrant of George I two regular companies of field artillery, each 100 men strong, were raised at Woolwich. The title "Royal Artillery" (RA) was first used in 1720. On 1 April 1722 the two companies were increased to four and grouped with independent artillery companies at Gibraltar and Minorca to form the Royal Regiment of Artillery, commanded by Colonel Albert Borgard. In 1741 the Royal Military Academy was formed in the Royal Arsenal at Woolwich (RWA) to provide training for RA and Royal Engineers

(RE) officers. The regiment expanded rapidly and, by 1757, had 24 companies divided into two battalions, as well as a cadet company formed in 1741. During 1748, the presidential artilleries of Bengal, Madras and Bombay were formed. 1756 saw the creation of the Royal Irish Regiment of Artillery. In 1762 the Royal Artillery Band was formed at Minden—the oldest British military band. By 1771 there were 32 companies in four battalions, as well as two "invalid companies" comprising older and unfit men employed in garrison duties. During 1782, the regiment moved to the current Royal Artillery Barracks (front parade) on Woolwich Common. In January 1793, two troops of Royal Horse Artillery (RHA) were raised to provide fire support for the cavalry, augmented by two more in November 1793. All RHA personnel were mounted. The Royal Irish Artillery was absorbed into the RA in 1801. During 1805, the Royal Arsenal was moved to Woolwich Common. In 1819, the Rotunda was given to the regiment by the Prince Regent to celebrate end of the Napoleonic Wars. (It was originally built in St. James's Park as the outer casing of the tent in which the Prince Regent entertained the Allied sovereigns in 1814). In 1832, the regimental mottoes were granted.

The regiment was under the control of the Board of Ordnance until the board was abolished in 1855. Thereafter the regiment came under the War Office along with the rest of the army. The School of Gunnery established at Shoeburyness, Essex in 1859. In 1862 the regiment absorbed the artillery of the British East India Company – 21 horse batteries and 48 field batteries – which brought its strength up to 29 horse batteries, 73 field batteries and 88 heavy batteries.

On 1 July 1899, the Royal Artillery was divided into three groups: the Royal Horse Artillery of 21 batteries and the Royal Field Artillery of 95 batteries comprised one group, while the coastal defence, mountain, siege and heavy batteries were split off into another group named the Royal Garrison Artillery of 91 companies. The third group continued to be titled simply *Royal Artillery*, and was responsible for ammunition storage and supply. Which section a gunner belonged to was indicated by collar badges (R.A., R.F.A., R.H.A., or R.G.A.). The RFA and RHA also dressed as mounted men, whereas the RGA dressed like foot soldiers. In

1920 the rank of Bombardier was instituted in the Royal Artillery. The three sections effectively functioned as separate corps. This arrangement lasted until 1924, when the three amalgamated once more to became one regiment. In 1938, RA Brigades were renamed Regiments.

There used to be hundreds of regiments within the Royal Artillery-at the end of the Second World War, the RA was larger than the Royal Navy. In 1947 the Riding Troop RHA was renamed The King's Troop RHA and, in 1951, the title of the regiment's colonel-in-chief became Captain General.

The Royal Horse Artillery, which has always had separate traditions, uniforms and insignia, still retains a separate identity within the regiment, however, and is considered (by its members at least) to be an élite.

Before the Second World War, Royal Artillery recruits were required to be at least 5 feet 4 inches (1.63 m) tall. Men in mechanised units had to be at least 5 feet 8 inches (1.73 m) tall. They initially enlisted for six years with the colours and a further six years with the reserve or four years and eight years. They trained at the Royal Artillery Depot in Woolwich.

THE ROYAL ARTILLERY TODAY

The Royal Artillery is equipped with a variety of equipment and performs a wide range of roles, including:

- Surveillance and Target Acquisition
- Commando and Airborne artillery
- Self Propelled Artillery
- Multiple Launch Rocket Systems
- Air defence.

The Captain General of the regiment is Queen Elizabeth II. The post was previously known as Colonel-in-Chief until King George VI expressed the desire to be known as Captain General. The head of the regiment is the Master Gunner, St. James's Park. The Royal Regiment of Artillery comprises both Regular (full-time) and Territorial (part-time) units. The current regiments of the Royal Artillery are:

Regular Army

The Royal Regiment of Artillery comprises the Royal Artillery and the Royal Horse Artillery. The Regular Army units are:

Regular regiments of the Royal Horse Artillery

- King's Troop, Royal Horse Artillery is a ceremonial unit equipped with 13 pounder guns for firing salutes, and is located in St John's Wood near Regent's Park.
- 1st Regiment Royal Horse Artillery-equipped with AS90 self-propelled artillery at Assaye Barracks in Tidworth
- 3rd Regiment Royal Horse Artillery (The Liverpool and Manchester Gunners) are equipped with the AS90 self-propelled artillery, based at Caen Barracks in Hohne, Germany.
- 7th (Parachute) Regiment Royal Horse Artillery-(The Airborne Gunners) Equipped with L118 105MM light gun and are currently part of 16th Air Assault Brigade based in Colchester

Regular regiments of the Royal Artillery

- 4th Regiment Royal Artillery-(The North East Gunners) are equipped with AS90 self-propelled artillery at Alanbrooke Barracks in Topcliffe
- 5th Regiment Royal Artillery-(The North, East & West Yorkshire Gunners) are equipped with Surveillance and Target Acquisition and based at Marne Barracks in Catterick, North Yorkshire
- 12th Regiment Royal Artillery-(The Lancashire and Cumbrian Gunners) are equipped with Starstreak HVM and are based at Baker Barracks, Thorney Island
- 14th Regiment Royal Artillery-are the Training and Support Regiment based at Stirling Barracks in Larkhill
- 16th Regiment Royal Artillery-(The London and Kent Gunners) are equipped with Rapier and are based at St George's Barracks North Luffenham, in Leicestershire
- 19th Regiment Royal Artillery-(The Highland Gunners) are equipped with AS90 self-propelled artillery at Assaye Barracks in Tidworth

- 26th Regiment Royal Artillery-(The West Midland Gunners) are equipped with AS90 self-propelled artillery at Mansergh Barracks in Gütersloh
- 29th Commando Regiment Royal Artillery-(The Commando Gunners) are equipped with the (L118 105MM light gun, and are currently part of 3 Commando Brigade, with most batteries based at the Royal Citadel in Plymouth, and one battery (148 (Meiktila) Battery) based at RM Poole
- 32nd Regiment Royal Artillery-are equipped with Surveillance and Target Acquisition and Unmanned Air Vehicles and are based in Roberts Barracks in Larkhill
- 39th Regiment Royal Artillery-(The Welsh Gunners) are equipped with MLRS and GMLRS and are based at Newcastle, Tyne and Wear, their recruiting area is Wales.
- 40th Regiment Royal Artillery-(The Lowland Gunners) are equipped with L118 105MM light gun at Thiepval Barracks in Lisburn, Northern Ireland
- 47th Regiment Royal Artillery-(The Hampshire and Sussex Gunners) are equipped with Starstreak HVM and are based at Baker Barracks, Thorney Island.

THE TERRITORIAL ARMY

- Honourable Artillery Company (Surveillance and Target Acquisition) (London) (Not part of the Royal Regiment of Artillery).
- 100th (Yeomanry) Regiment Royal Artillery (Armoured/ Field/Airborne Artillery)
- 101st (Northumbrian) Regiment Royal Artillery (Volunteers) (STA & MLRS)
- 103rd (Lancashire Artillery Volunteers) Regiment Royal Artillery (Field Artillery) (Lancashire Artillery Volunteers Band)
- 104th Regiment Royal Artillery (Volunteers) (Surveillance and Target Acquisition-Unmanned Air Vehicles)
- 105th Regiment Royal Artillery (Volunteers) 'The Scottish & Ulster Gunners' (Field Artillery)

- 106th (Yeomanry) Regiment Royal Artillery (Air Defence Artillery).

The Royal Artillery's traditional home has been Woolwich, in south-east London but much of the training activity takes place at the Royal School of Artillery at Larkhill on Salisbury Plain in Wiltshire. The Royal Regiment of Artillery is unique in that it has sub-units that often move between regiments, or are placed into suspended animation.

Equipment

Air Defence

The Royal Artillery is equipped with two main weapons in the air defence mission;

- Rapier FSC-Rapier is the standard Low Level Air Defence (LLAD) weapon in the British Army. In the Royal Artillery, it equips 16 Regiment, and a battery of 106 Regiment RA(V).
- Starstreak HVM-Starstreak is a continuation of the Blowpipe and Javelin series. In the RA it can be used as a shoulder-launched weapon, in the Lightweight Multiple Launcher (LML) or mounted on a Stormer armoured vehicle. The weapon equips 12 Regiment, 47 Regiment, 104 Regiment RA(V), 105 Regiment RA(V), and two batteries of 106 Regiment RA(V).

Close Support

In the support mission, the Royal Artillery has three types of weapon;

- MLRS-the Multiple Launch Rocket System equips the "heavy" regiments of the Royal Artillery, 39 Regiment and 101(V) Regiment.
- AS90-the AS90 is a self-propelled gun that equips five field regiments, 1 RHA, 3 RHA, 4 Regiment, 19 Regiment and 26 Regiment.
- Light gun-the Light Gun is a 105 mm gun used in the close support mission in support of light or specialist forces. It equips three Regular regiments, 7 (Para) RHA, 29

(Commando) Regt RA and 40 Regiment RA, as well as three Territorial Army Regiments-100 Regt RA(V), 103 Regt RA(V) and 105 Regt RA(V).

Surveillance and Target Acquisition

- COBRA, MAMBA, ASP-the COunter Battery RAdar (Cobra), Mobile Artillery Monitoring Battlefield Asset (Mamba) and Advanced Sound ranging Program (ASP) are the main pieces of equipment used in the battlefield surveillance mission by 5 Regiment & 101 Regt RA(V).
- Phoenix UAV-the Phoenix Unmanned Aerial Vehicle is utilised in the surveillance mission by 32 Regiment.
- Desert Hawk UAV-the Desert Hawk Unmanned Aerial Vehicle is a smaller, more discreet vehicle. Also operated by 32, 47 and 12 Regiment.

Miscellaneous Facts

- The Royal Artillery does not carry colours. Its guns are its colours and are saluted on parade.
- Many Regular Army batteries bear an honour title (in parentheses) commemorating an exceptional act of service.
- Battalions and Companies were renamed Brigades and Batteries in 1859.
- Until 1794, the Royal Artillery hired civilian horses and drivers to haul its guns. In that year, the Corps of Captains' Commissaries and Drivers was formed to provide these services. This was reformed as the Corps of Gunner Drivers in 1801. In 1806 these became the Royal Artillery Drivers. In 1822 these were disbanded and from that date all men enlisted into the Royal Artillery as "Gunner and Driver"; until 1918, when they simply became Gunners. None of this applied to the Royal Horse Artillery, which had always had its own drivers.
- On 1 April 1947, all Royal Artillery units (except the Royal Horse Artillery) were placed on a single roll. This meant that each battery and regiment carried a unique number (whereas before there could have been, for instance, a 10th Field Battery, 10th Heavy Battery, 10th Coastal Battery

etc.). The numbers of the batteries within a regiment bear no relation to the regiment or each other. Royal Horse Artillery batteries (and batteries that used to be RHA) bear letters instead of numbers.

- All British coast-defence artillery units were disbanded in the 1950s.
- When on parade with its guns, the Royal Horse Artillery takes precedence over every other regiment and corps in the British Regular Army (and parades at the right of the line). Otherwise it immediately follows the Household Cavalry. The rest of the Royal Artillery takes precedence immediately after the regiments of the Royal Armoured Corps. If the Territorial Army were included in the parade, the honour of parading at right of the line of the Territorials would fall to the HAC as the oldest regiment which has guns as colours. The Territorial Army itself ranks after Regular units in precedence.
- In 1871 the Royal Regiment formed two batteries of garrison artillery which became the Royal Canadian Horse Artillery.
- During World War II, the Royal Artillery created a new type of formation, the Army Group Royal Artillery to command artillery assets at levels higher than division.
- In recognition of its history, 25/170 (Imjin) Battery of 47 Regiment wears the United States Distinguished Unit Citation that was awarded to 170 Battery for its service at the Battle of the Imjin River during the Korean War.

2

Indian Navy

The Indian Navy is the naval branch of the armed forces of India. It currently has approximately 56,000 personnel on active duty, including 5,000 members of the naval aviation branch, 2,000 marine commandos and 1,000 Sagar Prahari Bal soldiers., making it the world's sixth largest navy. The Indian Navy currently operates more than 155 vessels, including the aircraft carrier INS *Viraat*, along with operational jet fighters.

Though the primary objective of the navy is to secure national maritime borders, India also uses its navy to enhance its international relations through joint exercises, port visits and humanitarian missions, including disaster relief. In recent years, the Indian Navy has undergone extensive modernization and expansion with an intention to increase its capabilities as a recognized blue-water navy. Role The Indian Navy sees several principal roles for itself:

- In conjunction with other armed forces of the union, act to deter or defeat any threats or aggression against the territory, people or maritime interests of India, both in war and peace;
- Project influence in India's maritime area of interest, to further the nation's political, economic and security objectives;
- In cooperation with the Indian Coast Guard, ensure good order and stability in India's maritime zones of responsibility.
- Provide maritime assistance (including disaster relief) in India's maritime neighbourhood.

- To play a key role as part of 'a pluralistic security order' for a better world.

ENLISTED PERSONNEL

ORGANIZATION

The Indian Navy is divided into the following broad categories:

- Administration
- Logistics and Material
- Training
- The Fleets
- The Naval Aviation
- The Submarine Arm

COMMANDS

The Indian Navy operates four Commands. Each Command is headed by a Flag Officer Commanding-in-Chief in the rank of Vice Admiral.

Commands	HQ Location	Current FOC-in-C
Western Naval Command	Mumbai	Vice Admiral Vinod Bhasin
Eastern Naval Command	Visakhapatnam	Vice Admiral Anup Singh
Southern Naval Command	Kochi	Vice Admiral K N Sushil
Far Eastern Naval Command	Port Blair	Vice Admiral Vijay Shankar

The Far Eastern command, a joint Navy, Army and Air force command was set up in the Andaman and Nicobar Islands in 2001 as a strategic area of defence.

It was created to safeguard India's strategic interests in Southeast Asia and the Strait of Malacca. The Indian Navy plays a major role in patrolling the area with the Indonesian Navy, Royal Malaysian Navy and Royal Thai Navy. India and Australia signed an agreement to provide maritime security in the Asia Pacific region.

Bases

In 2005, the Indian Navy commissioned *INS Kadamba* at Karwar, 100 km from Goa. This is the third operational naval base after Mumbai and Vishakapatnam and the first to be controlled exclusively by the Navy. (The other bases share port facilities with civilian shipping, but this one is for purely naval use.) Built under Phase I of the multi-billion dollar 'Project Seabird', it is the largest naval base in the region. Asia's largest Naval academy INS Zamorin, was inaugurated at Ezhimala, in January 2009 by the Prime Minister of India.

Another naval base is being planned for the eastern shores, near Vishakapatnam at a cost of USD 350 million. The base, which will be located fifty km south of Vishakapatnam in Rambilli Mandal, will have comprehensive anti-aircraft, anti-submarine and amphibious capability. The Indian Navy is setting up a Naval Station in Madagascar, to monitor and patrol the coast of Mozambique as well as the Southern Indian Ocean. The Indian Navy also has berthing rights in Oman.

Marine Commando Force

The Marine Commando Force (MCF), also known as *MARCOS*, is a special forces unit that was raised by the Indian Navy in 1987 for direct action, special reconnaissance, amphibious warfare and counter-terrorism. In 1988, the MARCOS successfully rescued several hostages, including Maldives' then-Minister of Education, aboard a ship hijacked by PLOTE mercenaries during Operation Cactus. The MARCOS are also deployed to prevent infiltration through the Jhelum and Wular Lake and are involved in covert counter-terrorism operations in and around lakes and rivers in Jammu and Kashmir. The MARCOS were also involved in the rescue mission of hostages captured by the terrorists in Taj Mahal Palace & Tower luxury hotel in Mumbai as part of a large terrorist attack in Mumbai metropolis in November 2008.

Ships

The names of all commissioned ships (and Naval Bases) of the Indian Navy are prefixed with the letters INS, designating *Indian Naval Ship* or *Indian Navy Station*. The fleet of the Indian

Navy is a mix of domestic built and foreign vessels and is expanding with new inductions. India often build destroyers, frigates and corvettes.

Destroyers

The Indian Navy currently operates the *Delhi* and *Rajput* class guided-missile destroyers. The next-generation, *Kolkata* class vessels are expected to be commissioned starting in 2012.

Frigates

The guided-missile frigates currently in service are the *Talwar* class, *Brahmaputra* class and *Godavari* class. The *Nilgiri class* (variants of the British Leander class) vessels have all been decommissioned. The 3 *Advanced Talwar* class frigates (Krivak IV) are also scheduled for delivery by 2012 The next-generation *Shivalik* class vessels, which will have a lot of stealth features incorporated into them are planned for commissioning in 2010.

Corvettes

The Indian Navy currently operates the *Kora, Khukri, Veer* and *Abhay* class corvettes. The next-generation Project 28 and Project 28A class of corvettes are expected to be commissioned starting in 2012.

Amphibious Warfare Vessels

The Indian Navy has an Amphibious transport dock of the Austin class, re-christened as INS Jalashwa in service.

Aircraft Carriers

The Indian Navy presently has one aircraft carrier in active service — INS *Viraat*. The carrier is planned for decommissioning after the induction of the first domestically built *Vikrant* class aircraft carrier. The Indian Navy will also induct the Russian-built INS *Vikramaditya* in 2014.

SUBMARINES

Diesel Submarines

The Indian Navy currently maintains a fleet of diesel-electric submarines, primarily of the Sindhughosh and Shishumar classes. India signed a deal for six Scorpène class submarines with MESMA air-independent propulsion and construction has begun. These submarines will join the Indian Navy from 2012 onwards. The Indian Navy may arm its *Kilo* class submarine fleet with the BrahMos cruise missiles after successfully completing test launches from the submarine. India will issue request for proposals for another six submarines in financial year 2008-09.

Unmanned Submarines

The National Institute of Oceanography has developed the Autonomous Underwater Vehicle (AUV) that has applications in the field of Oceanographic research. Also an Autonomous Surface Vehicle (ASV) has been developed.

Nuclear Powered Submarines

In January 1988, India leased for three years an ex-Soviet Charlie class nuclear powered guided missile submarine with eight Ametist (SS-N-7 Starbright) anti-shipping missile launchers. In the Indian Navy, the vessel was christened INS *Chakra,* and the submarine was manned by an Indian crew. Upon expiration of the ship leasing term in 1991, the submarine was returned to Russia and joined the Pacific Fleet of the Russian Navy. India's indigenously designed and built nuclear-powered ballistic missile submarines of the Arihant class are expected to be commissioned starting in 2011. The lead vessel of the class, INS Arihant, was launched for sea-trials on July 26, 2009 in Visakhapatnam.

Planned Acquisitions

The Navy is purchasing from Russia the Kiev class aircraft carrier *Admiral Gorshkov* (INS *Vikramaditya*), which will be delivered to India by 2012. The Indian Navy is also negotiating with Russia for the acquisition of further *Advanced Talwar* class frigates, and six conventional submarines. India started a program in 1985 to develop indigenous technologies for building a nuclear-powered submarine, known as the Advanced Technology Vessel (ATV) project. The first Advanced Technology Vessel is called INS Arihant, was launched on July 26, 2009. The hull for the vessel has been built by Larsen & Toubro at its A naval version of a nuclear reactor has been developed at the Indira Gandhi Centre For Atomic Research, Kalpakkam and will be deployed on the submarine's hull after miniaturization. The Prototype Testing Centre (PTC) will be used to test the submarine's turbines and propellers. A similar facility is operational at Vishakapatnam to test the main turbines and gear box.

Once the vessel is completed, it may be equipped with K-15 as well as Sagarika/Agni-III ballistic missiles and advanced Indian made sonar systems. According to defence sources, the ATV is expected to be commissioned in 2010. Each unit will cost one billion U.S. dollars. Government has given approval for constructing the follow on SSBN's which will be larger than the Arihant class submarines. Approval has also been given for the construction of SSN's which will escort the SSBN's.

India is reportedly paying two billion dollars for the completion of two Akula-II class submarines which were 40-60% completed. Three hundred Indian Navy personnel are being trained in Russia for the operation of these submarines. India has finalized a deal with Russia, in which at the end of the lease of these submarines, it has an option to buy them. According to report, the first submarine will be commissioned into the Indian Navy in September, 2009. The first submarine will be named INS Chakra, it is currently undergoing trials in the Pacific ocean.

Aircraft

The naval air-arm is an important component of the Indian Navy. The Indian Navy air arm consists of Sea Harrier jets that operate from the aircraft carrier INS *Viraat* and also from INS *Jalashwa*. Recently, the Harriers were modernized for Beyond Visual Range missile capability. The Kamov-31 provide the Airborne Early Warning cover for the fleet. In the anti-submarine role the Sea King, Ka-28 and the domestic built HAL Dhruv are used. The MARCOS use Sea King and HAL Dhruv helicopters while conducting operations. Reconnaissance operations are carried out by Tupolev 142, Ilyushin 38, Dornier Do 228 aircraft, as well as HAL Chetak helicopters. The Aircraft used for carrying out roles of a strategic bomber and as a maritime strike are carried out by 4(3 more on order) Tupolev Tu-22M, which is also capable of performing reconnaissance missions. The UAV arm consists of around 30 UAVs like Heron and Searcher-IIs that are operated from ships and shore for better surveillance. The Indian Navy also maintains a four aircraft aerobatic display team, the *Sagar Pawan*. The Sagar Pawan team will be replacing their present Kiran HJT-16 aircraft with the newly developed HJT-36 aircraft. The Indian Navy has also placed an order for 8 P-8I Poseidon long-range maritime reconnaissance (LRMR) aircraft.

In January 2004, the Indian Navy signed a contract for the delivery of 12 MiG-29K and 4 MiG-29KUB which will be operated from INS *Vikramaditya*. The first MiG-29KUB manufactured for the Navy took to the skies in May 2008.

The first four aircraft were delivered to India in February 2009. There were also reports that the Indian Navy would purchase an additional 30 MiG-29Ks and-KUBs for the Indigenous Aircraft Carrier. The Indian Air Force also has a maritime strike role, providing support to the Indian Navy. It operates SEPECAT Jaguar and Sukhoi Su-30MKIf. Aircraft in this role. The Jaguars are armed with the Sea Eagle missile, which will be replaced with the Harpoon missile. Su-30MKI and the Il-38 will be armed with the air-launched version of the Brahmos cruise missile.

Weapon Systems

The Indian Navy uses modern technology and weapon systems, most of which are imported from foreign countries. Others, like the BrahMos supersonic cruise missiles, are jointly developed with Russia-a major stride in defence research. There are reports on the joint development by India and Israel of the Barak-II missile system, an improved, longer range version of the Barak-I air defence missile which is operational on Indian Navy ships. The Barak-I is used on most of the main ships of the Indian Navy. The Indian Navy's nuclear deterrence capability is based on *Sukanya* class ships armed with the *Dhanush* ballistic missiles that has a range of 350 km.

India has a number of foreign made cruise missile systems, including the Klub SS-N-27. It also has its own Nirbhay cruise missile systems under development. The Sagarika (Oceanic) submarine launched ballistic missile (SLBM), which has a range of at least 700 km (some sources claim 1000 km) forms part of India's nuclear triad. Another successful program has been the adaptation of the Yakhont anti-ship missile system into the BrahMos by the NPO and the DRDO. The BrahMos has been tailored to Indian needs and uses a large proportion of Indian-designed components and technology, including its fire control systems, transporter erector launchers, and its onboard navigational attack systems. The successful test of Brahmos from INS Rajput (D51) provides Indian Navy with precision land attack capability.

Electronic Warfare and Systems Management

Sangraha is a joint electronic warfare program of the Defence Research and Development Organisation (DRDO) and the Indian Navy. The system comprises a family of electronic warfare suites, such as Ajanta and Ellora, for use on different naval platforms capable of intercepting, detecting, and classifying pulsed, carrier wave, pulse repetition frequency agile, frequency agile and chirp radars.

The systems employ a modular approach facilitating deployment on various platforms like helicopters, vehicles, and small ships. Certain platforms, apart from ESM (electronic support measures), have ECM (electronic countermeasure) capabilities. Advanced technologies like multiple-beam phased array jammers are employed in the system for simultaneous handling of multiple threats.

The Indian Navy also relies on information technology to face the challenges of the 21st century. The Indian Navy is implementing a new strategy to move from a platform centric force to a network-centric force by linking all shore-based installations and ships via high-speed data networks and satellites. This will help in increased operational awareness. The network is referred to as the Navy Enterprise Wide Network (NEWN). The Indian Navy has also provided training to all its personnel in Information Technology (IT) at the Naval Institute of Computer Applications (NICA) located in Mumbai. Information technology is also used to provide better training, like the usage of simulators and for better management of the force.

Fleet Reviews

The President of India is entitled to inspect his fleet, as he is the supreme commander of the Indian Armed Forces. The first President's fleet review by India was hosted by Dr. Rajendra Prasad on October 10, 1953. President's reviews usually take place once in the President's term. In all, nine fleet reviews have taken place, the most recent being in February 2006, when President Dr. APJ Abdul Kalam took the review. The Indian Navy also conducted an International fleet review named *Bridges of Friendship* in February 2001 in Mumbai. Many ships of friendly Navies from all around the world participated, including two from the U.S. Navy. Once in two years navies from the Indian Ocean region meet at the Andaman and Nicobar Islands and the event is named as *MILAN* (Sanskrit: Get together).

NAVAL EXERCISES AND COOPERATION

India often conducts naval exercises with other friendly countries designed to increase naval interoperability and also to strengthen cooperative security relationship. Some such exercises take place annually like the *Varuna* with the French Navy, *Konkan* with the Royal Navy (UK), *Indra* with Russian Navy, *Malabar* with the U.S. Navy and *Simbex* with the Republic of Singapore Navy. The Indian Navy also conducted exercise with the People's Liberation Army Navy in 2003 and will send ships to the South China Sea to participate in the fleet review.

In 2007, the *TROPEX* (Theatre-level Readiness Operational Exercises) was held during which Indian Navy experimented the doctrine of influencing a land and air battle to support the Indian Army and the Indian Air Force. Apart from the Indian Ocean, India has steadily gained influence in the Pacific Ocean. In 2007, Indian Navy conducted naval exercise with Japan Maritime Self-Defence Force and U.S Navy in the Pacific and also signed an agreement with Japan in October 2008 for joint naval patrolling in the Asia-Pacific region.

Naval aircraft from Indian and US Navy flying in formation over Indian Navy aircraft carrier *INS Viraat* during Malabar 2007.

India has also held naval exercise with Vietnam, Philippines and New Zealand.

In 2007, India and South Korea decided to conduct annual naval exercise and India participated in the South Korean international fleet review. In addition, Indian Navy will also be increasing naval cooperation with other allies, particularly with Germany and Arab states of the Persian Gulf including Kuwait, Oman, Bahrain and Saudi Arabia. India held the first Indian Ocean Naval Symposium (IONS) with an objective to provide a forum for all the littoral nations of the Indian Ocean to cooperate on mutually agreed areas for better security in the region. The Indian Navy is increasingly used in international diplomacy. Since 2000, the Indian naval ships have made port calls in Israel, Turkey, Egypt, Libya, Greece, Oman, Thailand, Indonesia, Australia, New Zealand, Tonga, South Africa.

Kenya, Qatar, Oman, United Arab Emirates, Bahrain, Kuwait and other countries in 2005-2007.

The first Atlantic Ocean deployment of the Indian Navy happened in 2009. During this deployment, the Indian Naval fleet will conduct exercise with the French, German, Russian and British Navies.

Exploration

The Indian Navy regularly conducts adventure expeditions. The sailing ship and training vessel INS *Tarangini* began circumnavigating the world on 23 January 2003, intending to foster good relations with various other nations; she returned to India in May of the following year after visiting 36 ports in 18 nations. INS Tarangini returned to port, after a ten month long overseas voyage named Lokayan 07. Lt. Cdr. M.S. Kohli led the Indian Navy's first successful expedition to Mount Everest in 1965; the Navy's ensign was again flown atop Everest on 19 May 2004 by a similar expedition. Another Navy team also successfully scaled Everest from the north face, the technically more challenging route. The expedition was led by Cdr Satyabrata Dam, belonging to the elite submarine arm. Cdr. Dam is a mountaineer of international repute and has climbed many mountains including the Patagonias, the Alps among others. This team's record is unmatched by any other navy. The Navy was also the first to send a submariner to summit Everest.

An Indian Navy team comprising 11 members successfully completed an expedition to the Arctic pole. To prepare, they first travelled to Iceland, where they attempted to summit a peak. The team next flew to eastern Greenland; in the Kulusuk and Angmassalik areas, they used Inuit boats to navigate the region's ice-choked fjords. They crossed northward across the Arctic Circle, reaching seventy degrees North on skis. The team scaled an unnamed peak of height 11,000 feet and named it "Indian Peak".

The Indian Naval ensign first flew in Antarctica in 1981. The Indian Navy succeeded in Mission Dakshin Dhruv 2006 by traversing to the South Pole on skis. With this historic expedition, they have set the record for being the first military team to have successfully completed a ski traverse to the Geographic South Pole. Also, three of the ten member team-the expedition leader-Cdr. Satyabrata Dam, leading medical assistants Rakesh Kumar and Vikas Kumar are now amongst the few people in the world to have visited the two poles and summited Mt. Everest. Indian Navy became the first organization to reach the poles and Mt.Everest. A solo circumnavigation voyage named 'Sagar Parikrama' is underway by Cdr. Dilip Donde.

Ongoing Expansion

In 2004, India bought the Russian aircraft carrier, *Admiral Gorshkov* for the equivalent of US$1.5 billion. It will cost an additional US$1.5 billion to refit, and is expected to join the Indian Navy in 2012 as INS *Vikramaditya.* A further US$700 million will be spent to purchase 12 single-seat MiG-29K and four dual-seat MiG-29KUB fighters, six Kamov-31 attack and reconnaissance anti-submarine helicopters; also included are training facilities for pilots and technical staff, delivery of simulators and spare parts, and establishment and maintenance of Indian Navy facilities. Upgrades include removing missiles from the carrier foredeck to make way for a 14.3-degree ski-jump. The Mig-29's will be delivered to the Indian Navy in 2009.

In April 2007, India began construction of a 40,000 tonne *Vikrant* class aircraft carrier at a cost of $800 million and scheduled to operate 30 aircraft, including Naval LCA, MiG-29K, and Sea Harrier combat aircraft, as well as HAL Dhruv, Ka-31, and Sea

King Mk.42 helicopters. Four turbine engines will power the ship. The carrier is being constructed by state-run Cochin Shipyard Limited. and will be commissioned by 2012-13. The Indian Minister of State for Defence, Pallam Raju, went on record in September 2006 stating that the aircraft carrier is likely to be commissioned by 2011. There are plans to build more aircraft carriers domestically.

The Indian Navy is currently undergoing rapid expansion and modernisation. Yantar, a plant in Kaliningrad, Russia, was awarded a US$1.56 billion contract to build three additional 1135.6 frigates. The increased price is due to more sophisticated armaments such as BrahMos cruise missiles. The Navy has government approval for an additional eight warships.

The Indian Navy has signed a deal with Boeing to supply eight P-8 Poseidon Anti Submarine Warfare/Maritime Surveillance Aircraft. The first aircraft will be delivered 4 years after the signing of the contract, that is 2012.

INDIAN NAVAL AIR ARM

The Indian Naval Air Arm is part of the Indian Navy which is tasked to provide an aircraft carrier based strike capability, fleet air defence, maritime reconnaissance, and anti-submarine warfare. To undertake these tasks, the Indian Navy employs an aircraft carrier and a variety of manned and unmanned aircraft and helicopters.

The INS Viraat carries a complement of Sea Harrier aircraft and Kamov, Sea King, Chetak and Dhruv helicopters. The Kamov Ka-31 provides AEW support for the fleet. In the anti-submarine role, the Sea King, Ka-28 and the indigenously-built HAL Dhruv are used. The MARCOS use Sea King and HAL Dhruv helicopters while conducting operations.

Reconnaissance operations are carried out by Tupolev Tu-142s, Ilyushin Il-38s, Dornier Do 228s and also by HAL Chetak helicopters. The UAV arm consists of around 30 UAVs, such as Heron and Searcher-IIs, that are operated from ships and shore for better surveillance. The Indian Navy also maintains an aerobatic display team, the Sagar Pawan. The Sagar Pawan team will be replacing the present HJT-16 Kiran with the HJT-36. The HJT-36 will also be used in training pilots.

History

The first naval air station, INS *Garuda,* was inaugurated in Cochin on 11 May 1953. This went hand-in-hand with the commissioning of the No.550 Squadron, utilizing Short Sealand aircraft. and Fairey Firefly aircraft. 1960 saw the No.300 White Tigers Squadron, consisting of Sea Hawks aircraft being commissioned.

In the very next year (1961), INS *Vikrant* (formerly HMS *Hercules*) was acquired by the Indian Navy. The *Vikrant*'s initial airwing consisted of British Hawker Sea Hawk fighter-bombers and a French Alize anti-submarine aircraft. On May 18, 1961, the first jet landed on board, piloted by Lieutenant (later Admiral) R H Tahiliani. That year, the No.310 Cobras Squadron (consisting of Alize aircraft) was commissioned. After playing an important role in several major Indian military actions, specifically the liberation of Goa and the India-Pakistan war in 1971, she was decommissioned in January 1997 and turned into a museum ship.

In 1976, the Indian Air Force handed over Super Constellation aircraft to the No.312 Albatross Squadron in Dabolim, Goa. Being fairly old aircraft at that point, these were withdrawn from active service by 1983. The No.315 Winged Stallions Squadron was commissioned in 1977 with the Ilyushin Il-38 aircraft.

Aircraft Carrier

INS Viraat was originally commissioned in the Royal Navy as the HMS Hermes on November 18, 1959. While in the Royal Navy, the Hermes was the flagship carrier during the Falkland Islands campaign. The vessal was acquired by the Indian Navy in April 1986 following an extensive refit at Devonport Dockyard. Another refit followed between 1999 and 2001, which is expected to extend her useful life till 2010. However, there is some uncertainty around this retirement date.. The second refit upgraded propulsion systems, added a package of sensors to sound emergency alerts, and introduced modern communication systems. In addition, long-range surveillance radar, weapon systems, and new hangar with fire curtains was installed. The lift system was revamped to reduce reaction time in the event of an attack and a new flood alarm system was installed. Another year of down time followed while the ship received the Israeli Barak surface-to-air missile system in 2004. In a wartime scenario, the INS Viraat can embark up to 18 combat aircraft. INS Viraat is ideally suited for two missions: supporting amphibious operations and conducting ASW operations. Despite its age and range considerations, INS Viraat can quite effectively project naval and air power anywhere in the South Asia region.

CURRENT INVENTORY OF THE NAVAL AIR ARM

AIRCRAFT

Mikoyan MiG-29K: The MiG-29K program was revived by Russia in response to the decision of the Indian Navy to acquire the Soviet aircraft carrier Admiral Gorshkov. On January 20, 2004, the Indian Navy signed a contract for 12 single-seat MiG-29K and 4 two-seat MiG-29KUB. The first MIG-29K for the Indian Navy took flight on January 22 2007. Though it is ready it is not yet in service. First four of the sixteen aircraft was expected to be delivered by September 2008. but has been delayed until the spring of 2009. The fighter plane is different from the Mig-29 flown by Indian Air Force. Modifications were made for Indian Navy requirement featured Zhuk-ME radar, RD-33MK engine, combat payload up to 5,500 kg, 13 hardpoints (inclusive of the multi-lock bomb carriers), additional fuel tanks situated in dorsal spine fairing and wing LERXs, increased total fuel capacity by 50% comparing to first variant of MiG-29 and updated 4-channel digital fly-by-wire flight control system. With special coatings MiG-29K radar reflecting surface is 4-5 times smaller than of basic MiG-29. Cockpit displays consist of wide HUD and 3 (7 on MiG-29KUB) colour LCD MFDs and French Sigma-95 satellite GPS module and Topsight E helmet-mounted targeting system. Compatible with the full range of weapons carried by the MiG-29M and MiG-29SMT. The MIG-29 KUB (double seat trainer) is more similar to the MIG-29K but with reduced operational range. The aircraft will be fielded on the aircraft carrier INS Vikramaditya.. A new squadron has been raised & is being christened "Black Panthers". It will get its first batch of four MiG-29K fighters later this year.

BAE Sea Harrier: The BAE Sea Harrier operates from the INS Viraat. The BAE Sea Harrier FRS Mk.51 / T Mk.60 fly with the

INAS 300 and INAS 552 squadrons of the Indian Navy. They were first acquired by the Indian Navy in the mid-1980s. After years of undergoing maintenance in the UK, the Indian Navy launched Project Ashok to set up a maintenance facility in Kochi in 1994. A mid-life upgrade in 1999 for these aircraft was cancelled when the decision was made to purchase MiG-29K air defence fighters, to be deployed aboard the INS Vikramaditya (formerly Admiral Gorshkov). The Sea Harriers are armed with the Matra Magic-II AAM and the Sea Eagle Anti-ship missiles. The aircraft were upgraded with the Elta EL/M-2032 radar and the Rafael Derby BVRAAM missiles. Though the Sea Harriers were expected to remain in service with the Indian Navy till 2012-15, limited upgrades are being performed on these Sea Harriers to extend the life of the aircraft by 15 years, indicating a retirement date of 2023. The upgrades are expected to be performed by Hindustan Aeronautics Limited (HAL).

Tupolev Tu-142: The Indian Navy operates eight Tu-142 aircraft. The aircraft was inducted into service in the year 1988. Upgrading of the aircraft are taking place, which helps to extend the service life of the aircraft by sixteen years. One the upgraded aircraft has been handed over to the Indian Navy. The aircraft operates from INS Rajali and INS Hansa. Two Tu-142 aircraft are being fitted with the air launched version of the Brahmos. The aircraft will be the test platform for the Brahmos cruise missiles. The integration and tests of the missile is expected to be completed by 2010. The eight aircraft will be fitted with the Brahmos cruise missiles.

UAV: The Indian Navy currently has one squadron (INAS 342) that operates the Heron and Searcher Mk-II UAVs. There are plans to have at least three squadron of UAVs. UAVs are operated from ships to increases the range of surveillance. There are plans to introduce rotary UAVs into the Indian Navy. These UAVs will have higher endurance and load carrying capability resulting in better reconnaissance capabilities.

HELICOPTERS

HAL Dhruv Developed by Hindustan Aeronautics Limited with MBB of Germany (now Eurocopter Deutschland), the Navy received its first Dhruvs on 28 March 2002. It is expected to receive a total of 120 units to replace the Chetak helicopters in service. The naval variant is fitted with the Super Vision-2000 maritime radar, capable of detecting targets with low radar cross section at a range of 200 km. The anti-submarine version of the helicopter is fitted with dunking sonar, torpedoes, depth charges. The helicopter may also be fitted with the missiles for anti-ship roles.

Kamov Ka-25 Hormone, Kamov Ka-28 Helix-A, and the Kamov Ka-31 Helix-B: The KA-25 was acquired by the Indian Navy in 1980 for anti-submarine warfare, but had severe technological limitations. The KA-28 were acquired in the mid-80s, and were said to be a quantum leap over their predecessors from an ASW standpoint. The KA-31 takes the Kamov capabilities even further by enabling real-time network-centric warfare for the Indian Navy.

Westland Sea King and the Sikorsky SH-3 Sea King: Used principally for anti-submarine warfare (ASW) and search & rescue roles, the helicopter fleet operate from INS Garuda (Kochi) as well as INS Kunjali-II (Mumbai) air stations. US sanctions on India in response to India's nuclear tests resulted in a large part of the Sea King fleet being grounded for want of spare parts. Seventeen of the Sea King helicopters will be upgraded. The upgrade will feature day and night capability, capability to work in adverse weather conditions, integration of two anti-ship missiles with a range of fifty kilometres and a new radar.

Aérospatiale SA 316 Alouette III: Also known as the Chetak, these choppers have seen active service in the Navy as well as the Coast Guard. They are carried on several combatant as well as non-combatant ships. They are also operated from and maintained at the INS Kunjali-II and INS Utkrosh Naval Air Stations in Mumbai and Port Blair respectively.

Future Aircraft Carriers

Vikrant class aircraft carrier:In April 2005, India began construction of a 40,000 tonne *Vikrant* class aircraft carrier at a cost of Rs.40 billion and scheduled to operate 30 aircraft, including Naval LCA, MiG-29K, and Sea Harrier combat aircraft, as well as HAL Dhruv, Ka-31, and Sea King Mk.42 helicopters. Four turbine engines will power the ship. The carrier is being constructed by state-run Cochin Shipyard Limited. and will be commissioned by 2012-13. The Indian Minister of State for Defence, Pallam Raju, went on record in September 2006 stating that the aircraft carrier is likely to be commissioned by 2011. There are plans to build more Indigenous aircraft carriers.

INS Vikramaditya: On January 20, 2004, after years of negotiations, Russia and India signed a deal for the sale of the ship, the then-Admiral Gorshkov. The ship was free, while India will pay US$800 million for upgrade and refit of the ship, as well as at least an additional $1bn for the aircraft and weapons systems. The Navy looked at equipping the carrier with the E-2D, but decided not to. The deal also includes the purchase of 12 single-seat MiG-29K 'Fulcrum-D' (Product 9.41) and 4 dual-seat MiG-29KUB aircraft (with an option for 14 more aircraft)$1bn, 6 Kamov Ka-31 "Helix" reconnaissance and anti-submarine helicopters, torpedo tubes, missile systems, and artillery units. Facilities and procedures for training pilots and technical staff, delivery of simulators, spare parts, and establishment maintenance on Indian Navy facilities are also part of the contract. The announced delivery date for INS Vikramaditya was August 2008, an ambitious schedule, but one that would allow the carrier to enter service in 2009, around the time as light carrier INS Viraat (formerly HMS Hermes, last of the Centaur class) was scheduled to retire. The new ship will berth at the new Indian Navy facility in Karwar, on India's west coast. The INS Viraat's retirement is now set for 2010-2012. The sea trials of INS Vikramaditya are expected to begin by 2010 and delivery is expected by 2012.

Aircraft Under Development and Future Aircraft

- HAL Tejas:The naval variant of the Tejas will have strengthened landing gear and other necessary modifications for service on an aircraft carrier. Two Naval prototypes will be built, the NP-1 (Naval Prototype-1) which will be a two seat variant and NP-2 (Naval Prototype-2), a single seat variant for carrier operations. The Tejas is expected to be delivered before 2012. The first flight of NP-1 is expected to take place by the end of 2008 but the carrier trials was delayed due to the delay in the delivery schedule of INS Vikramaditya. Hence the trials will have to be carried out at the SBTF (Shore-based Test Facility) under construction at the naval airbase INS Hansa in Goa. Indian Navy plans to operate two squadrons (40 aircraft) of carrier borne Tejas aircraft from the two aircraft carries. Indian navy has placed an order for six Naval LCAs. At an approximate cost of Rs 150 crore per aircraft, that will provide a Rs 900 crore infusion into the Naval LCA programme.

- Additional Fighter Aircraft:Indian Navy has issued RFI to various fighter aircraft manufacturers including Boeing for F-18 Super Hornet & Dassault for its Rafale fighters. These aircraft will be used for supplements to MIG29K's operating from Indigenous & Vikramaditya class aircraft carriers. These are ordered in order to reduce the delays in the procurement of fighter aircraft. Unknown number of fighters will be procured.
- Long Range Maritime Patrol Aircraft: The Indian Navy issued an RFP for eight maritime patrol aircraft. The plan is to induct up to thirty new maritime patrol aircraft by 2020. Out of all the bidders the P-8I Poseidon has won the contract. New Delhi and Boeing have inked a lucrative, $2.1 billion contract for the delivery of eight P-8 Poseidon sub hunters. The new aircraft will replace a fleet of outdated Russian-manufactured Tupolev-142M planes.
- Medium Range Maritime Reconnaissance Aircraft: The Indian Navy issued an RFP for six medium-range maritime reconnaissance (MRMR) aircraft. Contenders are ATR-72MP/ ATR-42MP, EADS C-295MPA/C-235MPA, Dassault's Falcon 900MPA and Embraer P-99A platforms.
- E-2D Advanced Hawkeye
- 17 Hawk Trainer
- HAL HJT-36
- 20 ASW Helicopters (to replace Sea King) Extended to 60 helos
- 15 NAL Saras aircraft have been ordered, mostly to replace the Dornier Do-228.

- 40 Unmanned helicopters. This helicopter is under development and will be based on the HAL-built Cheetah helicopters.
- Rustom UAV.

Personnel and Structure

The 5000-person Naval Air Arm is headed by Rear Admiral Vijay Shankar, Assistant Chief of Naval Staff (Air). The current Chief of Naval Staff, Admiral Sureesh Mehta was in the Naval Air Arm and flew the Hawker Sea Hawk from the INS Vikrant earlier on in his career. He also held command of the INS Garuda air station in Kochi, Kerala.

Western Command

Established in 1986, the Flag Officer Naval Aviation (FONA) is headquartered in Goa, and is responsible for all naval aviation aspects. The Directorate of Naval Air Staff at Naval HQ has centralized functions like laying down the general principles of operational deployment, organisation, administration and operational/training standards for the flying units. On the other hand, FONA controls training, maintenance and other functions of naval aviation. Aircraft yards at Kochi, Kerala and Dabolim, Goa are responsible for maintaining the fleet's air arm. An exclusive base, INS Shikra for helicopters was commissioned in Mumbai.

Eastern Command

To protect and preserve India's growing trade with Southeast Asia and offer a bulwark against Chinese dominance in the Bay of Bengal, a new naval base is being built near Visakhapatnam. It is expected to be capable of harboring two aircraft carriers, including the new Vikrant-class aircraft carrier that is being planned.

Southern Command

It has at least one airfield.

Andaman & Nicobar Command

A fighter squadron is expected to be based in Port Blair in the future, to bolster the strength of the squadron of Mi-8 helicopters currently operating there.

Muscat (Oman)

A new airbase will be setup in Muscat, Oman to tackle piracy in the Gulf of Aden.

Other Naval Air Arm

- Fleet Air Arm Of U.K.
- United States Naval Aviator Of USA
- Aviation navale Of France
- Russian Naval Aviation.

INDIAN COAST GUARD

The Indian Coast Guard (ICG) is one of four branches of the Indian Armed Forces, tasked with the mission to guard the Republic of India's maritime interests. The Indian Coast Guard's organization is similar to that of other Para Military Forces of India. It was created on 18 August 1978 as an independent entity as per the Coast Guard Act. It operates under the effective control of the Ministry of Defence.

The ICG mission is to protect India's maritime interests, including its coastline, exclusive economic zone and shipping. It is also tasked with Indian maritime law enforcement relating to ocean resources, shipping, customs and revenue, maritime environment, protected species as well as narcotics. The coast guard works in close cooperation with the Indian Navy, Indian department of Fisheries, Department of Revenue (Customs) and the Central and State Police forces. The ICG is generally headed by a naval officer of the rank of Vice-Admiral.

History

The establishment of the Indian Coast Guard was first proposed by the Indian Navy to provide non-military maritime services to the nation. And it is considered as one of the best coast gaurds in the world In the 1960's, sea-borne smuggling of goods was threatening India's domestic economy. The Indian Customs Department frequently called upon the Indian Navy for assistance with patrol and interception in the anti-smuggling effort.

The Nag Chaudhri Committee was constituted with participation from the Indian Navy and the Indian Air Force to study the problem. In August 1971, the committee identified the need to patrol India's vast coastline, register fishing vessels in order to identify illegal activity and the need for a capable and well-equipped force to intercept illegal vessels. The committee also looked at the number and nature of the equipment, infrastructure and personnel required to provide these services.

By 1973, India had started a program to acquire the equipment and started deputing personnel from the Indian Navy for these anti-smuggling and law enforcement tasks, under the provisions of the Maintenance of Internal Security Act. The Indian Navy sensed that the nature of these duties diverged from its core mission as a military service. Based on the inputs from the Chief of Naval Staff, on August 31, 1974, the then Defence Secretary submitted a note the Cabinet Secretary outlining the need for the Coast Guard.

In September 1974, the Rustamji Committee was setup with participation from the Indian Navy and the Department of Revenue to examine the gaps in security and law enforcement between the roles of the Indian Navy and the central and state police forces. The discovery of oil off Bombay High further emphasized the need for a maritime law enforcement and protection service. The committee submitted its recommendation for the establishment of the Indian Coast Guard under the Ministry of Defence on July 31, 1975.

Bureaucratic wrangling followed, with the Cabinet Secretary making a recommendation to place the service under the Ministry of Home Affairs. Fortunately, Prime Minister Indira Gandhi overruled the Cabinet Secretary and decided to place the service under the Ministry of Defence.

An interim Indian Coast Guard came into being on February 1, 1977 equipped with two small frigates and five patrol boats deputed from the Indian Navy. The duties and functions of the service were formally defined in the Coast Guard Act, which was passed on 18 August 1978, and came into effect the next day. Vice Admiral V.A. Kamath of the Indian Navy was the founding Director General. Vice Admiral Kamath proposed a plan to develop the ICG into a potent force by 1984, but the full potential of this plan has not been realized due to a resource crunch.

The Indian Coast Guard conducts exercises with the other coast guards of the world. In 2006, the Indian Coast Guard conducted exercises with Japanese and Korean counterparts. In May 2005, the Indian Coast Guard agreed to set up liaison links with Pakistan Coast Guard which is formally known as the MSA Maritime Security Agency.

Major historic achievements of the service includes the first ever recapture of a pirated ship at high seas, the MV Alondra rainbow. After the 2008 Mumbai attacks, the Indian government has initiated a program to expand the ICG force, assets and infrastructure.

Rank Structure

Coast Guard Rank Structure	Equivalent Indian Navy Rank Structure
Director General	Vice Admiral
Inspector General	Rear Admiral
Deputy Inspector General+	Commodore
Deputy Inspector General	Captain
Commandant	Commander
Commandant (Junior Grade)	Commander
Deputy Commandant	Lieutenant Commander
Assistant Commandant	Lieutenant
Assistant Commandant†	Acting Lieutenant
Assistant CommandantÊ%	Midshipman

+ With three years seniority † Under training after completion of Phase III afloat training and during sub courses Ê% Under training after completion of Phase II afloat training

Organization

The Indian Coast Guard operations are split into 3 regions: Western Region headquartered in Mumbai, Eastern Region headquartered in Chennai and the Andaman & Nicobar Region headquartered in Port Blair. The force has a strength of 5440, including 633 officers.

The ICG is led by the Director General of Coast Guard, usually a commissioned officer of rank *Vice Admiral* from Indian Navy.

The current ICG DG is Vice Admiral Anil Chopra, AVSM. Each region is headed by an Inspector General (IG) or a Deputy Inspector General (DIG). The IG and DIG are commissioned Coast Guard Officers, often graduates of the Indian defence service colleges.

Each of the regions is further divided into multiple districts, typically covering a coastal state or a union territory.

Bases

The Indian Coast Guard operates:

- 29 Coast Guard Stations
- 2 air bases, in Daman and Chennai
- Air enclaves at Goa, Kolkata and Port Blair.

3

Indian Air Force

The Indian Air Force is the air arm of the armed forces of India. Its primary responsibility is to secure Indian airspace and to conduct aerial warfare during a conflict. It was officially established on October 8, 1932 as an auxiliary air force of the Indian Empire and the prefix *Royal* was added in 1945 in recognition of its services during the World War II. After India achieved independence from the United Kingdom in 1947, the Royal Indian Air Force served the Union of India, with the prefix being dropped when India became a republic in 1950.

Since independence, the IAF has been involved in four wars with neighboring Pakistan and one with the People's Republic of China. Other major operations undertaken by the IAF include Operation *Vijay*, Operation *Meghdoot* and Operation *Cactus*. Apart from conflicts, the IAF has been an active participant in United Nations peacekeeping missions.

The President of India serves as the Commander-in-Chief of the IAF. The Chief of Air Staff, an Air Chief Marshal (ACM), is a four star commander and commands the Air Force. There is never more than one serving ACM at any given time in the IAF. One officer has been conferred the rank of Marshal of the Air Force, a 5-star rank and the officer serves as the ceremonial chief. With strength of approximately 170,000 personnel and 1,700 aircraft, including 852 combat aircraft in active service, the Indian Air Force is the world's fourth largest.

In recent years, the IAF has undertaken an ambitious expansion and modernisation program to replace its aging Soviet-era fighter jets. Among the various expansion plans is the MRCA program under which the IAF plans to induct 126 fighter jets at a cost of US$12 billion.

Mission

The IAF's mission is defined by the Armed Forces Act of 1947, Constitution of India and the Air Force Act of 1950, in the aerial battlespace, as: *Defence of India and every part thereof including preparation for defence and all such acts as may be conducive in times of war to its prosecution and after its termination to effective demobilisation.* Moreover, the air force, along with the other branches of the Indian armed forces, can assist local and state governments; if assistance is sought by such government during natural disasters and for maintaining internal security.

History

The Indian Air Force was established as an auxiliary air force of the RAF with the enactment of the Indian Air Force Act of 1932 on October 8 that year. On April 1, 1933, the IAF commissioned its first squadron, No.1 Squadron, with four Westland Wapiti biplanes and five Indian pilots. The Indian pilots were led by Flight Lieutenant (later Air Vice Marshal) Cecil Bouchier. Until 1938, No. 1 Squadron remained the only squadron of the IAF, though two more flights were added. During the Second World War, the Air Force had grown to seven squadrons in 1943 and to nine squadrons in 1945. In recognition of the crucial role played by the IAF, King George VI conferred it the prefix *Royal* in 1945. Indian National Army youth cadets were trained by Imperial Japanese Army Air Force Academy in 1944. After Indian independence in 1947, Royal Indian Air Force (RIAF) was bifurcated. Three of the ten operational squadrons and facilities located within the borders of Pakistan were transferred to Royal Pakistan Air Force.

In 1947, when a conflict broke out over the control of erstwhile principality of Jammu & Kashmir, the Maharaja of the state decided to accede India in order to receive military help. The day after instrument of accession was signed, the RIAF was called upon to mobilise armed troops into the war-zone. This led to the eruption of full scale war between India and Pakistan without a formal declaration. During the war, the RIAF did not engage Pakistan

Air Force in air-to-air combat; however, it did provide effective transport and close air support to the Indian troops. When India became a Republic in 1950, the *Royal* title was dropped to become the Indian Air Force.

In 1960, when Belgium's 75-year colonial rule of the Congo ended abruptly, widespread violence and rebellion engulfed the nation. IAF aircraft arrived in Congo to support United Nations Operation in the Congo and started undertaking operational missions in November. The unit remained there until 1966, when the UN mission ended.

During the Sino-Indian War of 1962, India's military planners failed to deploy and effectively use the IAF against the invading Chinese forces. Three years after the Sino-Indian conflict, in 1965, India went to war with Pakistan again over Kashmir. Learning from the experiences of the Sino-Indian war, India decided to use its air force extensively during the war. This was the first time the IAF actively engaged an enemy air force. However, instead of providing close air support to the Indian Army, the IAF carried out independent raids against Pakistani Air Force (PAF) bases. These bases were situated deep inside Pakistani territory, making IAF fighters vulnerable to anti-aircraft fire. During the course of the conflict, the PAF enjoyed qualitative superiority over the IAF because most of the jets in IAF's fleet were of World War II vintage. Despite this, the IAF was able to prevent the PAF from gaining air superiority over conflict zones. By the time the conflict had ended, Pakistan claimed to have shot down 113 IAF aircraft while the Indians claimed that 73 PAF aircraft were downed. More than 60% of IAF's air combat losses took place during the disastrous battles over Kalaikunda and Pathankot; where most of the losses were on the ground.

After the 1965 war, the IAF underwent a series of changes. In 1966, the Para Commandos regiment was created. With an intention of increasing its logistics supply and rescue operations ability, the IAF inducted 72 Avro 748s which were built by Hindustan Aeronautics (HAL) under license from Avro. India started to lay more stress on indigenous manufacture of fighter aircraft. HAL HF-24 Marut, designed by the famed German aerospace engineer Kurt Tank, were inducted into the air force.

HAL also started working on a new improved version of the Folland Gnat, known as HAL Ajeet. At the same time, the IAF also started inducting Mach 2 capable Soviet MiG-21 and Sukhoi Su-7 fighters.

By late 1971, another war between India and Pakistan seemed inevitable because of the intensification of the independence movement in erstwhile East Pakistan. On November 22, 1971, 10 days before the start of a full-scale war, four Pakistani Air Force (PAF) F-86 Sabre jets attacked Indian and Mukti Bahini positions near the international border. Three of the four PAF Sabres were shot down by IAF's Folland Gnats. On December 3, India formally declared war against Pakistan following massive preemptive strikes by the PAF against Indian Air Force installations in Srinagar, Ambala, Sirsa, Halwara and Jodhpur. However the plan failed as the IAF had anticipated such a move and no major losses were suffered. The Indian Air Force was quick to respond to Pakistani air strikes, following which the PAF carried out mostly defensive sorties. Within the first two weeks, the IAF had carried out almost 2,000 sorties over East Pakistan and also provided close air support to the advancing Indian Army. IAF also assisted the Indian Navy in its operations against the Pakistani Navy and Maritime Security Agency in the Bay of Bengal and Arabian Sea. On the western front, the IAF destroyed more than 29 Pakistani tanks, 40 APCs and a railway train during the Battle of Longewala. The IAF undertook strategic bombing of West Pakistan by carring out raids on oil installations in Karachi, the Mangla Dam and a gas plant in Sindh. Similar strategy was also deployed in East Pakistan and as the IAF achieved complete air superiority on the eastern front, the ordnance factories, runways, and other vital areas of East Pakistan were severely damaged. By the time Pakistani forces surrendered, the IAF claimed that 94 PAF aircraft, including 54 F-86 Sabres. The IAF had flown over 6,000 sorties on both East and West fronts; including sorties by transport aircraft and helicopters. Towards the end of the war, IAF's transport planes dropped leaflets over Dhaka urging the Pakistani forces to surrender, demoralising Pakistani troops in East Pakistan.

In 1984, India launched Operation Meghdoot to capture the Siachen Glacier in the contested Kashmir region. IAF's Mi-8, Chetak and Cheetah helicopters airlifted hundreds of Indian troops to Siachen. Launched on April 13, 1984, this military operation was unique because of Siachen's inhospitable terrain and climate. The military action was successful, given the fact that under a previous agreement, neither Pakistan nor India had stationed any personnel in the area. The Indian forces, facing no opposition, took control over most of the heights on the glacier.

On May 20, 1999, the Indian Air Force was called in to provide close air support to the Indian Army at the height of the ongoing Kargil conflict. Because of Kashmir's high altitude and rigid terrain, the IAF initially expressed its reservations to deploy the slow-moving Mil Mi-8/17 helicopters which had a service ceiling of 10,000 feet. These concerns materialised when the Pakistani forces shot down an IAF Mi-8 helicopter and two fighter jets, MiG-21 and MiG-27, that had reportedly strayed into Pakistan's airspace. After the initial setbacks, the IAF deployed the Mirage 2000 which not only had better defence equipment compared to the MiGs, but also gave IAF the ability to carry out aerial raids at night. The Mirages successfully targeted enemy camps and logistic bases in Kargil and within days, their supply lines were severely disrupted. The IAF also deployed its radars and the MiG-29 fighter jets in vast numbers to keep check on Pakistani military movements across the border. The MiG-29s were also used extensively to provide fighter escort to the Mirage 2000. At the height of the conflict, the IAF was conducting over forty sorties daily over the Kargil region. The IAF's operations in Kargil not only boosted the morale of the Indian Army, but also paved the way for the early recapture of Muntho Dhalo and Tiger Hill. By July 26, the Indian forces had successfully liberated Kargil from Pakistani forces and Islamist militants. On August 10, 1999, IAF MiG-21s intercepted a Pakistan Navy Breguet Atlantic which was flying over the disputed region of Sir Creek. The aircraft was shot down killing all 16 Pakistani Navy personnel on board. India claimed that the Atlantic was on a mission to gather information on IAF air defence, a charge emphatically rejected by Pakistan which argued that the unarmed aircraft was on a training mission.

Since late 1990s, the Indian Air Force has been modernising its fleet to counter challenges in the new century. The fleet size of the IAF has decreased during this period because of the retirement of older aircraft. Still, India maintains the fourth largest air force. As new aircraft enter service and numbers recover, the IAF plans to have a fleet of 42 squadrons.

Structure of the IAF

The President of India is the Supreme Commander of all Indian armed forces and by virtue of that fact is the notional Commander of the Air Force. India's Ministry of Defence under the Defence Minister oversees the Air Force, by way of direct civilian leadership. The Prime Minister and the National Security Council provide indirect leadership by shaping government security policy. A Chief of the Air Staff with the rank of Air Chief Marshal commands Air Headquarters and provides military leadership. He is assisted by six officers: a Vice Chief of the Air Staff, a Deputy Chief of the Air Staff, the Air Officer in Charge of Administration, the Air Officer in Charge of Personnel, the Air Officer in Charge of Maintenance, and the Inspector General of Flight Safety. In January 2002, the government conferred the rank of Marshal of the Air Force on Arjan Singh making him the first and only *Five Star* rank officer with the Indian Air Force and ceremonial chief of the air force.

Commands and Structure

The Indian Air Force is divided into five operational and two functional commands. Each Command is headed by an Air Officer Commanding-in-Chief with the rank of Air Marshal. The purpose of an operational command is to conduct military operations using aircraft within its area of responsibility, whereas the responsibility of functional commands is to maintain combat readiness. Aside from the Training Command at Bangalore, the center for primary flight training is located at the Air Force Academy in Hyderabad, Andhra Pradesh, followed by operational training at various other schools. Advanced officer training for command positions is also conducted at the Defence Services Staff College; specialised advanced flight training schools are located at Bidar, Karnataka, and Hakimpet, Andhra Pradesh (also the location for helicopter training). Technical schools are found at a number of other locations.

Bases

The IAF operates over sixty air bases, with more being built or planned. Western Air Command is the largest Air Command. It operates sixteen air bases from Punjab to Uttar Pradesh. Eastern Air Command operates fifteen Air bases in Eastern and North-eastern India. Central Air Command operates seven Air Bases in Madhya Pradesh and surrounding states of central India. Southern Air Command, a strategically important Air command, in line with India's latest doctrine of protecting the vital shipping routes. It operates nine Air bases in Southern India and two in the Andaman and Nicobar Islands. South Western Air Command is the front line of defence against Pakistan, this important Command operates twelve air bases in Gujarat, Maharashtra and Rajasthan. India also operates the Farkhor Air Base in Tajikistan

Wings

A Wing is a formation intermediate between a Command and a Squadron. It generally consists of two or three IAF Squadrons and Helicopter Units, along with Forward Base Support Units (FBSU). FBSUs do not have or host any Squadrons or Helicopter units but act as transit airbases for routine operations. In times of war, they can become fully fledged air bases playing host to various Squadrons. In all, about 47 Wings and 19 FBSUs make up the IAF.

Squadrons

Squadrons are the field units and formations attached to static locations. Thus, a Flying Squadron is a sub-unit of an air force station which carries out the primary task of the IAF. All fighter squadrons are headed by a Commanding Officer with the rank of Wing Commander. Some Transport squadrons and Helicopter Units are headed by a Commanding Officer with the rank of Group Captain. Within this formation structure, IAF has several service branches for day-to-day operations. They are:

IAF Personnel

The IAF has a strength of 170,000 personnel. Its rank structure is based on that of the Royal Air Force. The highest rank attainable in the IAF is Marshal of the Indian Air Force, conferred by the President of India after exceptional service during wartime. MIAF Arjan Singh is the only officer to have achieved this rank. The head of the Indian Air Force is the Chief of the Air Staff, who holds the rank of Air Chief Marshal. The current Chief of the Air Staff is Air Chief Marshal P.V.Naik, appointed on May 1, 2009, following the retirement of Air Chief Marshal Fali Homi Major.

Officers

Anyone holding Indian citizenship can apply to be an officer in the Air Force as long as they satisfy the eligibility criteria. There are four entry points to become an officer. Male applicants, who are between the ages of 16½ and 19 and have passed high school graduation, can apply at the *Intermediate* level. Men and women applicants, who have graduated from college (three year course) and are between the ages of 18 and 28, can apply at the *Graduate* level entry. Graduates of engineering colleges can apply at the *Engineer* level if they are between the ages of 18 and 28 years. The age limit for the flying and ground duty branch is 23 years of age and for technical branch is 28 years of age. After completing a master's degree, men and women between the ages of 18 and 28 years can apply at the *Post Graduate* level. Post graduate applicants do not qualify for the flying branch. For the technical branch the age limit is 28 years and for the ground duty branch it is 25. At the time of application, all applicants must be single. The IAF selects candidates for officer training from these applicants. After completion of training, candidate are commissioned as Flying Officers.

Airmen

The duty of an airman in the Indian Air Force is to make sure that all the air and ground operations run smoothly. From operating Air Defence systems to fitting missiles, they are involved in all activities of an air base and give support to various technical and non-technical jobs. The recruitment of personnel below officer rank is conducted through All India Selection Tests and Recruitment Rallies. All India Selection Tests are conducted among 14 Airmen Selection Centres (ASCs) located all over India. These centres are under the direct functional control of Central Airmen

Selection Board (CASB), with administrative control and support by respective commands. The role of CASB is to carry out selection and enrolment of airmen from the Airmen Selection Centers for their respective commands.

Candidates initially take a written test at the time of application. Those passing the written test undergo a physical fitness test, an interview conducted in English, and medical examination. Candidates for training are selected from individuals passing the battery of tests, on the basis of their performance. Upon completion of training, an individual becomes an Airman. Some MWOs and WOs are granted honorary commission in the last year of their service as an honorary Flying Officer or Flight Lieutenant before retiring from the service.

Garud Commando Force

The Garud Commando Force is the Special Forces unit of the Indian Air Force. It was formed in September 2004 and has a strength of approximately 1500 personnel. The unit derives its name from *Garuda,* a divine bird-like creature of Hindu Mythology, but more commonly the word for eagle in Sanskrit. Garud is tasked with the protection of critical Air Force bases and installations; search and rescue during peace and hostilities and disaster relief during calamities. Presently, the GARUDs are deployed in Congo as part of the UN peace keeping operations.

Non Combatants Enrolled and civilians

Non Combatants Enrolled (NCs(E)) were established in British India as personal assistants to the officer class, and are equivalent to the *orderly* or *sahayak* of the Indian Army. Almost all the commands have some percentage of civilian strength which are central government employees. These are regular ranks which are prevalent in ministries. They are usually not posted outside their stations and are employed in administrative and technical work. More than 250 different designations exist.

Land-Based Air Defence

- Isayev SA-3 Goa: The Indian Air Force is considering upgrading its Pechora SA-3 missiles with Polish help whilst it waits for the Akash. According to Janes Missiles and

Rockets (December 2005), the IAF would like to conduct the Newa-SCM upgrade package upgrade to 20 S-125M Pechora-CC systems, using primarily the Tatra 8x8 chassis, which is licence-built in India. Installation on specially adapted heavy equipment trailers or Tatra 8x8 vehicles was studied at the request of the Indian Air Force. It incorporates a new ZNO-X digital transmitter/receiver block developed by the Przemyslowy Instytut Telekomunikacji (PIT) to replace the original magnetron-based hardware. The unit uses digital technology, including digital frequency synthesis, and has automatic built-in test facilities. While the ZNO-X is an expensive upgrade, it significantly improves system performance. Most of the upgrade work would be done in India, although the core elements of the upgrade would be delivered from Poland.Pechora SAM will be phased out by 2012. As of 2009, no firm SA-3 upgrade program has been signed for.

- SA-8 Gecko
- SA-10 Grumble/S-300. Reportedly 6 batteries were purchased in August 1995
- SA-16 Gimlet-MANPAD.

Aircraft Inventory

The Indian Air Force has a strength of over 1,915 (combat and non-combat) aircraft. Most are of Soviet/Russian origin. The Air Force also operates some aircraft from Britain and France. Hindustan Aeronautics Limited produces some of the Russian and British aircraft in India under licence. The exact number of aircraft in service with the Indian Air Force cannot be determined with precision from open sources. Various reliable sources provide notably divergent estimates for a variety of high-visibility aircraft.

Fighter and Multi-role Combat Aircraft

These aircraft are primarily for air defence and air superiority purposes. However, most of them have significant strike and close air support capabilities. The Sukhoi Su-30MKI is the IAF's prime air superiority fighter. The Su-30K variant was first acquired in 1996. That year, the IAF signed a US$1.6 billion contract with

Russia for the supply of 50 Su-30MKIs and the technology transfer and license to manufacture 140 Su-30MKIs by Hindustan Aeronautics Limited. The two-seat, multi-role fighter has a maximum speed of 2500 km/h (Mach 2.35) and a service ceiling of 20,000 meters. With one mid-air refueling, it can travel as far as 8000 km, making it a suitable platform to deliver strategic weapons..In 2007, the IAF spent US$700 million to upgrade its remaining 10 Su-30Ks and 8 SU-30MKs to MKI Std variant and signed a contract for the supply of 40 additional MKIs with Russia.

The MiG-29 (NATO: *Fulcrum*) is the IAF's dedicated air superiority fighter. It has a top speed of 2,445 km/h (Mach 2.3) and is armed with a 30 mm cannon along with R-60 & R-27 R missiles. The IAF began deploying MiG-29s in 1984, becoming the second air force to do so.. Since their induction, the IAF's MiG-29s have undergone a series of upgrades including more efficient and powerful radar (Zhuk-ME), weapons system, and engines. Mirage 2000s, capable of flying at 2,500 km/h (Mach 2.35), are the IAF's premier multirole fighter jet. These aircraft can carry a wide range of weaponry including two 30 mm integral cannon, two *Matra Super 530D* medium-range missiles, two *R550 Magic* close combat missiles and various ground attack munitions.

Since 1963, over 450 MiG-21 combat aircraft have served in the IAF. Most of these MiGs have been upgraded since induction. In 1996, India signed a US$300 million deal with Russia to upgrade 125 MiG-21 *Bis*, and a multi-million dollar deal was awarded to Israel's Elta for upgrading the avionics of the MiGs. Because of their frequent crashes, the MiG-21s have been dubbed *flying coffins* by the media. As of 2007, about 250 MiG-21s remain in service with the Indian Air Force and are planned to be replaced by the indigenously built HAL Tejas starting 2010. IAF has had problems in aircraft maintenance with many crashes in recent years. During the 2005-09 period, 32 MiG series fighters in service with the IAF crashed, resulting in the death of five pilots.

Strike, Attack and Close Support Aircraft

Squadrons of Jaguar (known as the *Shamsher* in Indian service) and MiG-27 aircraft serve as the IAF's primary ground attack force. The twin-engine Jaguar IB, with a top speed of Mach 1.6, is capable of carrying nuclear weapons. The IAF has 100 Jaguar IS and 8 maritime strike Jaguar IM aircraft. The single-seat MiG-27 carries one GSh-6-30 six-barreled 30 mm cannon, 4000 kg of general-purpose ordnance, SPPU-22 and SPPU-6 gun pods, and various guided air-to-surface missiles. In January 2009, India successfully completed the upgrade programs on the Air Force's MiG-27 ground attack variants. DRDO carried out the avionics upgrades on the fighter aircraft. In the upgraded MiG-27s, the avionics system is built around a modular mission computer termed Core Avionics Computer (CAC). The upgraded ground attack fighters are equipped with Inertial Navigation and Global Positioning System (INGPS) providing accurate navigation during aircraft sorties. To provide more accuracy to the aircraft's weapon systems, accurate ranging sensors such as Laser Designator Pod (LDP) and Laser Ranger and Marked Target Seeker (LRMTS) have been integrated in it also. To improve situational awareness of the pilot during air combat, a digital map generator has been integrated along with a digital video recording system, which helps in mission analysis and debrief support.

Airborne Early Warning Aircraft

In 2004, the IAF ordered 3 IAI Phalcon Airborne Early Warning radar system from Israel Aerospace Industries, which is considered to be the most advanced AEW&C system in the world. The air force will use 3 newly acquired Ilyushin Il-76 Phalcons as the platform for this radar. In May 2008, India appears to have ordered an additional three Phalcon radar-equipped IL-76s from Israel, pushing up the value of the deal from US$1.1 to 1.5 billion. An Indian defence delegation headed by Defence Secretary Vijay Singh, visited Israel in November 2008 to discuss the purchase of the planes and missiles from Israel Aerospace Industries (IAI). It has been reported that India has placed a follow-up order for 3 more Phalcon radar equipped IL-76 from Israel at a cost of $1.5 billion, pushing the total number to be acquired up to 6. The first Phalcons arrived in India on May 25, 2009 and are expected to be commissioned into service by 2010. IAF Air Chief said that it would take a year and a half to get each and every combat plane in IAF to link with Phalcon.

Transport Aircraft

The IAF operates 25 Ilyushin Il-76s for military transport duties such as heavy lift at all operational levels. The Il-76 MD is a strategic air-lifter with a payload of 95,000 lb and a range of over 5,000 km (2,700 nm; 3,100 statute miles). In 2003, the IAF orderd 6 IL-78MKI aircraft from Uzbekistan and are fitted with aerial refueling pods from Israel. India took delivery of the tankers in 2004.

IAF has a fleet of 64 Avro 748 which has a payload of 5,136 kg (11,323 lb) and has a range of 1,715 km (926 nm; 1,066 mi). The air force also operates a fleet of 94 twin-engined turboprop Antonov An-32 and 73 Dornier Do 228 utility aircraft. In an effort to infuse fresh life into its transport fleet, the Indian Air Force will begin an upgrade programme for its Antonov An-32s and Dornier Do 228s in 2009.

Training Aircraft

The HPT-32 Deepak is IAF's basic flight training aircraft for cadets. Developed during the late 1970s, it has been in service with the IAF since 1984. The IAF uses the HAL HJT-16 Kiran mk.I for intermediate flight training of cadets, while the HJT-16 Kiran mk.II provides Stage II flight training. In 2004, the IAF placed an order for 66 BAE Hawk Mk 132 Advanced Jet Trainers in a deal worth over 1 billion GBP. Deliveries began in November, 2007 and induction in February, 2008. Pilot instructors and engineers were trained in the UK, and the aircraft is scheduled to replace the mk.II. HAL is developing the HJT-36 *Sitara* to replace the Kiran mk.I.

Helicopters

An important objective of the IAF is to support ground troops by providing air cover and by transporting men and essential commodities across the battlefield. For this purpose the Air Force maintains a fleet of helicopters. Helicopters in service with the IAF are:

Unmanned Aerial Vehicles

The primary role of unmanned aerial vehicles (UAVs) is to

provide aerial surveillance and reconnaissance. The IAF operates IAI Malat built Searcher II and Heron UAVs. Israel Aircraft Industries and Aeronautical Development Establishment (ADE). India's leading unmanned aerial vehicle research agency are also jointly developing three new UAVs.

UAVs can also be used as a *pilot-less target aircraft*. HAL *Lakshya*, indigenously developed pilotless target aircraft, was inducted into the IAF in July 2005. Another UAV, the HAL *Nishant* Remote Piloted Vehicle (RPV) has also been developed, with an endurance of over 3 hours. The UAV can be used to carry out ground attacks and aerial surveillance.

Ongoing Expansion

Future Aircraft

As of 2008, the Indian Air Force plans to induct 126 multi-role combat aircraft (with an option for an additional 74 aircraft), 280 Su-30MKI air superiority fighters (Ordered at cost of US$8.4 billion, 120 are already in service with the IAF), 220 HAL Tejas, 47 SEPECAT Jaguar combat aircraft. Additionally, the Indian Air Force has signed contracts for 66 BAE Hawk Mk.132 trainers (deliveries underway), 80+40 combat helicopters, 3 new Long Range UAVs, 6 mid-air refueling planes, 225+ HJT-36 Sitara Intermediate Jet Trainer aircraft and some additional medium-range transport aircraft. The Indian Air Force began the upgradation of its MiG-29 fleet in 2007. India awarded Russia a US$965 million contract to upgrade its multi-role MiG-29 into MiG-29SMT warplanes, on Monday March 10, 2008. According to the deal, Russia will re-arm the twin-engined MiG-29s with air-to-air missiles, and the upgraded MiGs will feature increased fuel capacity and state-of-the-art avionics.

Confirmed Sales

In early 2008, the IAF signed a deal to acquire 6 C-130J Super Hercules, modified for special mission roles, for US$1.06 billion. Lockheed Martin is expected to deliver the planes in 2011. In December 2008, India and Russia inked a deal for the supply of 80 Mi-17V-5 (also known as Mi-171) medium lift helicopters at a cost of US$1.2 billion. The two countries had earlier negotiated a price of $650 million, but early in 2008 Russia asked for a revision of the contract price. Russia is expected to deliver the Mi-171 to the IAF in 2010. The deal also envisages a US$405 million "offset" obligation by Russia. The new choppers, which have an 18,000 ft operational ceiling, will replace 50 Mi-8s currently in service with the IAF, some of which are over 35 years old, and boost IAF's capability to support high-altitude posts in Siachen and Ladakh sectors. The helicopter will come with the circuitry and hard points to carry weapons.

Under procurement

Because of delays in inducting the indigenous HAL Tejas, the IAF issued an Request of Intent (RoI) for the procurement of 126 multi-role combat aircraft to replace around 250 Cold War-era MiG-21 it operates. Contenders for the $10 Billion contract are the MiG-35 from Mikoyan of Russia, the Rafale from Dassault Aviation of France, the Eurofighter Typhoon, JAS 39 Gripen from Saab of Sweden, the F-16IN from Lockheed Martin and F/A-18E/F Super Hornet from Boeing. In May 2009, the IAF picked Airbus A330 multi-role tanker transport (MRTT) over Russia's Ilyushin Il-78 as the future tanker for the air force. The deal is worth approximately US$1 billion.

On May 26, 2009, the Indian Ministry of Defence invited bids for 22 combat helicopters and 15 heavy-lift helicopters in a deal worth US$2 billion. Companies which have expressed their interest in the tender include — Russia's Kamov and Mil Moscow Helicopter Plant, Europe's AgustaWestland and Eurocopter and United States' Bell Helicopter and Boeing. Boeing submitted its initial bid on Oct 23, 2009 offering the AH-64D Apache Longbow attack helicopter and the CH-47F Chinook heavy-lift, twin-rotor helicopters. On June 15, 2009, the IAF announced that it was interested in purchasing about 10 C-17 Globemaster III tactical military transport aircraft. The IAF will be sending a proposal to the Indian Defence Ministry to acquire these aircraft through US Government's Foreign Military Sales (FMS) route.

A tender for supply of 317 light helicopters will be floated by Ministry of Defence combining the requirements of Indian Air force (125) and Indian Army (197). Unnamed government official stated that Letters of Interest (LOI) have been sent to Kamov, Bell, Augusta Westland and Eurocopter. In February 2008, Bell withdrew from the race, citing differences in offset clause with the Government of India. HAL has also recently joined the race with its Light Observation Helicopter (LOH). Although it is still on the drawing board, HAL officials seem to be confident to deliver in time.

Under Development

HAL initiated the Light Combat Aircraft (LCA) programme in 1983 to develop a replacement aircraft for IAF's ageing MiG-21. After development during the 80s and 90s the first flight occurred in 2001. The aircraft has since been christened HAL Tejas. The IAF plans to induct 220 Tejas aircraft. It has ordered 28 limited production aircraft. These aircraft are expected to enter service in 2010.

In October 2007, India and Russia signed a pact to develop a Fifth Generation Fighter Aircraft. The Indian version will be a two-seater, air superiority fighter. Another agreement was signed between India's Hindustan Aeronautics and Russia's United Aircraft Corporation (UAC) in December 2008 which detailed the joint development and production the aircraft. Work on the program will start by mid-2009 and the program is expected to be completed by 2017. During this period, these companies will form a joint-venture for the development of a Multirole Transport Aircraft, which will replace the IAF's ageing fleet of Antonov An-32s. Both HAL and UAC will invest US$300 million each on the program.

HAL has also started design work on Medium Combat Aircraft (MCA) is a twin-engined 5th generation stealth multirole fighter. It will complement the HAL Tejas and the Sukhoi/HAL FGFA in the Indian Air Force. The main purpose of this aircraft is to replace the aging SEPECAT Jaguar & MiG-27.

In 2004, Defence Research and Development Organisation revived the Airavat Project, which was India's first attempt in developing an indigenous AEW aircraft. A $210 million deal signed with Brazil's Embraer in 2008 for the supply of three Embraer EMB-145 regional jets. India has sent a request for proposal to six vendors for the supply of Active Array Antenna Unit (AAAU) and various other sub-systems. These vendors include Israel's Elta, the European consortium EADS, France's Thales, Sweden's SAAB Erikson and the United State's Raytheon and Northrop Grumman.

HAL has developed HAL HJT-36 Sitara for the IAF which carried out its maiden test flight in 2003. These aircraft are scheduled to replace the aging HJT-16 Kiran mk.I as intermediate jet trainer. The company is developing an Light Combat Helicopter for the IAF based on HAL Dhruv. It is being designed to fit into an anti-infantry and anti-armour role and will be capable to operate from altitudes an 6,500 metre. First flight of HAL LCH (Light Combat Helicopter) is expected in 2009.

Aerospace Command

The IAF is setting up an aerospace command. This command will leverage space technology including satellites. The command will be utilised by all the three services of the Indian armed forces and also for civilian purposes by ISRO. On October 22, 2001, ISRO launched the Technology Experiment Satellite (TES). Its onboard 1-metre resolution camera was the testbed for Indian space based imagery intelligence. ISRO launched follow-up military satellite CARTOSAT-2A on 28 April, 2008. It carries a panchromatic camera (PAN) with a resolution less than 1-metre but lacks night time and cloudy weather observation capability. ISRO launched a sophisticated radar-imaging satellite on 20 April 2009 called RISAT-2. It is capable of imaging in all-weather conditions and has a resolution of one metre. ISRO has denied that the spacecraft is spy satellite; however, experts believe that the satellite will allow India's security agencies to monitor military activities and movements of suspected terrorists in neighboring countries as well as enable the IAF to carry out precise strikes against targets like terrorist training camps.

Surface to Air Missile Systems

- Barak SAM-India and Israel have agreed to expand their missile development cooperation with a longer-range version of their extended-range Barak ship defence system for the Indian Air Force.

- Trishul(Trident): Development of Trishul is complete. It has met the IAF requirements during its various developmental flight trials. DRDO is presently in dialogue with IAF for possible induction. Frontier India reports that Indian Air force is considering to induct small quantity to meet partial requirement of LLQRM (Low Level Quick Reaction Missile) System.. However it is not known if IAF has placed a formal order of Trishul SAM System.
- SPYDER (*S*urface-to-air *PY*thon and *DER*by): In June 2007, India signed a $250 million to purchase SPYDER mobile air defence missiles from Israel. The two countries signed an additional $4 billion deal for the joint-development of a medium range surface-to-air missiles. However, the procurement of SPYDER missiles was delayed because of an ongoing investigation against Israel Aerospace Industries and RAFAEL by Indian intelligence agencies for its alleged kickbacks in the Barak-I deal with the Indian Navy. In August 2008, a $2.5 billion deal was signed by India and Israel to develop an advanced version of the SPYDER.
- Maitri LLQRM (Low Level Quick Reaction Missile): DRDO is in talks with MBDA to develop Maitri LLQRM for Army, Air force and Navy. Sources said that DRDL is preparing feasibility report and is awaiting formal clearance from defence ministry.
- Akash: Indian Air force has approved the induction of Akash Missile System and had initiated the process of inducting the system. Akash has successfully demonstrated its performance through number of flight tests. DRDO and IAF jointly began a ten day intensive trial of Akash on December 13, 2007 aimed at making IAF familiar with the system.

IAF currently operates two squadrons of Akash. It is happy with the missile and is in the process of acquiring more squadrons for deployment in the North East.

Surface to Surface Missiles

- Prithvi II: 250 km Prithvi-II Ballistic Missile is under IAF service which could be used to target airfields, command and control centers etc.

Air to Surface Missiles

- DRDO-NPO Mashinostroeyenia Brahmos-Air launched version under Development

LIST OF REGIMENTS OF THE INDIAN ARMY

Indian Army Regiments

Infantry Regiments (29)

- Brigade of the Guards
- The Parachute Regiment
- Mechanised Infantry Regiment
- Punjab Regiment
- Madras Regiment
- The Grenadiers
- Maratha Light Infantry
- Rajputana Rifles
- Rajput Regiment
- Jat Regiment
- Sikh Regiment
- Sikh Light Infantry
- Dogra Regiment
- Garhwal Rifles
- Kumaon Regiment
- Assam Regiment
- Bihar Regiment
- Mahar Regiment
- Jammu & Kashmir Rifles
- Jammu & Kashmir Light Infantry
- Naga Regiment
- 1 Gorkha Rifles
- 3 Gorkha Rifles
- 4 Gorkha Rifles
- 5 Gorkha Rifles (Frontier Force)
- 8 Gorkha Rifles

- 9 Gorkha Rifles
- 11 Gorkha Rifles
- Ladakh Scouts.

Armoured Regiments (62)

- President's Bodyguard
- 1 Horse or Skinner's Horse
- 2 Lancers
- 3rd Cavalry
- 4 Horse or 'Hodson's Horse'
- 5 Armoured Regiment
- 6 Lancers
- 7 Cavalry
- 8 Cavalry
- 9 Horse or 'The Deccan Horse'
- 10 Armoured Regiment
- 11 Armoured Regiment
- 12 Armoured Regiment
- 13 Armoured Regiment
- 14 Horse or 'The Scinde Horse'
- 15 Armoured Regiment
- 16 Cavalry
- 17 Horse (The Poona Horse)
- 18 Cavalry
- 19 Armoured Regiment
- 20 Lancers
- Central India Horse (in 21st position)
- 40 Armoured Regiment
- 41 Armoured Regiment (India)
- 42 Armoured Regiment
- 43 Armoured Regiment-The only regiment in the Armoured Corps to hold the MBT Arjun as part of its standard weapons platform.
- 44 Armoured Regiment

- 45 Cavalry
- 46 Armoured Regiment
- 47 Armoured Regiment
- 48 Armoured Regiment
- 49 Armoured Regiment
- 50 Armoured Regiment
- 51 Armoured Regiment
- 52 Armoured Regiment
- 53 Armoured Regiment
- 61 Cavalry
- 62 Cavalry
- 63 Cavalry
- 64 Cavalry
- 65 Armoured Regiment
- 66 Armoured Regiment
- 67 Armoured Regiment
- 68 Armoured Regiment
- 69 Armoured Regiment
- 70 Armoured Regiment
- 71 Armoured Regiment
- 72 Armoured Regiment
- 73 Armoured Regiment
- 74 Armoured Regiment
- 75 Armoured Regiment-the only Indian armoured regiment to have been raised on foreign soil during the 1971 Indo-Pak war at Gadra Road (now in Pakistan)on 12 March 1972.
- 76 Armoured Regiment
- 81 Armoured Regiment
- 82 Armoured Regiment
- 83 Armoured Regiment
- 84 Armoured Regiment
- 85 Armoured Regiment
- 86 Armoured Regiment

- 87 Armoured Regiment
- 88 Armoured Regiment
- 89 Armoured Regiment
- 90 Armoured Regiment.

Units of the Regiment of Artillery

A few of the units of artillery are listed below:

- 37 (Coorg) Anti-Tank Regiment RIA
- 40 Field Regiment (Asal Uttar)
- 61 Medium Regiment
- 76 Field Regiment
- 216 Medium Regiment
- 163 Medium Regiment
- 168 Field Regiment
- 169 Field Regiment (Longewala)
- 195 Field Regiment (Banwat)
- 255 Field Regiment
- 286 Medium Regiment
- 311 Field Regiment
- 92 Medium Regiment
- 15 Medium Regiment
- 3342 msl regt
- 175 med regt=175 field regt
- [[70 Fd Regt(SAVIOURS)].

4

Indian Security Guards and Forces

NATIONAL SECURITY GUARDS

The National Security Guard is a Special Response Unit in India that has primarily been utilized for counter-terrorism activities and was created by the Cabinet Secretariat under the *National Security Guard Act* of the Indian Parliament in 1986. It works completely within the Central Paramilitary Force structure.

The NSG operates under the oversight of the Ministry of Home Affairs and is headed by the Director General of the Indian Police Service (IPS). The DG has always been an IPS officer whereas the recruitment is done from the Central Paramilitary Forces Of India and the Indian Armed Forces. The NSG members are also known as Black Cats because of the black nomex coveralls and balaclavas or assault helmets they wear.

FUNCTIONS

The NSG's roles include protecting VIPs, conducting anti-sabotage checks, rescuing hostages, neutralizing terrorist threats to vital installations, engaging terrorists and responding to hijacking and piracy.

The NSG is much sought after for VVIP security for high-risk VVIPs in India; this task is done by the Special Rangers Group of the NSG. The Special Action Group is the strike force in anti-terrorist and anti-hijack operations, supported by the SRG and others. The NSG's specific goals include:

- Neutralization of terrorist threats
- Handling hijacking situations in air and on land.

- Bomb disposal (search, detection and neutralisation of IEDs).
- PBI (Post Blast Investigation)
- Engaging and neutralizing terrorists in specific situations.
- Hostage Rescue.

The NSG has a total personnel strength of about 14,500. The NSG is modelled on Germany's GSG-9. It is a task-oriented force and has two complementary elements in the form of the *Special Action Group* (SAG) and the *Special Ranger Groups* (SRG). All the personnel are on deputation from Indian Armed Forces. The SAG is the offensive wing drawn from units of the Indian Army. The SRG consists of members from Central Police Organisations (CPOs) such as the Border Security Force (BSF), the Central Reserve Police Force (CRPF) and State Police forces and other units. The NSG Training Centre is a *Centre of Excellence* and the National Bomb Data Centre holds international conferences. Both are located at Manesar in Haryana. The NSG Headquarters Exchange is located at *Mehramnagar, Palam.*

History

The NSG was established under the *National Security Guard Act of 1986*. The NSG was formed after an analysis of 1984 Operation Blue Star. During this operation, in which the Indian Army removed Sikh militants who had seized control of the Golden Temple, there was significant civilian collateral casualties. The temple also suffered damages during that operation. The operation highlighted the need for a force specialising in counter-terrorist operations with greater efficiency.

The NSG commandos were first used to combat the insurgency movement in the Indian state of Punjab in 1986. They are now primarily utilised for counter-terrorist activities and have been continuing major combat operations in Jammu and Kashmir. NSG deployments are usually not made public, with most of its operations remaining classified.

Some of the NSG's known operations include:

- April 30, 1986-attack on Khalistani militants who took over the Golden Temple during Operation Black Thunder I

- May 12, 1988 — attack on Khalistani militants hiding in the Golden Temple during Operation Black Thunder II
- April 25, 1993 — rescue of hijacked plane Indian Airlines Boeing 737 by Islamic militants during Operation Ashwamedh
- October, 1998 — major combat missions in Jammu and Kashmir
- July 15, 1999 — rescue of 12 hostages held by armed terrorists who had stormed an apartment complex in Kashmir and killed 4 people
- September 25, 2002 — Operation Vajra Shakti to free hostages held by terrorists who had killed 96 worshippers at the Akshardham temple in Ahmedabad, Gujarat. They suffered their first combat death in this operation. A second commando, who was seriously injured and was in a coma, died after 18 months.
- November 26 2008 Mumbai attacks — Operation Black Tornado and Operation Cyclone to flush out terrorists & rescue hostages after multiple attacks across Mumbai, India. Major Sandeep Unnikrishnan and Hawaldar Gajender Singh Bisht of the Special Action Group lost their lives during the operations.

As on December 2008, Germany offered to give additional assistance and training to the NSG by the famous GSG-9. Criticism

There have been several occassions where the lack of proper transportation has hampered the response time of the unit. This was evident during the 1999 hijacking of Indian Airlines Flight 814 when the unit was stuck in rush hour traffic due to a lack of helicopters. During the Mumbai attacks, the unit was delayed due to lack of aircraft in Delhi and then lack of ground transportation in Mumbai.

In response to criticism of the time taken for the NSG commandos to arrive in Mumbai from their base in Manesar, Haryana during the November 2008 Mumbai attacks, the Government of India has decided to deploy NSG contingents in major cities across India like Mumbai, Kolkata, Hyderabad and Chennai. Most of the National Security Guards are assigned as bodyguards for various political leaders leaving a significantly lesser number of commandos who may be able to assist when the need arises.

Equipment

- SIG SG 551
- Heckler & Koch MP5
- Glock 17
- Glock 19
- Heckler & Koch PSG1
- Heckler & Koch 512

Upgrades after 26/11

- CornerShot Guns
- Wall Surveillance Radars
- Ghillie Suits
- Night Vision Devices
- Protective Goggles
- Thermal Imaging Cameras
- Mini Remotely Operated Vehicles
- by Indian Army Officer)

PARAMILITARY FORCES OF INDIA

The Paramilitary Forces of India (PMF) are those agencies of the Government of India which aid the operations of the law enforcement agencies of India and the Indian Armed Forces. With over a million personnel in active service, the PMF is one of the world's largest paramilitary organizations.

The Central Police Organizations (CPO) forms the first tier of the PMF while the Central Paramilitary Forces (CPF) forms the second tier. The primary difference between the two is that the CPO works independently or in coordination with the Indian Federal Agencies, State Police Forces and other Indian Law Enforcement Agencies, whereas the CPF works in close cooperation with the Indian Armed Forces (which includes the Indian Army, the Indian Navy and the Indian Air Force). During a war, the CPF would work directly under the control of the Armed Forces unlike the CPO. All branches of the PMF, excluding the Indian Coast Guard, are agencies of the Ministry of Home Affairs. The Coast Guard, a component of the CPF, is an agency of the Indian Defence Ministry and works in close coordination with the Indian Navy. Some of the administrative ranks of the paramilitary forces are shared with the Indian Police Service (IPS).

The PMF consists of several different components with a wide range of roles. Most of these forces, however, tend to share a broadly gendarmerie role and generally perform counter-insurgency or anti-terrorist missions. The Central Reserve Police Force, which primarily assists the Indian Police in maintaining law and order, is the largest of the paramilitary forces in India. Others, such as the Border Security Force (BSF) and Indo-Tibetan Border Police (ITBP), aid the Indian Army in guarding the international borders of India.

List of Central Police Organisations (CPO)

- Railway Protection Force-70,000 personnel who provide Police Security to Indian Railways (Headed by Indian Police Service Officer)
- Indian Home Guard: 600,000 personnel (Headed by Indian Police Service Officer)
- Civil Defence: 376,000 (Headed by Indian Police Service Officer)
- Special Protection Group: 3000 personnel (Headed by Indian Police Service Officer)
- The State Armed Police (Pradeshik)-450,000 persons who act as a mobile armed reserve maintained at key locations in some states and activated only on the orders from the Additional Commissioner of Police or higher-level. Armed constabulary are usually not in contact with the public until they are assigned to VIP duty or assigned to maintain order during fairs, festivals, athletic events, elections, and natural disasters. They may also be sent to quell outbreaks of student or labor unrest, organized crime, and communal riots; to maintain key guard posts; and to participate in antiterrorist operations. Depending on the type of

assignment, the Provincial Armed Constabulary may carry only lathis or they may be equipped with infantry weapons. (Headed by Indian Police Service Officer)

- Central Reserve Police Force: 250,000 personnel (210 battalions) (Headed by Indian Police Service Officer)
- Rapid Action Force-a 10 battalion semi-independent part of the CRPF trained to respond to sectarian violence. The Anti-Riot Police of the Indian Union. (Headed by Indian Police Service Officer)
- Commando Battalion for Resolute Action (COBRA): A 10,000 strong anti-Naxal force being raised under the command and control of the CRPF. (Headed by Indian Police Service Officer)

LIST OF CENTRAL PARAMILITARY FORCES (CPF)

- Border Security Force: 215,000 personnel (186 Battalions) (Headed by Indian Police Service Officer)
- National Security Guards: 7,500 personnel (Headed by Indian Police Service Officer)
- Central Industrial Security Force: 145,000 personnel (131 Battalions)(Headed by Indian Police Service Officer)
- Indo-Tibetan Border Police-60,500 (55 Battalions) (Headed by Indian Police Service Officer)
- Sashastra Seema Bal: 85,800 (78 Battalions) personnel which guard the Indo-Nepal and Indo-Bhutan Borders (Headed by Indian Police Service Officer)
- Special Frontier Force-10,000 personnel (Headed by Indian Police Service Officer)
- Rashtriya Rifles: 68,200 personnel (62 Battalions)(Headed by Indian Army Officer)
- Assam Rifles: 50,000 personnel (46 Battalions)(Headed by Indian Army Officer)

SPECIAL FRONTIER FORCE

The Special Frontier Force (SFF) is a paramilitary unit of India. It was conceived in the post Sino-Indian war period as a guerrilla force composed mainly of Tibetan refugees whose main goal was to conduct covert operations behind Chinese lines in case of another war between the People's Republic of China and India. Based in Chakrata, Uttarakhand, SFF is also known as the *Establishment* 22. The force was put under the direct supervision of the Intelligence Bureau, and later, the Research and Analysis Wing, India's external intelligence agency.

History

Ethnic Tibetans have been a part and parcel of the modern Indian Army for as long as it has existed. Independent formations of Tibetan (including Ladakhi, Bön, and Sikkimese) units were to patrol and police the lands they were native to. During the time of the Great Game, the British Indian Army began to employ Tibetans as spies, intelligence agents, and even covert militia in northern India and Tibet proper. At the time of Indian independence, the Northern Hills of India remained the most isolated and strategically overlooked territory of the subcontinent. When Tibet was invaded by the People's Liberation Army, India was in no position to militarily interfere. After the Chinese conquest of Tibet, Central Intelligence Agency and the Indian Intelligence Bureau established Mustang Base in Nepal, which trained Tibetans in guerilla warfare. The Mustang rebels were used to rescue the Dalai Lama from Chinese captivity, into exile in India.

Formation

After the Sino-Indian war and towards the end of 1962, after hectic lobbying by Intelligence Bureau (IB), the Nehru administration ordered the raising of an elite commando unit and specialized mountain divisions primarily composed of Tibetan resistance fighters. Chushi Gangdruk leaders were contacted for recruitment of Khampas into this new unit. An initial strength of 5000 men, mostly Khampas were recruited at its new Mountain Training Facility at Chakrata, Dehradun.

Established under the direct supervision of the Prime Minister, the unit under the operational command of IB and later R&AW, was designated the Special Frontier Force (SFF), and was primarily used for conducting clandestine intelligence gathering and commando operations along the Chinese Theatre. Initial training was conducted by the CIA paramilitary officers and the IB's own special operations unit. In 1968 SFF, with the help of the Aviation Research Centre which provided airlift facilities, became fully airborne-qualified and a dedicated mountain and jungle warfare unit. During this period the Indian government also formed the Ladakh Scouts and the Nubra Guards paramilitary force on similar lines. SFF was later incorporated in the Special Services Bureau (SSB) of R&AW.

The Organization

SFF is headed by the Inspector General (IG) who works under the supervision of Director General (DG) Security, Research and Analysis Wing (R&AW) who reports directly to the Director of R&AW. The current SFF force levels are around 10,000 men. Battalions have a strength of around 900, are composed of six companies each company consisting of 123 men. There is also a force of around 700 Gorkhas in the SFF at any given time. Transport is provided by the Indian Air Force's Sarasawa based 117 Helicopter Unit *Himalayan Dragons* which provides airlift capability with its HAL Dhruvs and Mi-17Sh Transport Helicopters. ARC also provides air surveillance facilities through the Chakrata Air Base near SFF HQ.

Training

Most training is still conducted at Chakrata, lasting nine months and is similar to India Army training, with extensive additional courses on guerrilla tactics, mountain and jungle warfare. All commandos are parachute qualified after five jumps, with three refresher jumps every year. SFF personnels are trained in four basic areas:

- Mountain: Experts in mountain and Arctic warfare, these men are trained to survive and fight in extreme conditions. Mountain troops' skills can be called on anywhere from the Siachen Glacier to the Himalayan ranges in the east. They are also known to have trained in the famed German Alpine Guides course at the Mountain Warfare School at Mittenwald and the High Altitude Warfare School at Gulmarg reaching proficiency levels that rival the best climbers in the world.

- Amphibious: This troop's combat divers are the outfit's amphibious experts. In essence, it provides a comparable amphibious warfare capability to the SFF as the MARCOS provide to the Indian Navy. While they have overlapping mission profiles, the Special Group clearly does not have as extensively maritime roles. There is close cooperation and cross-training between its amphibious troops and the MARCOS — and a rivalry exists between them.
- Air: Air Troop is the Special Group's free-fall parachuting specialists, tasked with jumping behind enemy lines, either on their own missions or to pave the way for other squadron troops. Air Troop also employ less conventional forms of air insertion such as micro-lites and powered parachutes. For HALO/HAHO combat jumps skydivers use square-type RAM parachutes which are more maneuverable also allow for softer, controlled landings than the standard round chutes.
- Jungle warfare: Jungle operations are considered to be one of the toughest in the world and more men here fall to nature than the enemy. The Special Group's Jungle troopers are the masters in jungle craft. They are skilled at carrying out deep interdiction and search and destroy operations for extended periods of time.

SFF Operations

SFF was raised with covert operations in mind, mainly along the Indo-China border, however SFF has been fielded by R&AW and the Indian government in various covert and overt operation theatres.

Current Roles

With warming of Indo-Chinese relations, SFF has moved out of covert operations to various other fields like counter-terrorism. The major functions of SFF in the present day scenario are as follows:

Counter-terrorism

One Squadron is responsible for counter-terrorism duties, with a team in a constant state of alert. The four squadrons rotate through this role on a six-monthly basis. Special Group teams regularly conduct CT operations in troubled Kashmir against militants on specific intelligence inputs.

Special Group

The Director General (DG) Security, Research and Analysis Wing (RAW) in 1982 dispatched 500 SFF operatives along with over 500 Indian Army special forces to Sarasawa for Counter Terrorist training. It is also thought that the selected troopers thereafter were sent to Israel for highly specialized training. These men formed the nucleus of an ultra-elite and highly classified new detachment, known as the *Special Group*.

The SFF Special Group is structured like the Special Air Service (SAS) Regiment, its headquarters supported by an Intelligence and Planning wing, a Training wing and a specialist Signals Troop which is solely responsible for support operations. Having four squadrons each made up of around 100 troopers, which are further divided into four troops. Each troop has a specialized role. The Special Group has a wide range of responsibilities, each requiring specific training and disciplines.Special Group is also the parent unit of elite National Security Guards(NSG). It is a volunteer force and persons are inducted only after a very tough probation and selection process.

Intelligence Gathering

Long Range Reconnaissance Patrols or Pathfinders must be able to remain hidden under the nose of the enemy for days or weeks on an end. The outfit was trained to do this against the Chinese but actually used the technique to great success in Pakistan-administered Kashmir and the fields of the northern state of Punjab.

Combat Air Control

With the emphasis on air power in modern warfare there comes a need for skilled combat air controllers, men on the ground calling in air strikes. There is usually a trooper specially trained to guide in attack aircraft for a strike, verbally or using Laser Designators. SFF Special Group troopers effectively demonstrated this capability during India's Kargil conflict with Pakistan in the summer of 1999.

Close Protection

The Special Group, along with the Special Protection Group (SPG) were the pioneers at close protection (CP) duties in India, having developed many of the protocols themselves, unique to the Indian subcontinent. Nowadays much of the VIP protection is the sole responsibility of the National Security Guards (NSG) and other specialized provincial units.

Training Foreign Military

Over the years, the Special Group has shared their expertise with a few friendly nations like Maldives and Nepal, training their own special forces. The government also gets political benefits from such arrangements.

SPECIAL PROTECTION GROUP

The Special Protection Group (SPG) is the executive protection agency of the Government of India. It is responsible for the protection of the Prime Minister of India, other top officials, and their immediate families. The force was established in 1985 after the assassination of Indira Gandhi. It is one of many Indian law enforcement agencies.

The work of the Special Protection Group was more organised after the assassination of Rajiv Gandhi on May 21, 1991, (who was, at that time, not under SPG cover since his term as Prime Minister had ended). After the Rajiv Gandhi assassination, there have been no successful attempts to attack the Prime Minister or the Prime Minister's family members.

The Special Protection Group has about 3,000 personnel. Recruits are drawn from police forces as well as National Security Guards commandos, who undergo training similar to that conducted by the United States Secret Service. The officer cadre is mainly Indian Police Service (IPS) officers from various state/ central cadres.

The Special Protection Group provides proximate security to protectees, including protection provided from close quarters, journey on foot, road, rail, aircraft, watercraft or any other means of transport, and includes places of functions, engagements, residence, etc. They comprise ring round teams, isolation cordons, the sterile zone, and the rostrum and access control to the person or members of his immediate family. The Special Protection Group, over a period of time, grew both in size as well as in specialisation.

Organisation

The SPG is divided broadly into the following four categories:

- Operations: Looks after the actual protection duties. In the Operations Branch, there are components like the Communications Wing, Technical Wing and Transport Wing.
- Training: Deals with the training of personnel on a continuous basis. The SPG imparts training in physical efficiency, marksmanship, anti-sabotage checks, communication and other operative aspects connected with close protection drills and having a bearing on VVIP security with a view to maintaining a high level of physical fitness and to fine-tune the operational skills of SPG Officers. The training programme is constantly reviewed and updated to effectively thwart threats from newer areas and in keeping with existing threat perception.
- Intelligence and Tours: Threat assessment, internal intelligence pertaining to personnel, verification of character and antecedents, tours and other allied jobs.
- Administration: Deals with personnel, procurement and other related matters.

History

Before 1981, the security of the Prime Minister of India at the Prime Minister's residence was the responsibility of the Special Security District of the New Delhi Police under the charge of Deputy Commissioner of Police (DCP). In October 1981, a Special Task Force (STF) was raised by the Intelligence Bureau (IB) to provide ring-round and escort to the Prime Minister in and out of New Delhi. After the assassination of Prime Minister Indira Gandhi in October 1984, a review was undertaken by a Committee of Secretaries and it was decided to entrust security of the Prime Minister to a Special Group under unitary and direct control of a designated Officer and the STF to provide immediate security cover both in New Delhi and outside. These decisions were taken as short-term measures.

Then on February 18, 1985, the Ministry of Home Affairs set up the *Birbal Nath Committee* to go into the issue in its entirety and submit its recommendation. In March 1985, the *Birbal Nath Committee* submitted its recommendations of raising a Special Protection Unit (SPU). On 30 March 1985, the President of India created 819 posts for the unit under the Cabinet Secretariat. The SPU was then re-christened *Special Protection Group* and the post of IGP was re-designated as Director.

The SPG came into being on 8 April 1985 when Dr. S. Subramaniam, then Joint Director (VIP Security) in the Intelligence Bureau assumed office. Creation of the SPG required an elaborate exercise in order to clearly delineate responsibility of various agencies concerned with the security of the Prime Minister. The provisions contained in the *Blue Book*, which lays down security guidelines for the protection of the Prime Minister, had to be harmoniously blended with this new concept of proximate security.

IB and the State/UT Police concerned were responsible for coordination, collection and dissemination of intelligence affecting VIP security. State/UT Police and the SPG were responsible for providing physical security arrangements for the Prime Minister, while the IB was to provide the required intelligence inputs to these operational agencies. The SPG functioned as a security group purely on the strength of an Executive Order for three years without a legislation, from April 1985 to June 1988.

The SPG was constituted and trained specially to provide protection to Prime Minister Rajiv Gandhi, in view of the threats to him from several sources. But, the organisation created for the proximate security of Prime Minister Gandhi, did not contemplate provision of protection to him when he ceased to be Prime Minister, and faced magnified threats. SPG cover for Rajiv Gandhi was withdrawn once he ceased to be Prime Minister. After the assassination of Rajiv Gandhi in May 1991, the *SPG Act* was amended in 1991 to provide security to former Prime Ministers and their immediate families for a period of 5 years from the date on which the former Prime Minister ceased to hold office.

The SPG cover for Sonia Gandhi & her children lapsed in December 1994, and has been extended for 10 years from the date Rajiv Gandhi was demitted from office as Prime Minister. An increase of about 40% was made in the 1997-98 Union Budget in the allocation for the SPG. The then-incumbent Union Finance Minister, P. Chidambaram, allocated Rs. 75.59 crores (755.9 million) for 1997-98, reflecting pressure on the SPG and expansion of the security cover provided by SPG.

CENTRAL RESERVE POLICE FORCE

The Central Reserve Police Force (CRPF) is a paramilitary security agency/Force functioning under the aegis of Ministry of Home Affairs(MHA), Government of India. The CRPF's primary role lies in assisting the State/Union Territories in police operations to maintain law and order and contain insurgency. It came into existence as the Crown Representative's Police on 27 July 1939. After Indian Independence, it became the Central Reserve Police Force on enactment of the CRPF Act on 28 December 1949.

Besides Law and Order and counter-insurgency duties, the role of CRPF in the General Elections, held repeatedly during the past few years, has been very significant and vital. This is especially true for the trouble-ridden states of J&K, Bihar and in the North East. During the Parliamentary elections of September 1999, the CRPF played a major role in the security arrangements. The CRPF is the largest paramilitary force in the world with 210 battalions besides various establishments. Of late, CRPF contingents are also being deployed in UN missions.

History

- The CRPF was derived from the CRP (Crown Representative Police) on 27 July 1939 with 2 Battalions in Nimach, Madhya Pradesh. Its primary duty at the time was to protect the British residents in sensitive states of India.
- In 1949, the CRP was renamed under the CRPF Act. During the 1960s, many state reserve police battalions were merged

with the CRPF. The CRPF has been active against foreign invasion and domestic insurgency.

- On 21 October 1959, Dy.S.P. Karam Singh and 20 soldiers were attacked by the Chinese army at Hot Springs in Ladakh resulting in 10 casualties. The survivors were imprisoned. Since then, 21 October is observed as Police Commemoration day.
- During the 1965 India-Pakistan War, two companies consisting of 150 men of the 2nd Battalion of the CRPF defeated an infantry brigade consisting of 1600 men of the Pakistan Army at Kanjar Kot in Gujarat.
- The CRPF guarded the India-Pakistan border until 1965, at which point the Border Security Force was created for that purpose.
- On 13 December 2001, the CRPF troopers killed all five terrorists who had entered the premises of the Indian Parliament at New Delhi. In 2005, the CRPF troops killed all terrorists who had stormed the Ram Temple at Ayodhya.
- In recent years, the Government of India has decided to follow up on recommendations of the Indian cabinet to use each security agency for its mandated purpose. As a result, the counterinsurgency operations in India has been entrusted to the CRPF.
- In 2008 a wing called Combat Battalions for Resolute Action (COBRA) was added to the CRPF to counter the Naxalite movement.
- On September 2 2009, 5000 CRPF soldiers were deployed for a search and rescue mission to find the then Andhra Pradesh chief minister Y. S. Rajasekhara Reddy whose helicopter went missing over the Nallamalla Forest Range in Andhra Pradesh.This was the largest search operation ever mounted in India.

Current Role and Strength

As of [2010], the CRPF is charged with securing the Kashmir valley except in some areas like Tral. The CRPF is headed by a Director general and is divided into ten administrative sectors, each headed by an Inspector General. Each Sector consists of one or more administrative and/or Operational Ranges, headed by an officer of the rank of Deputy Inspector General (DIG) of Police. Now, Group Centres are also headed by DIGs.

There are 210 CRPF battalions of approximately 720 constables each. Each battalion is commanded by an officer designated as Commandant, and consists of six CRPF companies, each comprising of roughly 120 constables. Each company is headed by an Assistant Commandant. The Home Ministry is planning to increase the strength of the force by adding 35 more battalions(30,000 personnel approx.) in the coming years.

The Rapid Action Force

The Rapid Action Force (RAF) is a specialised 10 battalion wing of the Indian Central Reserve Police Force. It was formed in October 1992, to deal with communal riots and related civil unrest. The battalions are numbered from 99 to 108.

Weapons

CRPF uses basic Infantry weapons such as:

1. FN 35 and Glock 17 9 mm pistols
2. Heckler & Koch MP5 replacing the Carbine 1A 9 mm sub-machine guns
3. INSAS 5.56 mm assault rifles replacing the FN FAL, 1A1, 1C, AKM and V.58 7.62 mm assault rifles
4. INSAS 5.56 mm light machine guns replacing the 7.62 mm FN MAG, Bren L4 and the.50 cal Browning M2HB machine guns
5. Dragunov, Mauser SP66 and Heckler & Koch MSG-90 7.62 mm sniper rifles
6. AGS-17 Plamya 30 mm automatic grenade launcher
7. M40 RCL 106 mm and Carl Gustav 84 mm recoiless rifles.

In addition to these, CRPF also uses land mine detectors, Light Machine-Guns and Heavy-Machine-Guns, sterling carbine9mm.

Women in the CPRF

The CRPF is the only Paramilitary Force in the world to have two battalions staffed entirely by women. The first battalion was raised in 1986 with its headquarters at New Delhi. The second battalion came into existence in 1996 at Gandhinagar, Gujarat.

The Green Force

Another specialised outfit of the CRPF is the Green Force. The force has been able to effectively check environmental degradation and sustain the regeneration of local flora and fauna. Every year Green Force personnel plant lakhs (one lakh = one hundred thousand) of trees in various parts of the country.

CENTRAL INDUSTRIAL SECURITY FORCE

It was set up under an act of Parliament on March 10, 1969 with a strength of 2,800. CISF was subsequently made an armed force of the Union of India by another act of Parliament passed on June 15, 1983. Its current strength is 105,000.The strength will be raised to 145,000 by 2-3 years.

It is directly under the federal Ministry of Home Affairs and its headquarters are at New Delhi.

The CISF provides security cover to 269 industrial units located all over India. Industrial Sectors like Atomic Power Plants, Space Installations, Defence Production Units, Mints, Oil Fields and Refineries, Major Ports, Heavy Engineering, Steel Plants, Barrages, Fertilizer units, Airports and Hydro electric/thermal power plants, Indian border, Plants producing Indian currency are protected by CISF. Most of these installations are located in difficult terrains of the country with harsh climatic conditions.

CISF also provides consultancy services to private industries as well as other organizations within the Indian government. The consulting wing has amongst its clients some of the renowned business houses and organisations of India including TISCO Jamshedpur; SEBI Hqrs. Mumbai; Vidhana Soudha,Bangalore; Orissa Mining Co.,Bhubaneswar; AP Assembly, Hyderabad; Bangalore Metropolitan Transport Corp., HIL Kerala, IARI, Delhi; NBRI, Lucknow and Electronics City, Bangalore. The scope of CISF's consulting practice includes security consulting and fire protection consulting.

Raising and Charter

It was set up under an act of the Indian Parliament on March 10, 1969 with a strength of around 2,800 personnel and as the name suggests, it was created for the better protection and security of Industrial Undertakings. There was a limitation though, that industries to be provided protection should be wholly owned by the Central Government, which has since been modified so that the industries can now be a joint venture with the Central Government. However the role of CISF has undergone a diversification and it now also protects airports, seaports, metro rail networks, government buildings, heritage monuments (including the Taj Mahal and others), Opium and alkaloids extractions, nuclear power plants, and space installations. It has also moved into the fields of VIP security as well as Disaster management.

CISF to protect private sector

The Indian Parliament on 25th February 2009 paved the way for providing Central Industrial Security Force security to private and cooperative establishments across the country for a fee with the passage of the CISF(Amendment) Bill, 2008. The Bill, which was passed by Rajya Sabha on February 19 and Lok Sabha on 25th February 2009, also provides for deployment of CISF to protect Indian missions abroad and its participation in the UN peacekeeping operations. CISF has started providing security to Infosys Bangalore office from July 31st 2009 for a fee.

Airport Security

The CISF controls airport security at all commercial airports in India. Airport security, in the past, was under the control of the Airport Police (under the State Government). However, following the hijacking of Indian Airlines Flight 814 in 1999, the topic of handing over security of the airports to the CISF was first proposed. While this proposal lay low for the next two years, the Central Government woke up to the security threat after the September 11, 2001 attacks in the United States of America and decided to implement the suggestion. The Jaipur Airport was the first airport that came under the CISF's control on 03rd feb 2000. Following this, majority of the commercial airports in India were brought under its purview.. As of now CISF is protecting a total of 54 international and domestic airports in the country.

Uniqueness

CISF is unique as a Force of its kind in that it has a well trained Fire Wing comprising 4625 Officers and personnel giving Fire Protection to 77 industries. As of 2006, it remains one of the largest *central paramilitary forces* in India with strength of nearly 105,000 with perhaps *no parallel* in the entire world for a Government agency providing security to such a large number (269) industries with thousands of million rupees worth of assets. It is shaping up as an elite Force protecting the *critical infrastructure* of India. It is unique due to multifunctional duties and best performance

INDIAN POLICE SERVICE

The Indian Police Service, simply known as Indian Police or IPS, is one of the three All India Services of the Government of India; other two being the Indian Administrative Service (IAS) and Indian Forest Service (IFS). In 1948, a year after India gained independence from Britain, the Imperial Police (IP) was replaced by the Indian Police Service. The IPS is not a law enforcement agency in its own right; rather it is the body to which all senior police officers belong regardless of the agency for whom they work.

Objectives

The First Police Commission, appointed on 17th August, 1860, contained detailed guidelines for the desired system of police in India and defined police as a governmental department to maintain order, enforce the law, and prevent and detect crime. The Indian Police Service is not a force itself but a service providing leaders and commanders to staff the state police and all-India Para-Military Forces. Its members, who are all at least university graduates, are the senior officers of the police. With the passage of time Indian Police Service's objectives were updated and redefined, the roles and functions of an Indian Police Service Officer are as follows:

- To fulfill duties based on broader responsibilities, in the areas of maintenance of public peace and order, crime prevention, investigation, and detection, collection of intelligence, VIP security, counter-terrorism, border policing, railway policing, tackling smuggling, drug trafficking, economic offences, corruption in public life, disaster management, enforcement of socioeconomic legislation, bio-diversity and protection of environmental laws etc.

- Leading and commanding the Indian Intelligence Agencies like Research and Analysis Wing (RAW), Intelligence Bureau (IB), Central Bureau of Investigations (CBI),Crime Investigation Department (CID) etc., Indian Federal Law Enforcement Agencies, Civil and Armed Police Forces in all the states and union territories.
- Leading and commanding the Para-Military Forces of India (PMF) Central Police Organisations (CPO) like Border Security Force (BSF), Central Reserve Police Force (CRPF), Indo-Tibetan Border Police (ITBP), National Security Guard (NSG), Rashtriya Rifles, Central Industrial Security Force (CISF), Vigilance Organisations, Indian Fedral Law Enforcement Agencies, Assam Rifles, etc.
- Serve at head of the departments in policy making in the Ministries and Departments of Central and State Governments and public sector undertakings both at centre and states, Government of India.
- To interact and coordinate closely with the members of other All India Services and Central Civil Services and also with the Indian Armed Forces.
- Last but not the least, to lead and command the force with courage, uprightness, dedication and a strong sense of service to the people.
- Endeavour to inculcate in the police forces under their command such values and norms as would help them serve the people better.
- Inculcate integrity of the highest order, sensitivity to aspirations of people in a fast-changing social and economic milieu, respect for human rights, broad liberal perspective of law and justice and high standard of professionalism.

History

Reforms ordered by the Supreme Court (1996-2006)

Prakash Singh, one of the former Director Generals of Police of the states of Assam and subsequently Uttar Pradesh and finally Director General of the Border Security Force, initiated a Public Interest Litigation (PIL) in the Supreme Court of India, asking the court to investigate measures to reform the police forces across India in order to have the proper rule of law and significantly improve security across India.

Several measures were identified in order to professionalize the police in India:

- A mid or high ranking police officer must not be transferred more frequently than 2 years
- The state government cannot ask the police force to hire someone nor can they choose who the Chief Commissioner will be
- There must be separate departments and staff for investigation and a separate one for patrolling

3 new authorities will be created in each state, to prevent political interference in the police and also to make the police accountable for their heavy-handedness, which will include the creation of:

- A State Security Commission for policies and direction
- A Police Establishment Board, which will decide the selection, promotions and transfers of police officers and other staff
- A Police Complaints Authority, to inquire into allegations of police misconduct.

In 2006, due to a lack of action by all the state governments in India, the supreme court ordered the state governments to report to it why the reform measures outlined were not implemented.

After being questioned in front of the judges of the Supreme Court of India, the state governments are finally starting to reform the police forces and give them the operational independence they need for fearless and proper law enforcement.

Examination and Training

To serve in the IPS one has to pass the Civil Services Examination or be elevated from the state cadre, which is conducted by the Union Public Service Commission, every year. This examination is a common examination conducted for selection to the other one of the other All India Services, as well as various other Group A and Group B services under the Central Government. Taking the Civil Services Examination, a three-stage competitive selection process consisting of a preliminary exam, a main exam, and an interview is the only way to get in to IPS as with many other civil service bodies. This Civil Services Examination is administered by the Union Public Service Commission once a year.

At stage one, there is an objective type examination called the Preliminary examination. This is a qualifying examination and only the candidates who clear this can appear for the next stage called the Main examination. In the Main examination each candidate has to select two optional subjects, apart from which all candidates have to take a General Studies, Essay and compulsory language paper and English paper. Preliminary examination consists of General Studies & Optional 1. On clearing this candidate would be allowed to write mains, which consists of nine papers.

After being selected for the IPS, candidates are allocated to their Cadres. There is one cadre in each Indian state, except for three joint cadres: Assam-Meghalaya, Manipur-Tripura, and Arunachal Pradesh-Goa-Mizoram-Union Territories (AGMUT).

Each state and union territory of India has a state police force, headed by the Commissioner of Police (State) or Director General of Police (DGP). It is controlled by the Chief Minister and Home Minister of the state/union territory.

The state police is responsible for maintaining law and order in townships of the state and the rural areas. States such as Tamil Nadu and Maharashtra have taken steps to get their police force trained by advanced police training schools notably the Atlanta City Police of the USA and the World Police Academy of Canada. The Tamil Nadu state police is at the forefront of advancement with the Tamil Nadu Police Academy which now is seeking university status. The advanced training that the Tamil Nadu Police undergo vary from fraud investigation to advanced patrol training. This training when completed will make the Tamil Nadu Police one of the most advanced police forces in India. The World Police Academy and the Atlanta City Police USA are known across the world for their excellence in police training.

The World Police Academy Canada has been spoken of as being nation specific and is therefore focused on the specific requirements of the Indian Police. City Police Services on the other hand are known for their one lesson fits all attitude. The Indian Police Forces are to be commended for their determination and focus at securing the best possible training provided to their officers.

Ranks and insignia of Non-Gazetted Officers

- Three stars with a red and blue ribbon at the outer edge of the shoulder straps (Same insignia as a Junior Commissioned Officer in the Indian Army who wears a red and yellow ribbon bar, but perhaps more closely equivalent to the rank of Subedar-Major who dons the national emblem with similar ribbons)
- Inspector of Police
- Two stars with a red and blue ribbon at the outer edge of the shoulder straps (Same insignia as a Subedar in the Indian Army)
- Sub-Inspector of Police
- One Star with a red and blue ribbon at the outer edge of the shoulder straps (Same insignia as a Naib Subedar in the Indian Army)
- State Police Service Probationary Rank
- State Police Officers are first appointed as ASIs when in probationary period (a time span of 2 years) and in the 3rd year officers are promoted to the rank of Deputy Superintendent of Police (DySP) or Assistant Commissioner of Police (ACP) immediately as their probationary period ends.
- Assistant Sub-Inspector not in charge of sub-division with less than 2 years service

- Three chevrons points facing downwards / Navy Blue colored epaulettes with three golden stripes on the Shoulder (Same insignia as a Havildar in the Indian Army)
- Head Constable or Police Sergent.
- Two chevrons points facing downwards / Navy Blue colored epaulettes with two golden stripes on the Shoulder (Same insignia as a Naik in the Indian Army)
- Senior Police Constable or Police Constable (Selection Grade) or Police *Naik.*
- No rank insignia (equivalent to Sepoy in the Indian Army)
- Police Constable

INDIAN CAVALRY CORPS

The Indian Cavalry Corps was a formation of the British Indian Army in World War I. It was formed in France in December 1914. It remained in France until March 1916, when it was broken up. The high number of officer casualties suffered early on had an effect on its later performance. British officers that understood the language, customs, and psychology of their men could not be quickly replaced, and the alien environment of the Western Front had some effect on the soldiers.

The corps consisted of the 1st Indian Cavalry Division and the 2nd Indian Cavalry Division, and together with the Indian Corps formed 2nd Indian Cavalry Division

History

The 2nd Indian Cavalry Division was a regular division of the British Indian Army. The division sailed for France from Bombay on October 16, 1914, under the command of Major General G A Cookson. During the war the Division would serve in the trenches as infantry due to the difference on troop levels each Cavalry Brigade once dismounted formed a dismounted regiment. In March 1916 the 2nd Indian Cavalry Division was attached to the British Fourth Army. On July 1, 1916 the Secunderabad Cavalry Brigade moved into a reserve position on the Somme, ready to exploit any breakthrough. The same Brigade was sent up again on July 14, to Montauban to support the attack on the Bazentin-Longueval ridge. At 17.30 the leading two regiments were ordered to advance between High Wood and Delville Wood. The British 7th Dragoon Guards and the Indian 20th Deccan Horse galloped forward to a position between the woods. But little could be achieved. At 03.30 on July 15, they returned to Montauban, having suffered casualties of 74 men and 110 horses.

Cavalry units were again brought forward on September 15, to support the attack on Flers Courcelette, but were not drawn into the fighting and played no further part in the Battle of the Somme, except as labour units in reserve.

The high number of officer casualties suffered early on had an effect on its later performance. British officers that understood the language, customs, and psychology of their men could not be quickly replaced, and the alien environment of the Western Front had some effect on the soldiers. The 2nd Indian Cavalry Division was renamed the 5th Cavalry Divisions on 26 November 1916 and attached to the 5th Army.

FORMATION

5TH (MHOW) CAVALRY BRIGADE

6th (Inniskilling) Dragoons
2nd Lancers (Gardner's Horse)
38th King George's Own Central India Horse
Signal Troop

3RD (AMBALA) CAVALRY BRIGADE

13th Hussars
3rd Skinner's Horse
18th King George's Own Lancers
Signal Troop

9TH (SECUNDERABAD) CAVALRY BRIGADE

7th (Princess Royal's) Dragoon Guards
20th Deccan Horse
34th Prince Albert Victor's Own Poona Horse
Signal Troop

CANADIAN CAVALRY BRIGADE

Joined the Division June 1916
Royal Canadian Dragoons
Lord Strathcona's Horse
Fort Garry Horse
Canadian Cavalry Brigade Machine Gun Squadron
The Indian Expeditionary Force A.

THE 1ST INDIAN CAVALRY DIVISION IN 1914-1918

The history of the 1st Indian Cavalry Division

A Division of the Indian Army which was renamed as the 4th Cavalry Division in November 1916. The Division arrived in France on 7 October 1914 and remained on the Western Front in France and Flanders, taking part in the many engagements before being broken up in February 1918, but principally:

1917

The German Retreat to the Hindenburg Line (14 March-5 April 1917)

The Battle of Cambrai (20 November-30 December 1917)

INDIAN ARMY MEDICAL CORPS

Very little is known of the medical organisations that existed in the various Armies in this country in the ancient times. However, Kautilya's Arthashastra shows that during battles, physicians with surgical instruments (Sastra, medicines and drugs in their hands besides women with prepared food and beverages) used to stand behind the fighting men. Similarly, from Sushruta Samhita, it is seen that a physician fully equipped with Medicines would live in a camp not remote from the royal pavilion and there the persons wounded by arrows and other war projectiles, or those who had imbibed poison used to be treated. A physician in the King's service used to adopt certain measures to protect the life of his royal highness from secret poisoning. The physician well versed in technical sciences and with knowledge of other allied branches of study was held in high esteem by the King and others.

The Army Medical Corps came into existence as a homogeneous corps of officers and men on the pattern of the Royal Army Medical Corps on 03 Apr 1943 by the amalgamation of the Indian Medical Service, the Indian Medical Department and the Indian Hospital Corps. The Corps was formed as a wartime necessity for attracting suitably qualified men for service in a rapidly expanding army.

INDIAN MEDICAL SERVICE

The history of the Indian Medical Service (IMS) dates back to 1612 when on the formation of the East India Company into a joint stock business, the Company appointed John Woodall as their first Surgeon General. Under him, medical Corps officers (mainly civilians) were recruited more or less on individual contracts. The company expanded activities in various part of the country which necessitated the formation and maintenance of regular bodies of troops in India. As a consequence, they commenced employing Military Surgeons from 1745 onwards. It was not until 1764 that these Surgeons were made into regular establishment of the company's armies. Thus the Bengal Medical Service was formed in 1764, the Madras Medical Service in 1767 and the Bombay Medical Service in 1779 for the three Presidency Armies of Bengal, Madras and Bombay respectively. Three medical services were in due course combined into one Indian Medical Services (IMS) in Apr 1886 under a Surgeon General to the Govt of India. The designation was later changed into the Director General, Indian Medical Service. In 1913, the appointment was designated as the Director of Medical Services in India.

Until the First Word War the IMS was pre-dominantly civil in character, but gradually from 1912 onwards those employed in civil duties became less and less in number. Indianisation of this service commenced from 1915 onwards. Sarjoo Coomar Goodeve Chauckerbutty was the first Indian to enter the service as Assistant Surgeon on 24 Jan 1855. Until Burma was separated in 1935, the IMS was catering for the civil and military needs of Burma also. During this period, the IMS was assisted by the members of the Indian Medical Department (IMD) and Indian Hospital Corps (IHC).

The idea of re-organising the medical services into a separate Medical Corps exclusively for the Defence Services was first conceived in 1939 with the out break of World War II and with the formation of Indian Army Medical Corps in 1943, the extinction of the IMS as such was merely a matter of time. On 14 Aug 1947 the service was finally wound up.

Indian Medical Department

The history of the Indian Medical Department (IMD) dates back to 19th century. Initially starting as compounders and dressers in the three Presidency Medical Services they became Sub Surgeons and later on as Indian Medical Assistants in Indian Regiments. In 1868, they were redesignated as Hospital Assistants. In 1900, the Senior Hospital Assistants were granted the rank of Viceroy's Commissioned Officers and in 1910 the designation was finally changed to Sub Assistant Surgeons of IMD. They were primarily for work with the Indian troops.

Indian Hospital Corps

The Indian Hospital Corps was formed on 01 June 1920 by combining the Army Hospital Corps and Army Bearer Corps and the subordinate personnel of Indian Station Hospitals, comprising persons of categories then considered necessary for hospitals, field ambulances and other medical units.

Army Hospital Corps

In the days of the East India Company there were no regular formations or units charged with the task of looking after the health of troops. In 1881 the British Regimental Hospitals gave way to British Station Hospitals and they needed subordinate persons.

So in 1981, the Army Hospital Native Corps was formed of menials of the disbanded British Regimental Hospitals, Compounders, dressers, ward coolies, barbers, shop coolies, cooks, bhistis and sweepers and were designated as, Hospital Attendants. With the abolition of the Presidency Armies by the Government and the evolution of the Army into 10 Divisions, the Army Hospital Native Corps was re-organised into 10 Companies as Army Hospital Corps.

Army Bearer Corps

It was not until 1901 that the necessity for a proper corps of bearers was accepted by the Government and in this year, Dooly Bearers and Kahars were enlisted in the newly formed Army Bearer Corps, which came under the Medical Department. The Army Hospital Corps persons did the menial service in British Station Hospitals and the Army Bearer Corps provided persons for the carriage of the sick and wounded. In 1903, the Army Bearer Corps was re-organised into 10 Division Companies and the duties of these Companies in war were to carry stretchers and doolies, and in peace for general work in hospital.

Station Hospitals

Indian troops had no station hospital facilities until 1918, and had to depend entirely on their regimental hospitals. In October 1918, Station Hospitals for Indian troops were sanctioned. Ward orderlies and followers came from Army Hospital Corps and bearers were provided by the Army Bearer Corps.

The IHC initially was divided into 10 Division Companies corresponding to the 10 existing Military Divisions in India and Burma and they were located at Peshwar, Rawalpindi, Lahore, Quetta, Mhow, Poona, Meerut, Lucknow, Secunderabad and Rangoon. The whole corps was re-organised on command basis during the year 1929-32 and thus there were five companies of the IHC in 1932, No 1 Company at Rawalpindi, No 2 Company at Lucknow, No 3 Company at Poona. No 4 Company at Quetta and No 5 Company at Rangoon. On separation of Burma in 1935, No 5 Company of IHC was formed as Burma Hospital Corps and this left four companies of IHC.

Indian Army Medical Corps

World War II was responsible for rapid developments. The idea of having a homogeneous corps by amalgamating IMS, IMD gradually took shape and Indian Army Medical Corps (IAMC) came into being on 03 Apr 1943. On the formation of the IAMC, the IHC HQs at Poona became the Administrative Headquarters of the IAMC in May 1943. After Independence of the country, the Corps has made a steady progress. The men enjoy combatant status. The post of Director General Armed Forces Medical Services was created in 1949 as coordinating head of the med services of the Army, Navy and Air Force.

Army Medical Corps

The IAMC was re-designated as Army Medical Corps with effect from 26 January 1950.

Military abbreviations applicable to the Medical Corps

Within the military, Medical officers could occupy a number of roles that were dependent on experience, rank and location. Within military documentation numerous abbreviations were used to identify these roles of which the following are some of the most common:

- ADMS = Assistant Director Medical Services
- DADMS = Deputy Assistant Director of Medical Services
- DDGMS = Deputy Director General Medical Services
- DDMS = Deputy Director Medical Services
- DG = Director General (Medical Services)
- DGAMS = Director General Army Medical Services (at War Office, London)
- DGMS = Director General Medical Services
- DMS = Director Medical Services
- EMO = Embarkation Medical Officer
- GDMO = General Duties Medical Officer (a junior army doctor attached to a field unit before commencing higher specialist training)
- MCD = Military Clinical Director (a senior army Consultant)
- MO = Medical Officer
- OMO = Orderly Medical Officer
- PMO = Principal Medical Officer
- RMO = Regimental Medical Officer (normally an army General Practitioner with additional training in Pre-Hospital Emergency Care and Occupational Medicine)
- SMO = Senior Medical Officer (normally a senior army General Practitioner)

5

Royal Engineers and Tank Regiment

The Corps of Royal Engineers, usually just called the Royal Engineers (RE), and commonly known as the Sappers, is one of the corps of the British Army. It provides military engineering and other technical support to the British Armed Forces. It is headed by the Chief Royal Engineer. The Regimental Headquarters and the Royal School of Military Engineering are in Chatham in Kent, England. The corps is divided into several regiments, barracked at various places in the United Kingdom of Great Britain and Northern Ireland and Germany.

HISTORY

The Royal Engineers trace their origins back to the military engineers brought to England by William the Conqueror and claim over 900 years of unbroken service to the crown. Engineers have always served in the armies of the Crown; however, the origins of the modern corps, along with those of the Royal Artillery, lie in the Board of Ordnance established in the 15th century. In 1717, the Board established a Corps of Engineers, consisting entirely of commissioned officers. The manual work was done by the Artificer Companies, made up of contracted civilian artisans and labourers. In 1782, a Soldier Artificer Company was established for service in Gibraltar, and this was the first instance of non-commissioned military engineers. In 1787, the Corps of Engineers was granted the *Royal* prefix and adopted its current name and in the same year a Corps of Royal Military Artificers was formed, consisting of non-commissioned officers and privates, to be officered by the RE. Ten years later the Gibraltar company, which had remained separate, was absorbed and in 1812 the name was changed to the Corps of Royal Sappers and Miners.

In 1855 the Board of Ordnance was abolished and authority over the Royal Engineers, Royal Sappers and Miners and Royal Artillery was transferred to the Commander-in-Chief of the Forces, thus uniting them with the rest of the Army. The following year, the Royal Engineers and Royal Sappers and Miners became a unified corps as the Corps of Royal Engineers. In 1862 the corps also absorbed the British officers and men of the engineer corps of the East India Company.

In 1911 the Corps formed its Air Battalion, the first flying unit of the British Armed Forces. The Air Battalion was the forerunner of the Royal Flying Corps and Royal Air Force.

The Corps has no battle honours, but its motto *Ubique* (Everywhere), awarded by King William IV in 1832, signifies that it has seen action in all the major conflicts of the British Army and quite a few of the little ones too. A second motto is *Quo Fas et Gloria ducunt* (Where right and glory lead). The Royal Engineers Museum of Military Engineering is in Gillingham in Kent.

A point of some pride to the Sappers is that their name takes the form Corps of Royal Engineers rather than, for example, Royal Engineer Corps. The distinction, they say, is that every Sapper is Royal in his own right, rather than simply being a member of a Royal Corps (such as the Royal Corps of Signals or the Royal Regiment of Artillery).

Before the Second World War, Royal Engineers recruits were required to be at least 5 feet 4 inches tall (5 feet 2 inches for the Mounted Branch). They initially enlisted for six years with the colours and a further six years with the reserve or four years and eight years. Unlike most corps and regiments, in which the upper age limit was 25, men could enlist in the Royal Engineers up to 30 years of age. They trained at the Royal Engineers Depot in Chatham or the RE Mounted Depot at Aldershot.

SPORT

Football

The famous Royal Engineers A.F.C. won the FA Cup in 1875

and were the pioneers of the modern passing football game. Most notably the Engineers were the first team to show the benefit of cooperative teamwork, in particular ball passing. The following contemporary account from 1870 is the earliest description of ball passing in football: "Lieut. Creswell, who having brought it up the side then kicked it into the middle to another of his side, who kicked it through the posts the minute before time was called" The Engineers were the first team renown for "playing beautifully together".

Rugby

The Army were represented in the very first international by two members of the Royal Engineers, both playing for England, Lieutenant Charles Arthur Crompton RE and Lieutenant CW Sherrard RE.

Trades

All members of the Royal Engineers are trained combat engineers and all sappers (privates) and non-commissioned officers also have another trade. Women are eligible for all Royal Engineer specialities.

Sappers can join the Royal Engineers in one of the following trades:

- Bricklayer and Concretor
- Building and Structural Finisher
- Carpenter and Joiner
- Command, Communications and Information Systems Specialist
- Construction Materials Technician
- Draughtsman (Design)
- Draughtsman (Electrical and Mechanical)
- Driver RE
- Electrician
- Fabricator (Welder)
- Fitter (Air Conditioning and Refrigeration)
- General Fitter
- Geographical Technician

- Heating and Plumbing Engineer
- Pioneer
- Plant Operator Mechanic
- Resources Specialist
- Specialist Equipment Driver/Operator
- Surveyor (Engineering)
- Surveyor (Topographical)
- Armoured

Later, sappers can specialise in further trades and specialities, including:

- Bomb Disposal and Specialist Search
- Amphibious Engineer
- Clerk of Works (Construction)
- Clerk of Works (Electrical)
- Clerk of Works (Mechanical)
- Commando Engineer
- Diver
- Military Plant Foreman
- Parachute Engineer
- Regimental Signals Instructor

Senior NCOs who have passed the appropriate Clerk of Works course can be commissioned as Garrison Engineers (Construction, Electrical or Mechanical).

UNITS

The Royal Engineers comprises units of both the Regular Army and the Territorial Army. There is also a higher engineer formation:

THEATRE TROOPS

- 8 Force Engineer Brigade
    - o 12 (Air Support) Engineer Group (25, 39, 71 and 73 Regiments, 529 STRE)
    - o 29 (Land Support) Engineer Group (33 and 101 Regiments)

- o 170 (Infrastructure Support) Engineer Group (previously Military Works Force)
  - — HQ Works Group
  - — Royal Engineers Specialist Advisory Team (RESAT)
  - — Technical Information Centre Royal Engineers
  - — 62 Works Group [water]
  - — 519 STRE (Works)
  - — 523 STRE (Works)
  - — 520 STRE (Water Development)
  - — 521 STRE (Water Development)
  - — 63 Works Group [electricity]
  - — 518 STRE (Works)
  - — 528 STRE (Power)
  - — 535 STRE (Works)
  - — 64 Works Group [fuel]
  - — 516 STRE (Fuels)
  - — 517 STRE (Fuels)
  - — 524 STRE (Works)
  - — 527 STRE (Works)
  - — 66 Works Group (formed 2008)
  - — 522 STRE (Works)
  - — 530 STRE (Materials)

REGIMENTS

- 21 Engineer Regiment
  - o 7 Headquarters & Support Squadron
  - o 1st Armoured Engineer Squadron
  - o 4 Armoured Engineer Squadron
  - o 73 Armoured Engineer Squadron
- 22 Engineer Regiment
  - o 6 Headquarters & Support Squadron
  - o 3 Armoured Engineer Squadron
  - o 5 Armoured Engineer Squadron

  - o 52 Armoured Engineer Squadron (2008)
- 23 Engineer Regiment (Air Assault)-part of 16 Air Assault Brigade
  - o 12 (Nova Scotia) Headquarters and Support Squadron (Air Assault)
  - o 9 Parachute Squadron
  - o 51 Parachute Squadron
- 24 Commando Engineer Regiment-(Attached to 3 Commando Brigade, Royal Marines).(based at Chivenor)
  - o 59 Commando Squadron
  - o 54 Commando Headquarters and Support Squadron
  - o 56 Commando Field Squadron
  - o 131 Commando Squadron (TA)

NB: As part of the restructuring of the armed forces in 2004, it was announced that the engineering support for 3 Commando Brigade would be increased to a full regiment, with 24 (Commando) Engineer Regiment to be formed.

- 25 Engineer Regiment
  - o 43 Headquarters & Support Squadron (Air Support)
  - o 34 Field Squadron (Air Support)
  - o 53 Field Squadron (Air Support)
- 26 Engineer Regiment
  - o 38 Headquarters & Support Squadron
  - o 8 Armoured Engineer Squadron
  - o 30 Armoured Engineer Squadron
  - o 33 Armoured Engineer Squadron (2008)
- 28 Engineer Regiment
  - o 64 Headquarters & Support Squadron
  - o 23 Amphibious Engineer Squadron + 412 tp(V) TA
  - o 42 Field Squadron
  - o 45 Field Support Squadron
  - o 65 Field Support Squadron
- 32 Engineer Regiment
  - o 2 Headquarters & Support Squadron

  - o 26 Armoured Engineer Squadron
  - o 31 Armoured Engineer Squadron
  - o 39 Armoured Engineer Squadron
- 33 Engineer Regiment(EOD)
  - o 22 Headquarters and Support Squadron (EOD)
  - o 17 Field Squadron (EOD)
  - o 21 Field Squadron (EOD)
  - o 49 Field Squadron (EOD)
  - o 58 Field Squadron (EOD)
  - o 61 Field Squadron
- 35 Engineer Regiment
  - o 44 Headquarters and Support Squadron
  - o 29 Armoured Engineer Squadron
  - o 37 Armoured Engineer Squadron
  - o 77 Armoured Engineer Squadron
- 36 Engineer Regiment
  - o 50 Headquarters & Support Squadron
  - o 20 Field Squadron
  - o 69 Gurkha Field Squadron, Queen's Gurkha Engineers
  - o 70 Gurkha Field Support Squadron, Queen's Gurkha Engineers
- 38 Engineer Regiment
  - o 32 Headquarters & Support Squadron
  - o 11 Field Squadron
  - o 15 Field Support Squadron
  - o 25 Field Squadron
- 39 Engineer Regiment
  - o 60 Headquarters and Support Squadron (Air Support)
  - o 10 Field Squadron (Air Support) based at RAF Leeming
  - o 48 Field Squadron (Air Support)
- 42 Engineer Regiment (Geographic)
  - o 13 Geographic Squadron
  - o 14 Geographic Squadron (based in Moenchengladbach)

  - o 16 Geographic Support Squadron
- 62 Cyprus Support Squadron Royal Engineers (British Forces Cyprus)

TRAINING UNITS

- Royal School of Military Engineering
  - o Combat Engineer School
    - — 3 Royal School of Military Engineering Regiment
    - — 55 Training Squadron Royal Engineers
    - — 57 Training Squadron Royal Engineers
    - — 63 Training Support Squadron Royal Engineers
    - — Battlefield Engineering Wing
    - — United Kingdom Mine Information and Training Centre
    - — Communication Information Systems Wing
  - o Construction Engineer School
    - — 1 Royal School of Military Engineering Regiment
    - — 24 Training Squadron Royal Engineers
    - — 36 Training Squadron Royal Engineers
    - — Command Wing
    - — Civil Engineering Wing
    - — Electrical and Mechanical Wing
    - — National Search Centre
  - o Defence Explosive Ordnance Disposal School
  - o Royal School of Military Survey (until 1 April 2006)
- 28 Training Squadron, Army Training Regiment (Bassingbourn)
- Diving Training Unit (Army), (DTU(A))
- Band of the Corps of Royal Engineers

TERRITORIAL ARMY

- Royal Monmouthshire Royal Engineers (Militia)
  - o 100 Field Squadron [Cwmbran/Bristol/Cardiff]
  - o 101 Headquarters Troop [Monmouth]
  - o 108 (Welsh) Field Squadron [Swansea/Gorseinion]

  - o 225 Field Squadron [Birmingham]
  - o The Jersey Field Squadron [St Helier]
- 71 Engineer Regiment (Volunteers) (Air Support)
  - o 102 (Clyde) Field Squadron (Air Support) [Paisley/ Barnsford Bridge]
  - o 124 Field Squadron (Cumbernauld)
  - o 236 Field Squadron [Elgin]
  - o Headquarters Troop [RAF Leuchars]
  - o 10 Orkney Field Troop [Orkney Islands]
- 72 Engineer Regiment (Volunteers) Close Support
  - o 103 (Tyne Electrical Engineers) Field Squadron (Air Support) [Newcastle/Sunderland]
  - o 106 (West Riding) Field Squadron [Sheffield/Bradford]
  - o 299 Para Field Squadron [Wakefield/Hull/Gateshead]
- 73 Engineer Regiment (Volunteers) (Air Support)
  - o 129 Headquarters and Support Squadron [Nottingham]
  - o 350 Field Squadron (Air Support) [Nottingham]
  - o 575 (Sherwood Foresters) Field Squadron (Air Support) [Chesterfield]
- 75 Engineer Regiment (Volunteers) (Field)
  - o 107 (Lancashire and Cheshire) Field Squadron [Birkenhead/St Helens]
  - o 125 (Staffordshire) Field Support Squadron [Stoke-on-Trent]
  - o 143 Plant Squadron [Walsall]
  - o 201 Headquarters Squadron [Manchester]
- 101 Engineer Regiment (EOD) (V)
  - o 217 (London) Field Squadron (EOD) [Holloway]
  - o 221 Field Squadron (EOD) [Rochester/Catford]
  - o 579 Field Squadron (EOD) [Tunbridge Wells]
- 131 Independent Commando Squadron Royal Engineers (Volunteers) [London/Bath/Plymouth/Birmingham] *to form 24 Commando Regiment Royal Engineers in early 2007*

- 135 Independent Geographic Squadron Royal Engineers (Volunteers) [Ewell]
- Engineer and Logistic Staff Corps (Volunteers)
- 170 (Infrastructure Support) Engineer Group (previously Military Works Force)
    - o 62 Works Group [Regular]
        - — 506 STRE (Water Infrastructure)
    - o 63 Works Group [Regular]
        - — 504 STRE (Power Infrastructure)
    - o 64 Works Group [Regular]
        - — 503 STRE (Fuels Infrastructure)
    - o 65 Works Group
        - — 507 STRE (Railway Infrastructure)
        - — 509 STRE (Ports Infrastructure)
        - — 508 STRE (Works)
        - — 525 STRE (Works)
        - — 526 STRE (Works)
- 591 Independent Field Squadron
    - o Is the only Royal Engineer TA Unit in Northern Ireland.

SUCCESSOR UNITS

Several units have been formed from the Royal Engineers.

- The Air Battalion Royal Engineers (formed 1911) was the precursor of the Royal Flying Corps (formed 1912) which evolved into the Royal Air Force in 1918.
- The Telegraph Battalion Royal Engineers became the Royal Engineers Signals Service, which in turn became the independent Royal Corps of Signals in 1920.
- The Royal Engineers were responsible for railway and inland waterway transport, port operations and movement control until 1965, when these functions were transferred to the new Royal Corps of Transport.
- In 1908, the Army Postal Corps (formed in 1882) and the Royal Engineers Telegraph Reserve (formed in 1884) amalgamated to form the Royal Engineers Postal Section.

This later became the Army Postal and Courier Service and remained part of the RE until the formation of the Royal Logistic Corps in 1993.

The Royal Engineers from just after the Second World War until the early 1970s also had 4 Plant Troops located in the United Kingdom which were RE reinforced Plant & Engineering troops attached to various Home Commands. The Command Plant Troops were initially set up in the late 40s to clear up the beach defences around the coast and remove the minefields and were equipped with Armoured Bulldozers. In the 1950s once all this work was complete they took responsibility of maintaining and building all Army Ranges and various civil works in support of the civilian population and in support of civilian organisations in the event of natural disasters and crises such as the Torrey Canyon disaster where the Southern Command Plant Troop was deployed to the West Country to clean up the mess on the beaches caused by the large volume of oil that floated ashore. The 4 Command Plant Troops were based in various locations across the United Kingdom with Southern Commend Plant Troop initially based in Tidworth, then Perham Down in Wiltshire and eventually Longmoor in Hampshire. The Midlands Plant Squadron was based in Walsall and the Northern Command plant troop was based in Ripon. The other command plant troop was based in Scotland. In Germany there was an Entire Engineering group based in Willich near Düsseldorf called the Military Civilian Plant & Engineering group that had a similar large scale Engineering, Plant and Support role for British Army of the Rhine. Each Command Plant Troop was commanded by an RE Major supported by a Military Plant Foreman.

In 1969, it was decided to amalgamate all of the Command Plant Troops into one large Squadron which had 4 troops, an HQ Troop and a large REME Attachment to it and the Squadron-66 Plant Squadron became the largest squadron in the entire Royal Engineers, in terms of Plant Engineering and Equipment as well as staff. Its last home was in Longmoor Hampshire-Engineer Stores Depot attached to Longmoor Military Camp, which was also home to a Field Support Squadron. Longmoor Military Railway was from 1901 until the late 1960s the preserve of the

Royal Engineers but subsequently Royal Corps of Transport and eventually Royal Logistic Corps Railway Training Centre. Its role also changed with a much wider role to support Military operations throughout NATO.

In late 1976 a Mr Trotter in Parliament asked the Secretary of State for Defence which units, apart from 66 Plant Squadron Royal Engineers, are specialists in heavy plant; whether he still intends to disband this squadron; if so, what unit will take its place; and what will be the reduction in the engineers' heavy plant capacity.

In answer to Mr Trotter 's question Mr. Robert C. Brown replied...There is no directly comparable regular unit containing a similar concentration of specialist plant expertise, but specialist capability exists in parts of various regular field and base units in the United Kingdom, BAOR and elsewhere. In addition, there are two TAVR plant squadrons. As a consequence of the Defence Review, 66 Plant Squadron, Royal Engineers will disband by early 1978, but most of its heavy equipment will be taken over by other engineer units notably in the TAVR. As a result, there will be some reduction in the capacity of the Royal Engineers to plan and conduct major projects in peacetime.

EQUIPMENT

- Chieftain Armoured Vehicle Royal Engineer (ChAVRE)
- Chieftain Armoured Vehicle Layer Bridge (ChAVLB)

These are being replaced by 66 Armoured Support Vehicles

- TROJAN is a minefield breaching vehicle. It prepares routes, mark safe routes using an Obstacle Marking System, breach complex obstacles and provide short dry and wet gap crossing utilising its excavator arm, earth moving blade and a midi fascine. It will plough through minefields, build trenches and dig defensive ditches
- TITAN will carry and lay the current range of In-Service Close Support bridges laying them faster, and in a wider variety of terrain conditions, than previous equipment. TITAN can lay a bridge over a 26 metre gap in two minutes,

making it the fastest Support Vehicle in the world at this task. This gives commanders a potential battle winning edge and allows them to choose from a more flexible range of armoured vehicles.

Both vehicles which weigh over 60 tonnes and are capable of speeds of up to 56 km/h, are designed to mount and tow the current range of in-service Royal Engineer equipment (PYTHON, AVRE Trailer, Track/Full Width Mineploughs and earth moving blades). They have purpose designed hulls, will incorporate Special to Role equipment and have major assemblies common to the Challenger 2 Main Battle Tank.

ROYAL TANK REGIMENT

The Royal Tank Regiment (RTR) is an armoured regiment of the British Army. It was formerly known as the Tank Corps and the Royal Tank Corps. It is part of the Royal Armoured Corps and is made up of two operational regiments, the *1st Royal Tank Regiment* (1RTR) and the *2nd Royal Tank Regiment* (2RTR). The official regimental motto is *Fear Naught* while unofficial motto (signified also by the colours of the tactical recognition flash) is "From Mud, Through Blood to the Green Fields Beyond."

NOMENCLATURE

In the nineteenth-century (and before) British Army, regiments of infantry raised several battalions, which were often deployed separately. This practice remained into the modern era—in the First World War, it was common to see twenty or more battalions with a single regimental title. However, this practice did not hold for the cavalry regiments, which traditionally were only of limited size; in the modern era, this meant that each regiment would only constitute one battalion. As a result, it became traditional for a battalion-level unit of cavalry to be referred to as a "regiment". This was not as confusing as it may seem, since where other armies would use "regiment" for a unit of two to four battalions, the British Army used "brigade". Hence, an infantry brigade could consist of three battalions of infantry, but a cavalry brigade of equivalent size would have three regiments.

In the inter-war period, the British Army began to mechanise, with cavalry regiments giving up their horses in favour of armoured cars or light tanks. (The first regiment to do so was the 11th Hussars, in 1928; the last the Royal Scots Greys in 1941). As a result, it became common to refer to any armoured unit as a "regiment" rather than a "battalion"—the 11th Hussars were not merely an armoured-car battalion, but the whole of the regiment. In 1945, this usage became formal; all armoured battalions were henceforth referred to as regiments.

The Royal Tank Regiment is itself a regiment of the British Army, part of the Royal Armoured Corps. However, as a result of the above, both its "battalions" are formally titled regiments. This can cause some confusion, with the regiment currently being composed of two regiments.

World War I

The Royal Tank Regiment's formation followed the invention of the tank. Tanks were first used at Flers in September 1916 during the Battle of the Somme in World War I. At that time the six tank companies were grouped as the Heavy Branch of the Machine Gun Corps (MGC).

In November 1916 the eight companies then in existence were each expanded to form battalions still lettered A through H; another seven battalions, I through O, were formed by January 1918, when they all were converted to numbered units. On 28 July 1917 the Heavy Branch was by Royal Warrant separated from the rest of the MGC and given official status as the Tank Corps, meaning that by the beginning of 1918 the fifteen units were changed from letters to numbers as 1st Battalion to 15th Battalion, Tank Corps. More battalions continued to be formed, and by December 1918, 26 had been created. (At this time there were only 25 tank battalions, however; the 17th had converted to using armoured cars in April 1918). The first commander of the Tank Corps was Hugh Elles.

The Corps saw heavy action through 1917 and 1918, with special note being given to the Battle of Cambrai (1917), which the regiment continues to commemorate annually. During the war, four members of the Corps were awarded the Victoria Cross. However, heavy losses and recurrent mechanical difficulties reduced the effectiveness of the Corps, leading the Bovington

Tank School to adopt a doctrine that emphasised caution and high standards of maintenance in equal measure.

Interwar Period

After the war, the Tank Corps was trimmed down to a central depot and four battalions; the 2nd, 3rd, 4th and 5th Battalions, Tank Corps. In 1923 it was officially named *Royal* (making it the Royal Tank Corps) by Colonel-in-Chief King George V. It was at this time that the motto *Fear Naught*, the black beret and the unit badge were adopted. The word *Corps* was replaced in 1939 with *Regiment* to give the unit its current name, the Royal Tank Regiment.

In 1920, twelve Armoured Car Companies were set up as part of the Tank Corps, absorbing units from the Machine Gun Corps; eight were later converted into independent Light Tank Companies. All disbanded before the outbreak of the Second World War. In 1933 the 6th Battalion, Royal Tank Corps, was formed in Egypt by combining the personnel of two of these companies; in 1934, the 1st (Light) Battalion, Royal Tank Corps was formed in England with personnel from three of the existing battalions.With the preparations for war in the late 1930s a further two regular battalions were formed; the 7th in 1937 and the 8th in 1938. The 40th, 41st, 42nd, 43rd, 44th & 45th battalions were raised in 1938, being converted from Territorial Army infantry battalions; the 46th, 47th, 48th, 49th, 50th and 51st were likewise activated and converted in 1939. The twelve Yeomanry Armoured Car Companies of the RTR were all activated and transferred to the Royal Armoured Corps.

Before the Second World War, Royal Tank Corps recruits were required to be at least 5 feet 4 inches tall. They initially enlisted for six years with the colours and a further six years with the reserve. They trained at the Royal Tank Corps Depot at Bovington Camp, Dorset for about eight months.

World War II

At the outbreak of war, the Regiment consisted of eight regular battalions.

- 1st & 6th RTR was part of the Heavy Armoured Brigade (Egypt)

- 2nd, 3rd & 5th RTR were part of the 1st Heavy Armoured Brigade
- 4th 7th & 8th RTR were part of the British 1st Army Tank Brigade

In addition, there were a large number of territorial battalions, as well as hostilities-only battalions such as 9 RTR.

The regiment was again expanded such that there were numerous units of the RTR that took part in countless battles in World War II, including the Battle of Dunkirk, El Alamein and D-Day. Field Marshal Montgomery would frequently wear the Regiment's beret, with his Field Marshal's badge sewn on next to the Regimental cap badge, as it was more practical whilst travelling on a tank than either a formal peaked hat or the Australian slouch hat he previously wore. Higher-numbered battalions of the Regiment included the 40th, 41st, 42nd, 43rd, 44th, 45th, 46th, 47th, 48th, 49th, 50th, and 51st Royal Tank, and battalions were redesignated as regiments in 1945.

11 RTR formed part of 79th Armoured Division (aka Hobart's Funnies), equipped initially with CDL (tactical searchlight) tanks, but converted not long after D-Day to Buffalo (US LVT aka Amtrac), and participated in the assault crossing of the Rhine. Prime Minister Winston Churchill was ferried across the Rhine in a Buffalo from 'C' Squadron 11RTR.

Post-war Period

After World War II, the RTR was reduced through various amalgamations, first in 1959-60:

- 3RTR and 6RTR amalgamated as 3RTR
- 4RTR and 7RTR amalgamated as 4RTR
- 5RTR and 8RTR amalgamated as 5RTR

In 1969, 5RTR was disbanded, while under Options for Change, 4RTR amalgamated with 1RTR, and 3RTR with 2RTR. The current Colonel-in-Chief of the Royal Tank Regiment is Queen Elizabeth II.

Current Status

Today, there are two regiments, the 1st and 2nd Royal Tank Regiments (1RTR and 2RTR). Today, half of 1RTR forms part of the Joint CBRN Regiment (together with No. 27 Squadron RAF Regiment) at RAF Honington with the other half as a training unit at Harman Lines,Warminster while 2RTR retains its role as an armoured regiment as part of 1 Mechanised Brigade at Aliwal Barracks,Tidworth.

The Royal Tank Regiment has continued to see action, including playing a role in missions in Bosnia and Kosovo. Elements of 1RTR were deployed to Afghanistan in 2002 and both regiments were involved in the invasion of Iraq, with the 2RTR battlegroup playing an important role in the capture of the city of Basra. Squadrons of both Regiments are still deployed in Afghanistan and Iraq carrying out both Armoured and Infantry taskings.

Vehicles

The Royal Tank Regiment uses a variety of vehicles, including:

- Challenger 2 (introduced in 1998; the regiment's primary vehicle)
- FV107 Scimitar
- FV105 Sultan
- FV103 Spartan
- FV104 Samaritan
- HGV
- Land Rover
- Fuchs

Battle Honours

The Great War

- Somme 1916 '18, Arras 1917 '18, Messines 1917, Ypres 1917, Cambrai 1917, St. Quentin 1918, Villers Bretonneux, Amiens, Bapaume 1918, Hindenburg Line, Épéhy, Selle, France and Flanders 1916-18, Gaza

The Second World War

- North-West Europe 1940: Arras Counter Attack, Calais 1940, St. Omer-La Bassée, Somme
- North Africa 1940-43: Sidi Barrani, Beda Fomm, Sidi Suleiman, Tobruk 1941, Sidi Rezegh 1941, Belhamed,

Gazala, Cauldron, Knightsbridge, Defence of Alamein Line, Alam el Halfa, El Alamein, Mareth, Akarit, Fondouk, El Kourzia, Medjez Plain, Tunis

- Sicily 1943: Primosole Bridge, Gerbini, Adrano
- Italy 1943-45: Sangro, Salerno, Volturno Crossing, Garigliano Crossing, Anzio, Advance to Florence, Gothic Line, Coriano, Lamone Crossing, Rimini Line, Argenta Gap
- North-West Europe 1944-45: Odon, Caen, Bourguébus Ridge, Mont Pincon, Falaise, Nederrijn, Scheldt, Venlo Pocket, Rhineland, Rhine, Bremen
- Abyssinia 1940, Greece 1941, Burma 1942
- Korea 1951–53

Post War Years

Middle East 2003–date

- Al Basrah, Iraq 2003

Notable Former Members

- Jack Hargreaves
- John Le Mesurier
- Keith Floyd
- Chris Bonington
- Percy Hobart

Colonel-Commandants

- John Capper: 1923–?
- Ernest Swinton: 1934–1938

1st Royal Tank Regiment

The 1st Royal Tank Regiment (1 RTR) is an armoured regiment of the British Army. It is part of the Royal Tank Regiment, itself part of the Royal Armoured Corps. It was originally formed as 1st (Light) Battalion, Royal Tank Corps in 1934.

In 1993, it amalgamated with the 4th Royal Tank Regiment without change of title. It incorporated both the original regiment's traditional recruiting areas of Merseyside and Scotland. The new regiment also adopted the strong Scottish connections of the 4th RTR, taking on the former regiment's pipes and drums, which wear the Hunting Rose tartan. The Regiment Colours symbolise the phrase "From the Mud(brown), Through the blood(red) to the green fields beyond." In 1999, two squadrons were split off as part of the Joint Chemical, Biological, Radiation and Nuclear regiment amalgamating with n0.27 sqadron RAF Regimentand two squadrons of the royal yeomanry. The Regimental March is Lippe Dotmed.

2 Royal tank Regiment

The 2nd Royal Tank Regiment (2 RTR) is an armoured regiment of the British Army. It is part of the Royal Tank Regiment, itself part of the Royal Armoured Corps. It originally saw action as B Battalion, Tank Corps in 1917.

In 1992, it amalgamated with the 3rd Royal Tank Regiment without change of title.

The Regiment has seen action most recently in Kosovo, Iraq and Afghanistan. After a long period in Fallingbostel, Germany, the regiment moved back to the UK and Aliwal Barracks in Tidworth in July 2007. All four of the Regiment's Sabre Squadrons were deployed in 2006/7 with EGYPT providing the Challenger 2 armoured punch on Op TELIC 9 who were then replaced on TELIC 10 by CYCLOPS with BADGER operating in Warrior tracked armoured vehicles. FALCON have recently returned from Op HERRICK in Afghanistan where they conducted numerous operations on the new Mastiff armoured vehicle. As of June 2009 EGYPT are back in Afghanistan operating on the Viking armoured vehicle.

The Regiment had a busy training year with AFV Ranges followed by BATUS towards the end of the year. On 25 June 2008 at Buckingham Palace both Regiments were presented with their new Standard by The Queen which included the new Battle Honour of Al Basra 2003.

3rd Royal Tank Regiment

The 3rd Royal Tank Regiment (3 RTR) was an armoured regiment of the British Army until 1992. It was part of the Royal

Tank Regiment, itself part of the Royal Armoured Corps. It originally saw action as C Battalion, Tank Corps in 1917.

In 1939 it was retitled from 3rd Royal Tank Corps. In 1940, it was preparing to go to France as part of 1st Armoured Division when it was diverted at short notice to Calais. It fought during the four-day Siege of Calais. All its tanks were lost, and many personnel killed or taken prisoner, but some escaped to Dunkirk or were evacuated from Calais before the port fell.

The unit was subsequently rebuilt in the UK as part of 3rd Armoured Brigade, its original parent formation. Shipped to the Middle East, it was part of the British 1st Armoured Brigade when it went to Greece to try and stem the German invasion in 1941.

In 1942, it briefly amalgamated with the 5th Royal Tank Regiment, as the 3rd/5th Royal Tank Regiment, returning to its previous title a month later. It formed part of 8th Armoured Brigade, fighting at El Alamein, and in Tunisia and Sicily. It later joined 29th Armoured Brigade and fought in Normandy, Holland and Germany as part of 11th Armoured Division.

In 1959, it amalgamated with the 6th Royal Tank Regiment without change of title. In 1992, it amalgamated with the 2nd Royal Tank Regiment.

6

Indian Rifles and Regiments

RASHTRIYA RIFLES

The Rashtriya Rifles (if fully translated, *National Rifles*) is a counterinsurgency force in India. It is a Ministry of Defence paramilitary force deployed in Jammu and Kashmir.

CREST

The Rashtriya Rifles crest consists of two crossed AK-47 rifles with fixed bayonets atop which is the coveted Ashoka Chakra. Beneath, in a banner, is emblazoned the motto of this force-*dridhta aur virta*. The AK-47 is the main personal weapon of this force.

HISTORY

It was raised by General B C Joshi in 1990 specifically for fighting insurgency in Kashmir, to complement the weak local security forces in the area. By 1994 it had 5,000 troops, all of whom served in Jammu and Kashmir. Some observers expected the force to grow to thirty battalions, with around 25,000 personnel. In March 1995, Indian television referred to the Delta Force of the "fledgling" Rashtriya Rifles. It was reported that the force was operating against terrorists and foreign mercenaries in Doda District in south-central Jammu and Kashmir.

MISSION

The main role of the formation is to allow the Indian Army to ensure its primary task of defending the borders and the state's territory unhindered by action from Pakistani-backed terrorists and guerrillas.

ORGANIZATION

The Rashtriya Rifles comprises 63 battalions. The efficacy of an RR battalion arises from the fact that unlike conventional Army battalions, it has six rifle companies instead of four they possess and has kept its heavy weapons — useless in their sphere of activities — back at their bases.

Originally comprising a total of four Counterinsurgency Forces, each responsible for an area of the Kashmir Valley and Jammu, the RR raised a fifth force 'Uniform' in 2003-04.:

- Counter Insurgency Force (CIF) R / Romeo Force-Rajouri and Poonch
- Counter Insurgency Force (CIF) D / Delta Force-Doda
- Counter Insurgency Force (CIF) V / Victor Force-Anantnag, Pulwama and Badgam
- Counter Insurgency Force (CIF) K / Kilo Force-Kupwara, Baramulla and Srinagar
- Counter Insurgency Force (CIF) U / Uniform Force-Udhampur and Banihal

RECRUITMENT

The RR was raised as a para-military force and it was envisaged that its personnel, like the Assam Rifles, would consist of regular Army volunteers on deputation, ex-servicemen and lateral inductees from various para-military forces and central police organisations. However, this never happened and the force has consisted only of regular Army officers and Jawans, especially from the various Infantry regiments, like the Rajputana Rifles, Gorkha Rifles, Maratha Light Infantry, Sikh Light Infantry and Sikh Regiment. Both officers and soldiers are sent to the RR on deputation for a period of 4-5 years. RR personell receive 25% more salary than regular Army personell, plus additional benefits, that is why it is often a coveted deputation.

ASSAM RIFLES

The Assam Rifles are one of the Paramilitary forces of India. The unit can trace its lineage back to a paramilitary police force that was formed under the British in 1835 called *Cachar Levy*. Since then the Assam Rifles have undergone a number of name changes before the name *Assam Rifles* was finally adopted in 1917. Over the course of its history, the Assam Rifles and its predecessor units have served in a number of roles, conflicts and theatres including World War I where they served in Europe and the Middle East, and World War II where they served mainly in Burma. In the post World War II period the Assam Rifles has expanded greatly as has its role. There are currently 46 battalions. of Assam Rifles under the control of the Indian Ministry of Home Affairs (MHA) and they perform many roles including the provision of internal security under the control of the army through the conduct of counter insurgency and border security operations, provision of aid to the civil power in times of emergency, and the provision of communications, medical assistance and education in remote areas. In times of war they can also be used as a combat force to secure rear areas if needed.

History

The present day Assam Rifles can trace its origins back to a paramilitary force known as *Cachar Levy* which was established by the British in 1835 in the Assam region. With approximately seven hundred and fifty men, this force was formed as a police unit to protect settlements against tribal raids and other assaults as British rule slowly moved towards the north east parts of India.

Despite problems with equipment and training, the contribution of this force in opening the region to administration and commerce was nevertheless quite significant and over time they have become known as the "...right arm of the civil and [the] left arm of the military" in the region. In 1870 these existing elements were merged into three Assam Military Police battalions which were spread out in the Lushai Hills (later 1st battalion), Lakhimpur (2nd battalion) and Naga Hills (3rd battalion). A fourth battalion was later formed Imphal in 1915.

Since then the name of the force has undergone a number of changes, as have the roles that it has been required to perform.

World War I and after War Years

During World War I, men from what was then known as the

Assam Military Police were part of the Indian forces that fought in Europe and the Middle East. Over three thousand men from the force were provided to the Gorkha regiments of the Indian Army in this time, earning seventy-six gallantry awards during the conflict including seven Indian Order of Merit awards and five Indian Distinguished Service Medals. These men performed with such distinction that the name *Assam Rifles* was assigned in 1917 as recognition of their part in the war. Elements of the force were also utilised in India during the war, being used to maintain internal security in order to free up troops from the army for use overseas. During this time, the most notable action occurred in 1917 when columns of the Assam Rifles were despatched to Patna, to restore law and order in the riot-torn city.

After the war the force returned to northern India where they were used to maintain security amidst growing civil unrest and disorder. In concert with the British Indian Army, they also undertook a number of expeditions into remote tribal areas along the northeast frontier and into Burma. In 1924 they were sent to Malabar, which was then still part of the Madras Presidency, to carry out operations against the Mopla rebels.

World War II

During World War II, the role of the Assam Rifles evolved once more as they were called upon to undertake even more varied tasks due to their status as both a police and military organisation. This time, however, their service would be undertaken closer to home. After the lightning Japanese advance in 1942, the Assam Rifles fought a number of independent actions behind enemy lines as the task of rear-area defence and rear-guard often fell to them during the Allies retreat into India. Later, as a large influx of refugees fled from the advancing Japanese into India, the Assam Rifles were given the task of managing and organising this mass of humanity.

They also organized a resistance group on the Indo-Burmese border to counter the Japanese invasion and to harass the enemy line of communications. This group became known as "Victor Force" (or sometimes V-Force), and the nucleus of it was formed from platoons made up of men from the Assam Rifles. As part of this force, Assam Rifles platoons were used as covering forces during the latter stages of the Burma Campaign. Other elements fought in the defensive "boxes" around Kohima, whilst another, from the 4th Battalion trained as airborne troops and were dropped near the Sittang River behind Japanese lines. The 1st Battalion, as part of Lushai Brigade was sent ahead of the rest of the force to provide resistance in the Chin Hills. As a testament to the performance of Assam Rifles men during the war, members of the unit received forty-eight gallantry awards. These included: 3 Members of the British Empire, 5 Military Crosses, 4 Orders of British India, 1 Indian Order of Merit, 13 Military Medals, 15 Indian Distinguished Service Medals and 7 British Empire Medals.

Post War Period

Following the end of the war the five Assam Rifles battalions became part of the civil police under the Assam Inspector General of Police. After independence, however, the Indian government assigned the Assam Rifles its own Director General. As the numbers of the force and the number of battalions gradually increased, the rank of the force commander was also upgraded until now it is that of Lieutenant General. The present Director General of the Assam Rifles, is Lieutenant General Karan Singh Yadava, of the 3rd Gorkha Rifles.

The role of the Assam Rifles continued to evolve when in 1950 a devastating earthquake hit the Assam region and the force was called in to assist in the reconstruction of the areas and help in the resettlement and rehabilitation of those affected by it. Later the force was once again called to undertake a combat role when, during the 1962 Sino-Indian War elements were used to delay the advancing Chinese forces so that the Indian Army could establish its defence lines. During this time and since then, the Assam Rifles also maintained their peacekeeping role in the northern areas of India in the face of growing tribal unrest and insurgency. In this environment the maintenance of law and order, countering insurgency and reassuring the people of the region became important tasks for the security forces and initially they fell to the Assam Rifles before the Army assumed control, and then later their experience and goodwill in the region was drawn upon in order to assist the army in conducting these tasks. In recognition of the unit's skill in counter insurgency operations, three battalions were deployed on Operation Pawan in Sri Lanka between December 1988 and February 1990. Through its deployment in what has become known as the "tribal belt", the Assam Rifles have developed an ethos that is based primarily upon the notion of extending the hand of friendship with the people of the region despite the troubles that have occurred there. This has resulted in their employment in a number of developmental activities in the region as they have worked to bring order and security to it. As such, their role has been further expanded to include the provision of medical assistance and basic education, assisting in reconstruction and agriculture and handling communications in remote areas. From a force of five battalions in 1947, the Assam Rifles has grown substantially over the years. In 1960 there were seventeen battalions, in 1968 there were twenty-one and now there are forty-six battalions today. In addition, the Force has several area HQs, a training centre that processes up to 1,800 recruits at time, and a number of logistics units.

Decorations

Members of the Assam Rifles have received the following military decorations since Indian independence:

Award	Times awarded
Ashoka Chakra	3
Vir Chakra	5
Kirti Chakra	31
Shaurya Chakra	120
Param Vishisht Seva Medal	5
Ati Vishisht Seva Medal	12
Sena Medal	188
Vishisht Seva Medal	74
Yudh Seva Medal	1
Mention in Dispatches	10

RAJPUTANA RIFLES

The Rajputana Rifles is the most senior rifle regiment of the Indian Army. It was originally raised in 1921 as part of the British

Indian Army, when six previously existing regiments were amalgamated together to form six battalions of the 6th Rajputana Rifles. In 1945 the numeral designation was dropped from the title and in 1947 the regiment was transferred to the newly independent Indian Army. Since independence, the regiment has been involved in a number of conflicts against Pakistan, as well as contributing to the United Nations Custodian Force in Korea in the 1950s and to the UN Mission to the Congo in 1962. Over the course of its existence the regiment has had the distinction of receiving six Victoria Crosses and one Param Vir Chakra as well as many other decorations and honours.

The Name

The name Rajputana Rifles is derived from the *Rajput* a hindu clan and Hindi word *Rajputana* which was the old name of Rajasthan. It is based on the Sanskrit word *Rajputra* meaning son of a king.

Lineage

The regiment's origins lie in the 18th century when the East India Company (HEIC) recruited Rajputs to protect its operations. The impressive performance of French local units which were composed of local recruits mixed with French officers, helped the HEIC to decide that it needed to do something similar. In January 1775, it raised its first local infantry units which included the 5th Battalion, Bombay Sepoys, which is considered to be the oldest rifle regiment of the Indian Army. The 5th Battalion was successively redesignated as 9th Battalion Bombay Sepoys in 1778; 2nd Battalion, 2nd Regiment of Bombay Native Infantry in 1796; 4th Regiment of Bombay Native Infantry in 1824, and then 4th Regiment Native Infantry (Rifle Corps) in 1881. It thus became the first Rifle Regiment of the British Indian Army. In 1899 the Battalion was once more renamed as 4th Regiment (1st Battalion Rifle Corps) Bombay Infantry and again in 1901 as 4th Bombay Rifles.

In Kitchener's 1903 reorganisation of the Indian Army, 4th Bombay Rifles became 104th Wellesley's Rifles, to commemorate the fact that the regiment had been commanded in 1800 by Arthur Wellesley (later the Duke of Wellington). In the further reorganisation in 1921, six regiments were brought together to form six battalions of the 6th Rajputana Rifles Regiment:

- 1st Battalion-104th Wellesley's Rifles
- 2nd Battalion-120th Rajputana Infantry
- 3rd Battalion-122nd Rajputana Infantry (God's Own)
- 4th Battalion-123rd Outram's Rifles
- 5th Battalion-125th Napier's Rifles
- 10th (Training) Battalion-13th Rajputs (The Shekhawati Regiment).

In 1945 the regiments of the British Indian Army dropped the numeral in their titles and so the Rajputanas assumed their current name. In 1947 the regiment was allocated to India and the newly formed Indian Army when the sub-continent became independent from the British Empire. In 1949, the 1st Battalion was elevated to the status of guards, becoming 3rd Battalion, Brigade of the Guards.

History

In 1817 the 4th Battalion met the Marathas at the Battle of Khadki. The defence earned the regiment the battle honour of "Khadki". In 1856–57 the 1st, 2nd and 4th Battalions were together in the Persian theatre of operations. In 1856 Captain J. A. Wood of the 2nd Battalion (then the 20th Bombay Native Infantry) was awarded the Victoria Cross for storming Reshire Fort. This was the first Victoria Cross to be won in an Indian unit. In the same battle Subedar Major Mohammed Sharief and Subedar Peer Bhatt were recommended for the Victoria Cross but were turned down as at that time the medal category was not open to Indians.

In 1878–1880, during the Second Afghan War, the 1st Battalion marched 145 miles in 5 days from Quetta to Kandahar and laid siege to the city. In 1900–1902, the 3rd Battalion was part of a force used to contain the Boxer rebellion in China.

The First World War saw the regiment fight in battlefields from France to Palestine. The 5th Battalion was in all theatres of the war and participated in General Allenby's march to recapture Jerusalem. In this march the units got the better of their German and Turkish opponents.

During World War II the regiment was expanded to thirteen battalions and served in the Middle East, Burma and Malaya. The 4th Battalion had the distinction of earning two Victoria Crosses during this conflict.

GORKHA REGIMENTS

The 1st Battalion of 1 Gorkha Rifles of the Indian Army take position outside a simulated combat town during a training exercise. Gorkha regiments have been serving in the Indian Army ever since independence in 1947, when the Tripartite Agreement was signed. The regiments have served gallantly under the Indian Army. Composed primarily of Nepalese soldiers, the regiments are famous for their use of the Khukri.

ORIGINS

Impressed by the fighting qualities displayed by the Gorkhas during the Gurkha War, Sir David Ochterlony was quick to realise the potential of the Gorkhas in the British Indian Army. Until then, Gorkha defectors were generally used as irregular forces. In April 1815, the first battalion of the Gorkha Regiment, was raised as the Nasiri regiment. This regiment later became the 1st King George's Own Gurkha Rifles, and saw action at the Maulun fort under Lieutenant Lawtie.

They were instrumental in the expansion of the British East India Company throughout the subcontinent. The Gorkhas took part in the Anglo-Sikh wars, Afghan wars, and in suppressing the Indian Rebellion of 1857. Throughout these years, the British continued to recruit the Gorkhas and kept increasing the number of Gorkha regiments.

By the time First World War started, there were 11 Gorkha regiments under the British Indian Army. The Gorkha regiments played a vital role in the Commonwealth armies during both the World Wars seeing action everywhere from Monte Cassino in the west to Rangoon in the east, earning Battle Honours everywhere. As a testament to the psychological factors of the Gorkha Regiments on its enemies, during the North African campaign, the German Afrika Corp accorded great respect to the brave khukris wielding Gorkhas.

Post Independence

Following India's independence, India, Nepal and Great Britain signed a Tripartite Agreement, and six regiments of the Gurkha Rifles joined the Indian Army. In 1950, when India became a republic, the Royal titles were dropped from the regiments that joined the Indian Army.

Following the divisions of the Gorkha regiments, the British Army decided that joining of the British Army would be entirely voluntary for the Gorkha soldiers and decided to hold a referendum. As a result, large numbers of men from the 7th Gurkha Rifles and the 10th Gurkha Rifles, which recruited predominantly from Eastern Nepal, decided not to join their regiments as part of the British Army. In order to retain a contingent from this area of Nepal, the Indian Army made the decision to re-raise the 11 Gorkha Rifles, which was disbanded after the 1922.

Since independence, the Gorkhas have fought in every major campaign involving the Indian Army being awarded numerous battle and theatre honours. The regiments have won many gallantry awards like the Param Vir Chakra and the Maha Vir Chakra. The 8 Gorkha Rifles, has the unique distinction of producing one of the two Field Marshals of the Indian Army, Field Marshal Sam Manekshaw. He was the commanding officer of the 3rd battalion of the 8 Gorkha Rifles, and is still considered the most revered officer of the regiment.

The 4/5 Gorkha Rifles (Frontier Force) fought in the Battle of Sylhet, earning the diistinction of being the first regiment of the Indian Army to be involved in a heliborne attack. Under the Indian Army, Gorkhas have served in Bangladesh, Sri Lanka, Siachen, and in the UN peacekeeping missions in Lebanon and Sierra Leone. Major Dhan Singh Thapa of the 1/8 Gorkha Rifles won the Param Vir Chakra for his heroic actions during the 1962 Sino-Indian conflict. The 1st battalion of the 11 Gorkha Rifles was involved in Operation Vijay where Lt. (acting Captain) Manoj Kumar Pandey won the Param Vir Chakra for his gallant actions.

Current Strength

Currently there are 7 Gorkha regiments serving in the Indian Army. Six regiments were transferred from the British Indian

Army, one regiment was formed after independence. The following is a list of the Gorkha Regiments currently serving in the Indian Army:

- 1 Gorkha Rifles previously 1st King George V's Own Gurkha Rifles (The Malaun Regiment);
- 3 Gorkha Rifles previously 3rd Queen Alexandra's Own Gurkha Rifles.
- 4 Gorkha Rifles previously 4th Prince of Wales's Own Gurkha Rifles
- 5 Gorkha Rifles (Frontier Force) previously 5th Royal Gurkha Rifles (Frontier Force).
- 8 Gorkha Rifles aka The Shiny Eight
- 9 Gorkha Rifles
- 11 Gorkha Rifles (Raised after the independence of India)

The individual Gorkha rifle regiments of India are collectively known for regimental purposes as the 'Gorkha Brigade' between themselves and are not to be confused with the Brigade of Gurkhas of the British Army.

ROYAL GURKHA RIFLES

The Royal Gurkha Rifles (RGR) is a regiment of the British Army, forming part of the Brigade of Gurkhas. The Royal Gurkha Rifles are now the sole infantry regiment of the British Army Gurkhas. Like the other Gurkha regiments of the British and Indian armies, the regiment is recruited from Gurkhas, a term for people from Nepal, which is a nation independent of the United Kingdom and not a member of the Commonwealth. The regiment was formed in 1994 from the amalgamation of the four separate Gurkha regiments in the British Army:

- 2nd King Edward VII's Own Gurkha Rifles (The Sirmoor Rifles)
- 6th Queen Elizabeth's Own Gurkha Rifles
- 7th Duke of Edinburgh's Own Gurkha Rifles
- 10th Princess Mary's Own Gurkha Rifles.

The Royal Gurkha Rifles are considered to be some of the finest soldiers in the world, as is evidenced by the high regard they are held in for both their fighting skill, and their smartness of turnout on parade. Their standard of drill is considered to be on a par with that of the Foot Guards and in July 1997 the regiment mounted the guard at Buckingham Palace.

In December 1995, Lieutenant-Colonel Bijaykumar Rawat became the commanding officer of the 1st Battalion, the first Nepalese to become a battalion commander in the RGR. He oversaw the departure of the battalion from Hong Kong just before that city's transfer to Chinese control, and the battalion's relocation to Church Crookham, Hampshire in 1996. Their motto is: *Better to die than live a coward.*

ORGANIZATION

- 1st Battalion, Royal Gurkha Rifles (1994-); formed by the amalgamation of the 1st Bn, 2nd King Edward VII's Own Gurkha Rifles and 1st Bn, 6th Queen Elizabeth's Own Gurkha Rifles.
- 2nd Battalion, Royal Gurkha Rifles (1994-); formed by renaming the 1st Bn, 7th Duke of Edinburgh's Own Gurkha Rifles.
- 3rd Battalion, Royal Gurkha Rifles (1994-1996); formed by renaming the 1st Bn, 10th Princess Mary's Own Gurkha Rifles. Amalgamated with the 2nd Bn, Royal Gurkha Rifles in 1996 as part of run down of British forces in Hong Kong.

The two battalions of the RGR are formed as light role infantry; they are not equipped with either armoured or wheeled vehicles. One battalion is based at Shorncliffe, near Folkestone in Kent as part of 52 Infantry Brigade, and is available for deployment to most areas in Europe and Africa. The other is based at the British garrison in Brunei as part of Britain's commitment to maintaining a military presence in SE Asia. The two battalions rotate in each role, usually for three years at a time.

As part of the restructuring of the infantry, the UK based battalion was transferred from 2 Infantry Brigade to 52 Infantry Brigade, to be given a more mainstream role. Together with the Royal Irish Regiment and the Argyll and Sutherland Highlanders (5 SCOTS), the UK based RGR battalion will rotate as part of 16 Air Assault Brigade—it will spend five years with this formation, followed by two years as a light infantry battalion with 52 Brigade. 2RGR will take on this role for the first time in 2010.

The proximity to Afghanistan has meant that the Brunei based battalion has been called upon to deploy as part of the British force. Twice during its most recent Brunei posting the 2nd Battalion was deployed as the Afghanistan Roulement Infantry Battalion, while the 1st Battalion deployed as part of 52 Infantry Brigade in late 2007. During this tour, Cornet HRH Prince Henry of Wales was attached for a period to the 1RGR battlegroup as a Forward Air Controller.

MARATHA LIGHT INFANTRY

The Maratha Light Infantry (MLI; also the *Ganpats*) is a light infantry regiment of the Indian Army. It was formed as the 103rd Maharattas in 1768, making it the most senior light infantry regiment of the Army. The regiment recruits from the Indian state of Maharashtra. Their regimental center is in Belgaum, Karnataka. The battle cry of Maratha Light Infantry is, *Bol Shri Chattrapati Shivaji Maharaj ki Jai!* ("Cry Victory to King Shivaji!"), in tribute to the Maratha conqueror Shivaji Bhosle.

Regimental insignia

The regimental insignia is a bugle and cords with a pair of crossed swords and a shield. The bugle represents the light infantry mode of combat skirmish, controlled by orders issued on the bugles. The insignia is worn with a red and green hackle.

History

One of the most famous regiments of the Indian Army, the history of MLI spans over 240 years.

Pre-independence

The Marathas were a potent force in 16th, 17th, and 18th century India. Their military qualities were brilliantly optimised in their historic campaigns against the Mughals and the British, under the leadership of King Shivaji and succeeding Maratha rulers.Maratha armies, comprising both infantry and light cavalry, with the Maratha naval power had dominated the military scene in India for three centuries. The 1st Battalion of the Regiment, otherwise known as *Jangi Paltan* (The fighting unit), was raised in August 1768 as the 2nd Battalion Bombay Sepoys, to protect the British East India Company's possessions on the islands of Bombay.

The second battalion known as *Kali Panchwin* followed the next year as the 3rd Battalion Bombay Sepoys. From then on the regiment grew from strength to strength. These two battalions were at the forefront of virtually every major engagement fought on the west coast from Surat to Cannanore during the last quarter of the 18th century. Prominent amongst these were the historic battles of Seedaseer and Seringapatam where in the words of Lord Wellesley their *conduct and success were seldom equaled and never surpassed.*

The turn of the century was witness to the expansion of the Regimental group with the raising of 3rd Battalion as 2nd Battalion the 5th (Travancore) Regiment of the Bombay Native Infantry in 1797. The Maratha Light Infantry Regimental Centre was raised in March 1800 as the 2nd Battalion the 7th Regiment of Bombay Native Infantry; the 4th Battalion in April 1800 as the 2nd Battalion the 8th Regiment Bombay Infantry and the 5th battalion from the Bombay Fencibles as the 1st Battalion the 9th Regiment of Bombay Native Infantry in December 1800.

In the second half of the nineteenth century, the battalions fought in various campaigns from the Middle East to China. In recognition of the gallant conduct of its detachments at the siege of Kahun and the defence of Dadar, in Baluch territory during the first Afghan War in 1841, the *Kali Panchwin* was created Light Infantry. Later, this honour was also bestowed on the 3rd and 10th Regiments of the Bombay Infantry (present 1 MARATHA LI and 2 PARA respectively) for their gallantry in Sir Robert Napier's Abyssinian Campaign of 1867-1868. The Regiment assumed the title 5th Mahratta Light Infantry in 1922.

During the Peninsular war of the British against the Napoleonic armies in the 18th century, special lightly armed troops noted for their courage were used for swift encircling movements to outflank the enemy. Each battalion had a light company and later, the title Light Infantry came to be bestowed as a mark of honour.

It was not without reason that only a few Regiments were given the unique distinction of becoming Light Infantry. There was historic symbolism in recognising a fact which has been the hallmark of Maratha soldiers since the days of Shivaji. Was it not the lightly equipped and fast moving Maratha soldiery which scaled lofty mountains and impregnable forts to batter the mammoth and unwieldy Mughal armies that were trying to overrun their country? No one knew this better than the British, at times to their discomfiture.

The true fighting qualities of the Marathas were discovered during the First World War (1914-1918) when, in the long drawn out Mesopotamia campaign, three Marhatta battalions the 103rd, 114th and 117th covered themselves with glory. In the ferocious battles that took place, the battalions at times lost 50 percent of their strength in casualties but never lost an inch of ground nor left their objectives uncaptured.

The gallantry and heroism of the 117th Marhattas (present 5 Maratha LI) was of an exceptionally high order. It was made into a Royal battalion for its conspicuously distinctive service during its campaign in Mesopotamia and particularly in the events leading to the capitulation after the bitter 146 day siege at Kut-el-Amara. No less distinguished was the conduct of the 114th Marhattas (present Regimental Centre) in the battle of Sharquat where it was awarded 28 gallantry awards, the highest earned by any unit in a single action. The other Maratha battalions the 105th Mahratta Light Infantry, 110th Maratha Light Infantry, 116th Mahrattas (present 2 Maratha LI, 2 PARA and 4 Maratha LI) also acquitted themselves in Palestine and Mesopotamia. After their return to India, these six battalions of the Bombay Army were merged to form a single group and designated as the 5th Mahratta Light Infantry in 1922. The redesignation also saw 114th Mahratta become the training battalion for the group and subsequently the Regimental Centre.

The Second World War saw the Marathas in the forefront in almost every theatre of operations from the jungles of South East Asia, to the deserts of North Africa, and the mountains and rivers of Italy. The war also saw the expansion of the regiment when thirteen new war service battalions were raised. Most of these were later demobilised after the war, whilst two were converted into artillery regiments. During the war the courage and determination of the Maratha soldier reached its pinnacle when Naik Yeshwant Ghadge and Sepoy Namdeo Jadhav were decorated with the Victoria Cross in the Italian campaign. The 130 other decorations awarded to the MLI was a tribute to the fighting qualities of its men. Apart from being the first light Infantry of the Indian Army,Kali Panchwin was the first Indian Battalion to participate in World War II,first to have lost its Commanding Officer in action,Col Chitty-battle of jebel Hamrin, 1917,First Maratha Battalion to participate in UN Mission. Later, it earned the Indian Army's first Ashoka Chakra in the North-East.

POST-INDEPENDENCE

The Indian independence saw the Regiment reverting back to the original five battalions, with the 3rd Maratha Light Infantry converting to the airborne role and becoming 2nd Bn, the Parachute Regiment in April 1952. With the integration of the erstwhile princely states, the 19th, 20th, 22nd battalions were amalgamated, from the state forces of Kolhapur, Baroda, and Hyderabad, with the Regiment. The expansion of the Indian Army to meet the omnipresent threat to its borders has seen the Regiment grow to its present total of 18 battalions and two TA battalions whilst the period also saw the conversion of 21st Bn into 21 Para (Special Forces) and the 115 Infantry battalion (TA) being grouped under the Mahar Regiment.

Since Independence, battalions of the MLI have taken part in every armed conflict – Jammu and Kashmir (J&K) operations in 1947-1948, entry into Junagarh, Liberation of Hyderabad, Goa, Daman and Diu, the Chinese aggression in 1961, conflicts with Pakistan in 1965 and 1971 against the Chinese on the Sikkim watershed in 1956, the operations in Sri Lanka, the on going operations in the Siachen glacier and in counter insurgency operations.

The conduct and performance of its troops in Korea, Laos and the Gaza strip as part of UN Peace keeping missions have drawn worldwide acclaim. The Regiment has conducted itself creditably whenever called upon for peacetime duties and combating insurgency and terrorism and reposed the confidence and faith.

The Ashoka Chakra awarded to Captain Eric Tucker(2 Maratha LI) and Colonel N. J. Nair(16 Maratha LI),Col Venugopal(9 Maratha LI), the five Mahavir Chakras and the numerous other war and peace time gallantry awards bear testimony to the frontline leadership and courage of the Regiment's Offrs, JCOs and men. Over the past two and a quarter centuries the Regiment has won a number of honours and awards.

Gen JJ Singh(9th and 5th) became the first Chief Of Army Staff from the Maratha Light Infantry in Feb.2005., a proud moment for the regiment indeed. Lt Col KS Gill, SM** from 1st battalion Maratha Light Infantry (Jangi Paltan) is holding the coveted appointment of Adjutant, National Defence Academy. The sight of the highly decorated officer astride his white charger 'WARRIOR' is enough to motivate whole new generation of young cadets to join the regiment.

BATTALIONS

- 1st Battalion(Jangi Paltan)
- 2nd Battalion (Kali Panchwin)
- 4th Battalion
- 5th Battalion
- 6th Battalion
- 7th Battalion
- 8th Battalion
- 9th Battalion
- 11th Battalion-AAKRAMAK AKRA [*The Aggressive/ Attacking Eleven*]
- 12th Battalion
- 14th Battalion
- 15th Battalion
- 16th Battalion
- 17th Battalion
- 18th Battalion
- 19th Battalion
- 22nd Battalion

- 26th Battalion
- 101 Infantry Battalion (TA)
- 109 Infantry Battalion (TA)
- 17 RR Maratha LI
- 27 RR Maratha LI
- 41 RR Maratha LI
- 56 RR Maratha LI.

Affiliations

Two special forces battalions of the Parachute Regiment (2 PARA (SF) & 21 PARA (SF), one mechanized battalion (10 Bn, Mechanised Infantry Regt), two Arty regiments (34 Medium Regiment & 36 Medium Regiment) one guided missile destroyer (INS Mumbai) and a fighter squadron (20 Sqn Air force) are also affiliated to the regiment.

SIKH LIGHT INFANTRY

The Sikh Light Infantry previously known as *"The Mazabhi and Ramdasia Sikh Regiment"* is a Regiment of the Indian Army. Its name was changed to the Sikh Light Infantry in 1944. The Sikh Light Infantry is the successor unit to the Mazhabi Sikh Pioneers 23rd, 32nd and 34th Sikh Pioneers. The Sikh Light Infantry inherited the battle honours, colours and traditions of the Mazhabi Sikh Pioneers on its merging with a few Ramdasia companies in 1941.

Regiment History

The Sikh Light Infantry comprises the Mazhabi and Ramdasia Sikh soldiers; well known for their dountless daring,courage, loyalty and tenacity, is one of the oldest Regiments of the Army. It traces its origin to the middle of the nineteenth century when the first Mazhabi soldiers were recruited into the British Indian Army. The first Corps of Mazhabi Sikh Pioneers, the fore bearer of the Sikh Light Infantry, was formed in 1850. The British had recognised the great fighting qualities and prowess of these soldiers in the Anglo-Sikh Wars. The stubborn and sustained resistance offered by them and their ability to maintain themselves frugally amazed them. The British had admiration for the mazhabi as they made *capital soldiers*. Maharaja Ranjit Singh also had a great admiration for their bravery and enlisted the mazhabis freely into the khalsa army; Which he nurtured into an excellent instrument of war. Being afraid, however, to form the mazhabis into a separate corps, he attached a mazhabi company to existing battalions.

Soldiering has been a way of life for the Sikhs of Punjab for centuries. After the Indian rebellion of 1857 the Bengal army regiments were replaced by the Punjabis as the major source of manpower for the British Army in India, but their loyalty had to be carefully nurtured. The British made many mistakes, at first failing even to recognize the religious significance of the Sikhs' beards and long hair. Performing well in World War I, the 23rd Sikh Pioneers, 32nd Sikh Pioneers and 34th Sikh Pioneers were then disbanded in 1933, a traumatic experience for the community. However, the Sikh Pioneers were re-raised for the second world war, becoming the Mazhabi and Ramdasia Sikh Regiment before being re-named the Sikh Light Infantry in 1944. The reconquest of Burma was essentially an Indian Army campaign. It was here that the Sikh Light Infantry was deployed. The fledgling regiment tasted blood and earned its first battle honours. Most of the Sikhs in the Light Infantry consist of mazhabi, and some Ramdasia sikhs.

The two homogeneous Sikh regiments are the Sikh Light Infantry and the Sikh Regiment, the former with 18 regular battalions and each contain approximately twenty battalions that account for a major element of the strike force in the main army divisions.

The Raising

In June 1857 a Regiment of Sikh Pioneers from the Mazhabi sikh soldiers drawn mainly from the Punjab and the adjacent areas was raised by Lt DC Home, VC. The regular Regiment 15th (Pioneer), was raised at Lahore on September 15, 1857 by Lt RH Shebbeare, VC. After a number of changes this 15th (Pioneer) Regiment came to be known as the 23rd Sikh Pioneers in 1908. (The 32nd Sikh Pioneers followed this). The 23rd and 32nd Regiments gave such an excellent account of themselves, establishing outstanding standards, that it was decided to raise another Regiment of Sikh Pioneers from the 34th Fatehgarh Levy, which had been raised from Mazbhi sikh Pioneers on March 28, 1887. Thus, the well-known trio of Sikh Pioneers that won fame through their deeds of glory was complete. Lt Gen Sir George Mac Munn, Commended the Regt for their memorable service, he wrote *"The sikh Pioneers were, for three quarters of a century, in the forefront of almost every campaign from the China Wall to the Flanders Rats."*

World War 1

During the First world war, the 23rd, 32nd and 34th Sikh Pioneers, which were originally one battalion regiments were developed into three battalions each. Soon these battalions were tramping over the battlefields of Egypt, Europe, Palestine and Mesopotamia leaving indelible imprints wherever they went. Once again a number of Battle Honours-"Egypt 1916-17"; "Gaza"; "Megiddo"; "Sharon"; "Nablus"; "Palestine 1917-18"; and "Aden" emblazoned the glorious record of the Sikh Pioneers. There were ten battalions of Sikh Pioneers (including the Training Battalion) when the armistice was declared in 1919.

The 1/34th Sikh Pioneers won the title of "Royal" during the Great War. They made a bronze screen from the driving bands of enemy shells. The unit armourer and blacksmith made this highly burnished screen, proudly displaying the magnificent achievements of the Sikh Pioneers as epitomized in their Battle Honors. The 34th Royal Sikh Pioneers presented this screen to King George V in 1933. It was through the personal intervention of Brig. F.R.L. Goadby (32nd Sikh Pioneers) and Lt Gen. Sir RA Savory, the first Colonel of the Regiment, that Queen Elizabeth II presented the historic screen back to the Regiment on October 4, 1975. The screen was unveiled by Brig AK Chatterjee, VSM, Colonel of the Regiment, at a special Durbar on April 9, 1977. Another remarkable victory was registered on December 21, 1919, when two companies of the 3/34th Sikh Pioneers, alone on a hill top (Black Hill) with no more than a knee-high wall and a few strands of barbed wire in front, gallantly faced and repelled waves of attacks on them by hordes of Mahsuds. There was grim hand-to-hand fighting with Capt. B. L. Gupta (he was awarded the Military Cross), the Indian Medical Officer with the Battalion, tending the wounded under constant enemy fire. The Battalion was awarded one DSO, two Military Crosses and a Bar to Military Cross. Twelve Indian Viceroy's Commissioned Officers and Other Ranks received well-merited decorations.

That night General Skeen published a complimentary Column Order announcing that in honour of the gallant action of the 3/34th Sikh Pioneers, a stone from the unfinished Black Hill Picquet be brought to the camp and formed as the base for the pioneer picuet memorial silverMess trophy. This trophy was presented by the 3/34th on their disbandment in June 1921, to the 1st Battalion of the 34th Royal Sikh Pioneers. When the Sikh Pioneers were disbanded in 1933, the curator of the British War Museum took this famous trophy. It was later given on a permanent loan to the SIKH LI and is housed in the Regimental Museum. As a result of the post-war reorganization of 1923, the battalions of the Sikh Pioneers were in 1929, reduced to a Corps HQ with one battalion from each of the three regiments.

Disbandment

Four years later, February 10, 1933, was a sad day for the Regiment as the Sikh Pioneers were disbanded after 75 years of glorious service. This was essentially a measure of economy especially as the Sappers and Miners were to be augmented with an increased number of Mazhabi Companies. A farewell parade was held at Sialkot on December 8, 1932, when the Sikh Pioneers paraded for the last time. Drawn up in line 1,600 strong were the 1st and 2nd Battalions, once the 23rd, 32nd and 34th, with the Corps Headquarters and the massed bands. At the saluting point was a crowd of spectators including many old bemedalled pensioners of the Sikh Pioneer regiments.

Re-Raising for World war II

After suspended animation of a little over eight years, the Sikh Pioneers were re-raised to meet the urgent and mounting demands of World War II. The 1st Battalion was raised at Jullundur on October 1, 1941. The 2nd and 3rd Battalions were raised at Peshawar and Sialkot on July 1, 1942 and August 15, 1942 respectively. Recruitment had been opend up to the Ramdasia sikhs. The re-raised Regiment was known as the *"Mazhbi and*

Ramdasia Sikhs" a nomenclature, which was found uninspiring. The Commander-in-Chief, General Sir Claude 'Auchinleck, wanted this changed and the Director General of Infantry, Maj Gen (later Lt Gen) Reginald Arthur Savory was tasked to find a suitable name for the Regiment. A committee was constituted at Army HQ, after some alternatives like the Sikh Fusiliers, the Sikh Rifles and the Sikh Grenadiers had been considered and examined, the Sikh Light Infantry was chosen. This became prevalent from June 23, 1944. The newly raised 1st Battalion joined the battlefronts of the 14th Army just a little after three years of being raised. The Battalion was flown to Meiktila (Burma) in February 1945 and became part of the 17th Division (Black Cat). The soldiers of the Battalion gave ample proof of, their valour, fighting in the jungles of Burma for eight months, they won the Battle Honours. "Defence of Meiktila": " Burma 1942-45; *"Rangoon Road"; "Pyabwe" and "Sittang 1945".*

Regimental Battalions

1st Battalion
2nd Battalion
3rd Battalion
4th Battalion
5th Battalion
6th Battalion
7th Battalion
8th Battalion
9th Battalion
10th Battalion
11th Battalion
12th Battalion
13th Battalion
14th Battalion
15th Battalion
16th Battalion
17th Battalion

18th Battalion
103 Inf Bn (TA) Sikh LI
158 Inf Bn (TA) (H&H) Sikh LI
163 Inf Bn (TA) (H&H) Sikh LI.

Historical Regiment Battles

The 1 Sikh Light Infantry

Israeli attacks on the 1st Sikh Light Infantry, which was part of the United Nations Emergency Force (UNEF), in the 1967 Arab-Israeli war cost the battalion more casualties than it suffered in its bloodiest engagement in the 1965 Indian-Pakistan war, Indian officers have charged. A United Nations spokesman in New York said 14 Indians were killed and 16 were wounded. On the first day of the Israeli-Egyptian fighting, an Indian convoy was en route from Camp Rafah to Gaza flying the U.N. flag from each jeep and truck. The convoy met an Israeli tank column on the road.

On 28 September 1965, 6 Sikh LI was ordered to take two important hill features as a preliminary to clearing a feature on Kalidhar in Jammu and Kashmir which Pakistani forces had, notwithstanding the cease-fire, encroached upon. With utter disregard for personal safety, the Battalion assaulted and captured both the preliminary objectives. The enemy brought down heavy artillery fire and counter-attacks three times. Two of the counter-attacks were beaten off with heavy casualties to the enemy. Due to heavy casualties and pressure of the enemy, our troops had to fall back from one of the two hill features. At this stage the Battalion halted the enemy's advance and stabilized the situation.

The 5 Sikh Light Infantry

In 1965, 5 Sikh Light Infantry was holding picket in Jammu and Kashmir. Pakistani troops had occupied a complex of hills called "OP Hill" in Mendar Sector. The complex dominated Road Mender Balnoi, thus isolating one infantry battalion and its administrative base at Balnoi. Earlier attempts to dislodge the enemy having failed, 5 Sikh L.I. was selected and moved to Mendar Sector to take part in a bridge attack on OP Hill. The battalion was new and its officers were very young, only one company commander had more than three years' service. The Commanding Officer decided to personally lead the assault. The approaches to the feature were heavily mined and, anticipating an attack, the enemy had ensured heavy concentration of artillery fire. The attack was launched before midnight on 2 November 1965. The morale of troops was very high and the Battalion captured its objective in a lightning move from a totally unexpected direction. Having surprised the enemy, the Commanding Officer, Lt. Col. Sant Singh (now Brig. Sant Singh, MVC, (Bar) (Retd.)) decided to exploit the advantage and ordered the capture of three more objectives which were assigned to another Battalion. The highest feature and the ground of tactical importance for the enemy was captured by midnight. The hills reverberated with the sound of the success signal-"Reveille on the bugle". Subsequently, two more objectives were captured, thus completing four attacks in one night. The highlights of the attacks were the enthusiasm displayed by men and launching of additional attacks without waiting for orders from the Brigade Commander. Throughout, the enemy put up a very tough fight and each bunker had to be cleared after hand-to-hand fighting. For taking most spectacular initiative in launching three additional attacks and for displaying conspicuous gallantry and inspiring leadership, the Commanding Officer (Lt Col. Sant Singh) was awarded Maha Vir Chakra. One more Maha Vir Chakra was awarded to Naik Darshan Singh (Posthumous). Besides these; one Vir Chakra (Posthumous), four Sena Medals (2 Posthumous) and five Commendation Cards were awarded. The Regiment was bestowed Battle Honour "Chuh-i-Nar 1965". In North East sector 5 Sikh L.I. was given a task of making new posts following Sino-India pact in 90s. Showing the valour, courage and great enthusiasm task was completed in most difficult terrain without the help of any engineering regiments. Four Commendation Cards were awarded and front post was named after Sohan Singh (Hony. Capt. Sohan Singh retd.)

The 6 Sikh Light Infantry

6 Sikh L.I. operated in Chamb Sector against Pakistani infiltrators and regular forces. The Battalion resisted every attempt by the enemy to infiltrate/raid/lay ambushes in the Battalion

Sector. The Battalion withstood worst ever shelling 15 August 1965 and stood out valiantly in their posts on the cease-fire line to the admiration of all troops despite intensive enemy shelling, disruption of communications and increased casualties. The stand of the battalion enabled 191 Brigade Group to reorganize, regroup and take offensive action to reoccupy posts vacated on 15–17 August 1965. 6 Sikh L.I. were ordered to retake lost posts of Maira and Nathan, with one company 3 Mahar and one troop 'C' squadron 20 Lancers under command, reoccupied both posts on 17 August 1965. Vigorious offensive action by all ranks kept the enemy at bay and delayed his offensive till 1 September 1965, by the time he was able to concentrate his armour, infantry, artillery, RCL, and MMG mounted on jeeps and infantry in greater strength to pierce through wide gaps between posts, outnumbered, outshelled, outgunned and threatened own posts on cease-fire line with encirclement and annihilation in details.

On 1 September 1965, the battalions artillery and air support failed, any communication or reinforcement ultimately disintegrated and it was no longer possible to hold out. Devastated but undeterred by Pakistan airforce and artillery, Battalion Headquarters with remnants of one company and 'C' squadron 20 Lancers underwent continuous shelling, withdrew before midnight on 1 September 1965 on orders from Headquarters 191 Infantry Brigade Group. The battalion fought with its back against the wall against innumerable odds and stood up well. It was indeed a great satisfaction that the battalion carried out the duty to its best ability. It was this feeling in fact that made the Battalion to quickly absorb reinforcement, re-equip and be operational to take on any task assigned to it culminating in the capture of Trig point 3776 (Kalidhar) on 4 October 1965. In this battle all ranks showed tenacity of purpose, determination, courage, devotion to duty and a spirit of self-sacrifice.

On the night of 3 October 1965 the Battalion was given the task of clearing the same objective with the help of a Mahar battalion. In the morning on 4 October 1965, 6 Sikh L.I. secured it objectives in spite of treacherous cliffish terrain, heavy enemy opposition and shelling, the battalion continued to advance up a very steep slope in the face of intensive enemy artillery fire and opposition by Infantry. Despite casualties and strong opposition, our troops continued to press forward and successfully secured three other important features by evening of the same day. The enemy staged three counter-attacks in heavy strength supported by artillery fire but they were all repulsed with heavy casualties.

The Battalion re-organized itself for the next assault on Kalidhar Trig Point 3776 despite heavy casualties and fatigue. The feature was finally cleared of the Pakistani intruders by mid-day on 5 October 1965. In this action the Battalion displayed remarkable courage, determination and self sacrifice for which one Maha Vir Chakra (Lt Col. PK Nandagopal), two Vir Chakras, four Sena Medals (two posthumous); five Mention in Despatches (three Posthumous) and one COAS's Commendation Card were awarded. The Regiment was also awarded the Battle Honour "Kalidhar 1965"

The 8 Sikh Light Infantry

11 December 1971 is a red letter day in the history of 8 Sikh L.I. Pak Fatehpur post, fortified on all four sides with high bunds, was a virtual fortress with innumerable automatic and anti-tank weapons deployed for its defence. Its diamond-like shape made it equally difficult to tackle from all side, on the night of 11 December the brave men of 8 Sikh Light Infantry discounted all difficulties and rushed forward on to this coveted objective, in the face of deadly small arms fire and devastating artillery shelling. Many a gallant soldier fell but others moved on undaunted. Not before long the enemy was either destroyed or in desperate flight, leaving behind large quantity of arms and ammunition. Apparently, the enemy had not accepted final defeat yet, he continued to plaster this position with accurate artillery and mortar fire from several directions. Two counter attacks attempted by the previously fleeing soldiers were disorganized and defeated by the 8 Sikh L.I.

In this battle, three officers, one JCO and 32 Ors sacrificed their life and approximately 100 others were wounded. A young battalion, within five years of its raising, had fought its maiden battle in masterly style and had come of age. The number of officers killed, wounded is tribute to the quality of glowing leadership provided by them.

8 Sikh L.I was awarded the Battle Honour "Fathepur" for this heroic action. Medals awarded for the battle include, one Mahavir Chakra, five Vir Chakras (2 posthumous), four Sena Medals (2 posthumous) and two Mention-in Despatches (Posthumous).

THE 10 SIKH LIGHT INFANTRY

10 Sikh L.I. spearheaded the advance of 85 Infantry Brigade Northward through the Sind Desert along the railway line Munabao-Naya Chor completing all the operational tasks given to it with distinction, right up to the day of cease fire, during the Indo-Pak operations in 1971. Kajlor the first objective, was overrun on 4 December 1971 and the second phase of the attack became redundant as the enemy flew helter-skelter without any loss to our troops. Next day advance was resumed and Khokh-Ropar Railway station saw the enemies blood turn to water with the battle cry of 'Bole so Nihal' the advance coming to a temporary halt at Bhitala as the administrative echelons had failed to negotiate the treacherous sand of the Sind desert.

The advance was maintained along Vasarbha railway station through December 5–7, 1971. By 1700 hrs on December 7, 10 Sikh L.I. reached Parche Jiveri station (now called Bahadur Nagar). The enemy strafed the battalion, wherein Sep. Kulwant Singh was killed while bringing down an enemy Sabre by his LMG fire and was awarded the Sena Medal for this brave deed. The Battalion firmed in on 8 December on approaching Naya Chor enemy defence. The key to the enemy defences was a dominating feature, Parbat Ali. The enemy brought down heavy artillery fire and country attacked twice but were beaten back and decided wisely to withdraw. The battalion firmed in and remained there till last light on 12 December.

10 Sikh L.I. was ordered to capture Village Parche Jiveri (Bahadur Nagar) and on the night of 14 December the battalion launched its attack. The assaulting companies ran into a mine-field and Maj Arora was severally wounded. Seeing the situation Commanding Officer Lt Col. Basant Singh left his post and himself moved up along with his Intelligence Officer, late Capt Bahadur Singh, Vir Chakra. While the Commanding Officer, was inspiring his troops, Capt Bahadur Singh, went up to the Artillery officer's

post and continued to direct artillery fire until hit by an enemy bullet in the head, and died on the spot. The attack went in through the minefields and heavy enemy fire. The enemy fled leaving behind 20 dead, two recoilless guns and a Jeep, besides vast quantities of ammunition. The battalion acquitted itself in an exemplary manner throughout this brief war and was awarded Battle Honour "Parbat Ali" and theatre honour "Sind 1971". Besides gallantry awards; five Vir Chakra, seven Sena Medals and three Mention-in-Despatches were awarded.

The 13 Sikh Light Infantry

13 Sikh Light Infantry battle at Kokkuvil, Sri Lanka, and the saga of the heroic fight put in by twenty-nine men have embedded themselves into the realms of history without an iota of doubt. The Battalion (less two companies) at Palali air fields in Sri Lanka, was tasked to capture LTTE military headquarters at Jaffna University.

At midnight the first Mi-8 helicopter of the 10th Battalion Parachute Regiment, Delta Company, took off for the landing zone, soon followed by the second Mi-8 helicopter. The platoon for Delta company led by late Maj. Birendra Singh, had to face tough resistance landing amidst heavy and accurate enemy machine gun fire.

The LTTE had intercepted radio communications allowing them advanced knowledge of the planned raid. The follow-up helicopters which were airborne were ordered to return to Palali, as three of the five helicopters having been hit resulted in no further landing behind the enemy lines in the LTTE strongest foothold. Amidst the confusing situation the remaining members of the Battalion was ordered to advance on vehicles to establish link with the beleaguered platoon of Delta Company. All communication had snapped, the last transmission from late Maj Birendra Singh of 13th Battalion, The Sikh Light Infantry Regiment, stating; "Not to worry, We'll hold on..."

SIKH REGIMENT

The Sikh Regiment is a regiment of the Indian Army. It is currently the highest decorated regiment in the Indian Army and was at one stage the highest decorated regiment in the British Empire. The Sikh Regimental Centre is located in Ramgarh Cantonment, 30 km from the Ranchi, which is the capital of the state of Jharkhand in India. The Centre was earlier located in Meerut in the state of Uttar Pradesh.

Over its life of more than 150 years, the regiment has participated in various actions and operations both in the pre and post-independence era in India and abroad, including the First and the Second World War. With a humble beginning of two battalions, today the fraternity has grown to a regiment of 1 training, 17 regular infantry and two reserve battalions strong. Enlisted soldiers are strictly recruited from the Sikh community, while officers are recruited from all regions and areas of India. The war cry of regiment, taken from Sikh scriptures is: *Jo Bole So Nihal, Sat Sri Akal* (He who cries God is Truth, is ever Happy)

Brief History

Maharaja Ranjit Singh brought the well built and courageous people, of the then Punjab, and other martial tribes and formed "Khalsa Army". Following numerous heroic and valiant battles by the Khalsa Army, XIV Ferozepur (1 Sikh, now 4 Mechanised Infantry), and XV Ludhiana (2 Sikh) were raised from the soldiers of the vanquished force on August 1, 1846.

The Sikh Regiment came into existence on 1 August 1846, with the raising of Regiment of Ferozepore Sikhs and Regiment of Ludhiana Sikhs by Captain G. Tebbs and Lieutenant Colonel P. Gordon respectively and were used in great effect in the 1857 Indian Rebellion.

The outcomes were extremely beneficial for the Sikhs, as their loyalty and fighting tenacity made them the backbone of recruitment for the British Indian Army. In this campaign the Sikhs were awarded their first two battle honours for operations conducted at the seige of Lucknow and the defence of Arrah.

In addition the Sikh Regiment were awarded a one rank seniority over other Indian Sepoys and awarded the authorisation to wear the converted red turban (which is still worn by the regiment today) opposed to the standard blue head dress worn by British Indian Army Units at the time. The Sikh Regiment was further used as a vanguard unit for the British Empire being used to garrison India internally, protect Indian frontiers (such as the North-West Frontier Province) and to serve in over seas deployments such as operations in Hong Kong. By 1914 Sikh Regiments were deployed as part of the British Indian Army for operations in World War I. The Regiment served in all theatres of operations and earning 28 battle honours.

In 1931 Adolf Hitler had seen the strength of the Sikh regiment in the war of France. Hitler had given a speech for the Sikhs to join the Nazis, but most of regiment had kept their loyalty towards the British because the empire had always given large amounts of land, money, and provided them to stay in other countries.

Sikhs make up 10–15% of all ranks in the Indian Army and 20% of its officers, whilst Sikhs only forming 1.87% of the Indian population, which makes them over 10 times more likely to be a soldier and officer in the Indian Army than the average Indian. The Sikh Regiment is one of the highest decorated regiment of the Indian Army, with 73 Battle Honours, 14 Victoria Crosses, 21 first class Indian Order of Merit (equivalent to the Victoria Cross), 15 Theatre Honours and 5 COAS Unit Citations besides 2 Param Vir Chakras, 14 Maha Vir Chakras, 5 Kirti Chakras, 67 Vir Chakras and 1596 other gallantry awards.The highest-ranking General in the history of the Indian Air Force is a Punjabi Sikh Marshal of the Air Force Arjan Singh. Advanced plans by the MOD to raise an Infantry UK Sikh Regiment were scrapped in June 2007 to the disappointment of the UK Sikh community and Prince Charles of Britain.

Fallen and Injured under the British

In the last two World Wars 83,005 turban wearing Sikh soldiers were killed and 109.045 were wounded. They all died or were wounded for the freedom of Britain and the World, enduring shell fire with no other protection but the turban, the symbol of their faith.

Operation Bluestar

Following Operation Bluestar, some of the recruits at Ramgarh mutinied. They shot and killed the Commandant of the Sikh

Regimental Center, Brigadier S.C. Puri and wounded some other officers. They then got hold of a number of trucks and started to proceed towards Punjab, but were stopped by army men in Bihar and Uttar Pradesh.

A part of 9 Sikh which was in the Ganganagar area of Rajasthan mutinied. This battalion was disbanded on April 1, 1985. Following Operation Bluestar, the then COAS, General Arun S. Vaidya wanted to have more mixed battalions. So he passed an order that single class battalions should begin recruiting other classes as well as their parent class. These mixed battalion came to be known as *Vaidya's Battalions.* The 13 Sikh is the Vaidya battalion and its class composition consists of a company each of Sikhs, Dogras, Garhwalis and South Indians.

Awards and Citations

The Museum of the Regimental Centre displays a record of the Sikh Regiment in four halls viz.,

- The Religious/motivational Hall,
- The Hall of Heritage,
- The Regimental Glory Hall
- The Peripheral Gallery.

The Chief of Army Staff (COAS) made a special instant award of "Unit Citation" to 8th Battalion, The Sikh Regiment for their meritorious and gallant performance during the isolation of Tiger Hill, which facilitated the capture of Tiger Hill top and battles of Helmet and India Gate, features to the West of Tiger Hill top, on night 07/8 July 1999, in Dras Sector.

During Operation *Vijay,* the unit displayed sterling performance marked with exceptional valour and grit in the face of the enemy.

In all, the Regiment has to its credit 1652 gallantry awards and honours including

- 2 Param Vir Chakra
    - o Lance Naik Karam Singh in 1948 during Kashmir operations.
    - o Subedar Joginder Singh during the Sino-Indian War of 1962.

- 14 Maha Vir Chakra (MVC)
- 68 Vir Chakra.
- 14 Victoria Crosses

In addition it has also earned:

- 73 battle honours
- 38 theatre honours besides four COAS Unit Citation, including
    - o the one bestowed upon 8 Sikh during the 1999 Kargil episode
    - o and two "Bravest of the Brave" citations.

7

Naval Aviation

Naval Aviation is the application of manned military air power by navies. Maritime Aviation is the operation of aircraft in a maritime role under the command of land based forces such as RAF Coastal Command or United States Coast Guard.

Naval aviation is typically projected to a position nearer the target by way of an aircraft carrier. Carrier aircraft must be relatively sturdy to withstand demanding carrier operations. They must be able to launch in a short distance and be sturdy and flexible enough to come to a sudden stop on a pitching deck; they typically have robust folding mechanisms that allow higher numbers of them to be stored in below-decks hangars. These aircraft are designed for many purposes including air-to-air combat, surface attack, submarine attack, search and rescue, materiel transport, weather observation, reconnaissance and wide area command and control duties.

In the United States military services, Marine Aviation is supported by Navy Amphibious assault ships and associated Navy personnel.

History

The foundations of naval aviation were set in June 1912, when Lieutenant Dimitrios Kamberos of the Hellenic Aviation Service flew with the "Daedalus", a Farman Aviation Works aircraft that had been converted into a seaplane, at an average speed of 110Km per hour, achieving a new world record. Then, on January 24, 1913 the first wartime naval aviation interservice cooperation mission, took place above the Dardanelles. Greek Army First

Lieutenant Michael Moutoussis and Greek Navy Ensign Aristedes Moraitines, on board the Maurice Farman hydroplane (floatplane/ seaplane), drew a diagram of the positions of the Turkish fleet against which they dropped four bombs. This event was widely commented upon in the press, both Greek and international.

In the United States, Captain Henry C. Mustin is often referred to as "The Father of Naval Aviation." He successfully designed the concept of the catapult launch, and in 1915 made the first catapult launching from a ship underway.

WWI and the First Carrier Strikes

The first strike from a carrier against a land target as well as a sea target took place in September 1914 when the Imperial Japanese Navy seaplane carrier *Wakamiya* conducted the world's first ship-launched air raids from Kiaochow Bay during the Battle of Tsingtao in China. The four Maurice Farman seaplanes bombarded German-held land targets (communication centers and command centers) and damaged a German minelayer in the Tsingtao peninsula from September until November 6, 1914, when the Germans surrendered. On the Western front the first naval air raid occurred on December 25, 1914 when twelve seaplanes from HMS' *Engadine*, *Riviera* and *Empress* (cross-channel steamers converted into seaplane carriers) attacked the Zeppelin base at Cuxhaven. The attack was not a success though a German warship was damaged.

Development in the Interwar Period

In the United States, Billy Mitchell's 1921 demonstration of the battleship-sinking ability of land-based heavy bombers made many United States Navy admirals angry. However, some men, such as Captain (soon Rear Admiral) William A. Moffett, saw the publicity stunt as a means to increase funding and support for the Navy's aircraft carrier projects. Moffett was sure that he had to move decisively in order to avoid having his fleet air arm fall into the hands of a proposed combined Land/Sea Air Force which took care of *all* the United States's airpower needs. That exact fate had befallen United Kingdom's two air services in 1918; the Royal Flying Corps had been combined with the Royal Naval Air Service to become the Royal Air Force, a condition which would remain until 1937. Moffett supervised the development of naval air tactics throughout the '20s.

Many British naval vessels carried float planes, seaplanes or amphibians for reconnaissance and spotting: two to four on battleships or battlecruisers and one on cruisers. The aircraft, a Fairey Seafox or later a Supermarine Walrus, were catapult-launched, and landed on the sea alongside for recovery by crane. Several submarine aircraft carriers were built by Japan. The French Navy built one large (but ineffective) aircraft carrying submarine, the Surcouf.

World War II

World War II saw the emergence of naval aviation as a significant, often decisive, element in the war at sea. The principal users were Japan, United States (both with Pacific interests to protect) and the United Kingdom. Other colonial powers, eg France and the Netherlands, showed a lesser interest. Other powers, such as Germany, Italy and the Soviet Union, did not develop naval aviation, for geographic or political reasons.

During the course of the war, seaborne aircraft were used in fleet actions at sea (Battle of Midway, Bismarck), pre-emptive strikes against naval units in port (Battle of Taranto, Attack on Pearl Harbor), support of ground forces (Battle of Okinawa, Allied invasion of Italy) and anti-submarine warfare (Second Battle of the Atlantic).

Experience showed that there was a need for widespread use of aircraft which could not be met quickly enough by the building of new fleet aircraft carriers. This was particularly true in the north Atlantic, where convoys were highly vulnerable to U-boat attack. The British authorities used unorthodox, temporary, but effective means of giving air protection such as CAM ships and merchant aircraft carriers, merchant ships modified to carry a small number of aircraft. The solution to the problem were large numbers of mass-produced merchant hulls converted into escort aircraft carriers (also known as "jeep carriers"). These basic vessels, unsuited to fleet action by their capacity, speed and vulnerability, nevertheless provided air cover where it was needed.

The Royal Navy had observed the impact of naval aviation and, obliged to prioritise their use of resources, abandoned battleships as the mainstay of the fleet. HMS *Vanguard* was therefore the last British battleship and her sisters were cancelled. The United States had already instigated a large construction programme (which was also cut short) but these large ships were mainly used as anti-aircraft batteries or for shore bombardment.

Roles

Strategic Projection

Carrier-based naval aviation provides a country's seagoing forces with air cover over areas that may not be reachable by land-based aircraft, giving them a considerable advantage over navies composed primarily of surface combatants.

In the case of the United States Navy during and after the Cold War, virtual command of the sea in many of the world's waterways allowed it to deploy aircraft carriers and project air power almost anywhere on the globe. By operating from international waters, U.S. carriers can bypass the need for conventional airbases or overflight rights, both of which can be politically difficult to acquire.

Anti-submarine

During the Cold War, the navies of NATO faced a significant threat from Soviet submarine forces, specifically Soviet Navy SSN and SSGN assets. This resulted in the development and deployment of light aircraft carriers with major anti-submarine warfare (ASW) capabilities by European NATO navies. One of the most effective weapons against submarines is the ASW helicopter, several of which could be based on these light aircraft carriers. These light carriers were typically around 20,000 tons displacement and carried a mix of ASW helicopters and BAe Sea Harrier or Harrier II V/STOL aircraft.

Naval Aviation Branches

- Argentine Naval Aviation
- Brazilian Naval Aviation
- Fleet Air Arm (RAN)

- Fleet Air Arm (Royal Navy)
- French Naval Aviation
- Indian Naval Air Arm
- Mexican Naval Aviation
- People's Liberation Army Naval Air Force
- Peruvian Naval Aviation
- Russian Naval Aviation
- United States Naval Aviation.

AIR TRAFFIC CONTROL

Air traffic control (ATC) is a service provided by ground-based controllers who direct aircraft on the ground and in the air. The primary purpose of ATC systems worldwide is to *separate* aircraft to prevent collisions, to organize and expedite the flow of traffic, and to provide information and other support for pilots when able. In some countries, ATC may also play a security or defence role (as in the United States), or be run entirely by the military (as in Brazil).

Preventing collisions is referred to as separation, which is a term used to prevent aircraft from coming too close to each other by use of lateral, vertical and longitudinal separation minima; many aircraft now have collision avoidance systems installed to act as a backup to ATC observation and instructions. In addition to its primary function, the ATC can provide additional services such as providing information to pilots, weather and navigation information and NOTAMs (*NOtices To AirMen*).

In many countries, ATC services are provided throughout the majority of airspace, and its services are available to all users (private, military, and commercial). When controllers are responsible for separating some or all aircraft, such airspace is called "controlled airspace" in contrast to "uncontrolled airspace" where aircraft may fly without the use of the air traffic control system. Depending on the type of flight and the class of airspace, ATC may issue *instructions* that pilots are required to follow, or merely *flight information* (in some countries known as *advisories*) to assist pilots operating in the airspace. In all cases, however, the pilot in command has final responsibility for the safety of the flight, and may deviate from ATC instructions in an emergency.

Although the native language for a region is normally used, the English language must be used on request, as required by the International Civil Aviation Organization (ICAO).

History

In 1919, the International Commission for Air Navigation (ICAN) was created to develop General Rules for Air Traffic. Its rules and procedures were applied in most countries where aircraft operated. The United States did not sign the ICAN Convention, but later developed its own set of air traffic rules after passage of the Air Commerce Act of 1926. This legislation authorized the Department of Commerce to establish air traffic rules for the navigation, protection, and identification of aircraft, including rules as to safe altitudes of flight and rules for the prevention of collisions between vessels and aircraft. The first rules were brief and basic. For example, pilots were told not to begin their takeoff until there is no risk of collision with landing aircraft and until preceding aircraft are clear of the field. As traffic increased, some airport operators realized that such general rules were not enough to prevent collisions. They began to provide a form of air traffic control (ATC) based on visual signals. Early controllers, like Archie League (one of the first system's flagmen), stood on the field, waving flags to communicate with pilots.

As more aircraft were fitted for radio communication, radio-equipped airport traffic control towers began to replace the flagmen. In 1930, the first radio-equipped control tower in the United States began operating at the Cleveland Municipal Airport. By 1935, about 20 radio control towers were operating. Increases in the number of flights created a need for ATC that was not just confined to airport areas but also extended out along the airways. In 1935, the principal airlines using the Chicago, Cleveland, and Newark airports agreed to coordinate the handling of airline traffic between those cities. In December, the first Airway Traffic Control Center opened at Newark, New Jersey. Additional centers at Chicago and Cleveland followed in 1936.

The early controllers tracked the position of planes using maps and blackboards and little boat-shaped weights that came to be called shrimp boats. They had no direct radio link with aircraft but used telephones to stay in touch with airline dispatchers, airway radio operators, and airport traffic controllers. In July 1936, en route ATC became a federal responsibility and the first appropriation of $175,000 was made ($2,665,960 today). The Federal Government provided airway traffic control service, but local government authorities where the towers were located continued to operate those facilities.

In 1941, Congress appropriated funds for the Civil Aeronautics Administration (CAA) to construct and operate ATC towers, and soon the CAA began taking over operations at the first of these towers, with their number growing to 115 by 1944. In the postwar era, ATC at most airports was eventually to become a permanent federal responsibility. In response to wartime needs, the CAA also greatly expanded its en route air traffic control system.

The postwar years saw the beginning of a revolutionary development in ATC, the introduction of radar, a system that uses radio waves to detect distant objects. Originally developed by the British for military defence, this new technology allowed controllers to see the position of aircraft tracked on visual displays. In 1946, the CAA unveiled an experimental radar-equipped tower for control of civil flights. By 1952, the agency had begun its first routine use of radar for approach and departure control. Four years later, it placed a large order for long-range radars for use in en route ATC.

In 1960, the FAA began successful testing of a system under which flights in certain positive control areas were required to carry a radar beacon, called a transponder that identified the aircraft and helped to improve radar performance. Pilots in this airspace were also required to fly on instruments regardless of the weather and to remain in contact with controllers. Under these conditions, controllers were able to reduce the separation between aircraft by as much as half the standard distance.

For many years, pilots had negotiated a complicated maze of airways. In September 1964, the FAA instituted two layers of airways, one from 1,000 to 18,000 feet (305 to 5,486 meters) above ground level and the second from 18,000 to 45,000 feet (13,716 m) above mean sea level. It also standardized aircraft instrument settings and navigation checkpoints to reduce the controllers' workload. From 1965 to 1975, the FAA developed complex computer systems that would replace the plastic markers for tracking aircraft thereby modernizing the National Airspace System. Controllers could now view information sent by aircraft transponders to form alphanumeric symbols on a simulated three dimensional radar screen. The system allowed controllers to focus on providing separation by automating complex tasks.

The FAA established a Central Flow Control Facility in April 1970, to prevent clusters of congestion from disrupting the nationwide air traffic flow. This type of ATC became increasingly sophisticated and important, and in 1994, the FAA opened a new Air Traffic Control System Command Center with advanced equipment.

In January 1982, the FAA unveiled the National Airspace System (NAS) Plan. The plan called for modernized flight service stations, more advanced systems for ATC, and improvements in ground-to-air surveillance and communication. Better computers and software were developed, air route traffic control centers were consolidated, and the number of flight service stations reduced. New Doppler Radars and better transponders complemented automatic, radio broadcasts of surface and flight conditions. In July 1988, the FAA selected IBM to develop the new multi-billion-dollar Advanced Automation System (AAS) for the Nation's en route ATC centers. AAS would include controller workstations, called "sector suites," that would incorporate new display, communications and processing capabilities. The system had upgraded hardware enabling increased automation of complex tasks. In December 1993, the FAA reviewed its order for the planned AAS. IBM was far behind schedule and had major cost overruns. In 1994 the FAA simplified its needs and picked new contractors. The revised modernization program continued under various project names. In 1999, controllers began their first use of an early version of the Standard Terminal Automation Replacement System, which included new displays and capabilities for approach control facilities. During the following year, FAA completed deployment of the Display System Replacement, providing more efficient workstations for en route controllers.

In 1994, the concept of Free Flight was introduced. It might eventually allow pilots to use on board instruments and electronics to maintain a safe distance between planes and to reduce their reliance on ground controllers. Full implementation of this concept would involve technology that made use of the Global Positioning System to help track the position of aircraft. In 1998, the FAA and industry began applying some of the early capabilities developed by the Free Flight program.

Current studies to upgrade ATC include the Communication, Navigation and Surveillance for Air Traffic Management System that relies on the most advanced aircraft transponder, a global navigation satellite system, and ultra-precise radar. Tests are underway to design new cockpit displays that will allow pilots to better control their aircraft by combining as many as 32 types of information about traffic, weather, and hazards.

Airport Control

The primary method of controlling the immediate airport environment is visual observation from the airport traffic control tower (ATCT). The ATCT is a tall, windowed structure located on the airport grounds. Aerodrome or Tower controllers are responsible for the separation and efficient movement of aircraft and vehicles operating on the taxiways and runways of the airport itself, and aircraft in the air near the airport, generally 2 to 5 nautical miles (3.7 to 9.2 km) depending on the airport procedures.

Radar displays are also available to controllers at some airports. Controllers may use a radar system called Secondary Surveillance Radar for airborne traffic approaching and departing. These displays include a map of the area, the position of various aircraft, and data tags that include aircraft identification, speed, heading, and other information described in local procedures.

The areas of responsibility for ATCT controllers fall into three general operational disciplines; Local Control or Air Control, Ground Control, and Flight Data/Clearance Delivery—other categories, such as Apron Control or Ground Movement Planner, may exist at extremely busy airports. While each ATCT may have unique airport-specific procedures, such as multiple teams of controllers ('crews') at major or complex airports with multiple runways, the following provides a general concept of the delegation of responsibilities within the ATCT environment.

Ground Control

Ground Control (sometimes known as Ground Movement Control abbreviated to GMC or Surface Movement Control abbreviated to SMC) is responsible for the airport "movement" areas, as well as areas not released to the airlines or other users. This generally includes all taxiways, inactive runways, holding areas, and some transitional aprons or intersections where aircraft arrive, having vacated the runway or departure gate. Exact areas and control responsibilities are clearly defined in local documents and agreements at each airport. Any aircraft, vehicle, or person walking or working in these areas is required to have clearance from Ground Control. This is normally done via VHF/UHF radio, but there may be special cases where other processes are used. Most aircraft and airside vehicles have radios. Aircraft or vehicles without radios must respond to ATC instructions via aviation light signals or else be led by vehicles with radios. People working on the airport surface normally have a communications link through which they can communicate with Ground Control, commonly either by handheld radio or even cell phone. Ground Control is vital to the smooth operation of the airport, because this position impacts the sequencing of departure aircraft, affecting the safety and efficiency of the airport's operation.

Some busier airports have Surface Movement Radar (SMR), such as, ASDE-3, AMASS or ASDE-X, designed to display aircraft and vehicles on the ground. These are used by Ground Control as an additional tool to control ground traffic, particularly at night or in poor visibility. There are a wide range of capabilities on these systems as they are being modernized. Older systems will display a map of the airport and the target. Newer systems include the capability to display higher quality mapping, radar target, data blocks, and safety alerts, and to interface with other systems such as digital flight strips.

Local Control or Air Control

Local Control (known to pilots as "Tower" or "Tower Control") is responsible for the active runway surfaces. Local Control clears aircraft for takeoff or landing, ensuring that prescribed runway separation will exist at all times. If Local Control detects any unsafe condition, a landing aircraft may be told to "go-around" and be re-sequenced into the landing pattern by the approach or terminal area controller.

Within the ATCT, a highly disciplined communications process between Local Control and Ground Control is an absolute necessity. Ground Control must request and gain approval from Local Control to cross any active runway with any aircraft or vehicle. Likewise, Local Control must ensure that Ground Control is aware of any operations that will impact the taxiways, and work with the approach radar controllers to create "holes" or "gaps" in the arrival traffic to allow taxiing traffic to cross runways and to allow departing aircraft to take off. Crew Resource Management (CRM) procedures are often used to ensure this communication process is efficient and clear, although this is not as prevalent as CRM for pilots.

Flight Data / Clearance Delivery

Clearance Delivery is the position that issues route clearances to aircraft, typically before they commence taxiing. These contain details of the route that the aircraft is expected to fly after departure. Clearance Delivery or, at busy airports, the Traffic Management Coordinator (TMC) will, if necessary, coordinate with the en route center and national command center or flow control to obtain releases for aircraft. Often, however, such releases are given automatically or are controlled by local agreements allowing "free-flow" departures. When weather or extremely high demand for a certain airport or airspace becomes a factor, there may be ground "stops" (or "slot delays") or re-routes may be necessary to ensure the system does not get overloaded. The primary responsibility of Clearance Delivery is to ensure that the aircraft have the proper route and slot time. This information is also coordinated with the en route center and Ground Control in order to ensure that the aircraft reaches the runway in time to meet the slot time provided by the command center. At some airports, Clearance Delivery also plans aircraft pushbacks and engine starts, in which case it is known as the Ground Movement Planner (GMP): this position is particularly important at heavily congested airports to prevent taxiway and apron gridlock. Flight Data (which is routinely combined with Clearance Delivery) is the position that is responsible for ensuring that both controllers and pilots have the most current information: pertinent weather changes, outages, airport ground delays/ground stops, runway closures, etc. Flight Data may inform the pilots using a recorded continuous loop on a specific frequency known as the Automatic Terminal Information Service (ATIS).

Approach and Terminal Control

Many airports have a radar control facility that is associated with the airport. In most countries, this is referred to as *Terminal Control*; in the U.S., it is often still referred to as a TRACON (Terminal Kadar Approach Control.) While every airport varies, terminal controllers usually handle traffic in a 30 to 50 nautical mile (56 to 93 km) radius from the airport. Where there are many busy airports in close proximity, one consolidated TRACON may service all the airports. The airspace boundaries and altitudes assigned to a TRACON, which vary widely from airport to airport, are based on factors such as traffic flows, neighboring airports and terrain. A large and complex example is the London Terminal Control Centre which controls traffic for five main London airports up to 20,000 feet (6,100 m) and out to 100 nautical miles (190 km).

Terminal controllers are responsible for providing all ATC services within their airspace. Traffic flow is broadly divided into departures, arrivals, and overflights. As aircraft move in and out of the terminal airspace, they are handed off to the next appropriate control facility (a control tower, an en-route control facility, or a bordering terminal or approach control). Terminal control is responsible for ensuring that aircraft are at an appropriate altitude when they are handed off, and that aircraft arrive at a suitable rate for landing.

Not all airports have a radar approach or terminal control available. In this case, the en-route center or a neighboring terminal or approach control may co-ordinate directly with the tower on the airport and vector inbound aircraft to a position from where they can land visually. At some of these airports, the tower may provide a non-radar procedural approach service to arriving aircraft handed over from a radar unit before they are visual to land. Some units also have a dedicated approach unit which can provide the procedural approach service either all the time or for any periods of radar outage for any reason.

En-route, Center, or Area Control

ATC provides services to aircraft in flight between airports as well. Pilots fly under one of two sets of rules for separation: Visual Flight Rules (VFR) or Instrument Flight Rules (IFR). Air traffic controllers have different responsibilities to aircraft operating under the different sets of rules. While IFR flights are under positive control, in the US VFR pilots can request flight following, which provides traffic advisory services on a time permitting basis and may also provide assistance in avoiding areas of weather and flight restrictions. In the UK, a pilot can request for "Deconfliction Service", which is similar to flight following.

En-route air traffic controllers issue clearances and instructions for airborne aircraft, and pilots are required to comply with these instructions. En-route controllers also provide air traffic control services to many smaller airports around the country, including clearance off of the ground and clearance for approach to an airport. Controllers adhere to a set of separation standards that define the minimum distance allowed between aircraft. These distances vary depending on the equipment and procedures used in providing ATC services.

General Characteristics

En-route air traffic controllers work in facilities called Area Control Centers, each of which is commonly referred to as a "Center". The United States uses the equivalent term Air Route Traffic Control Center (ARTCC). Each center is responsible for many thousands of square miles of airspace (known as a Flight Information Region) and for the airports within that airspace. Centers control IFR aircraft from the time they depart from an airport or terminal area's airspace to the time they arrive at another airport or terminal area's airspace. Centers may also "pick up" VFR aircraft that are already airborne and integrate them into the IFR system. These aircraft must, however, remain VFR until the Center provides a clearance.

Center controllers are responsible for climbing the aircraft to their requested altitude while, at the same time, ensuring that the aircraft is properly separated from all other aircraft in the immediate area. Additionally, the aircraft must be placed in a flow consistent with the aircraft's route of flight. This effort is complicated by crossing traffic, severe weather, special missions that require large airspace allocations, and traffic density. When the aircraft approaches its destination, the center is responsible for meeting altitude restrictions by specific points, as well as providing many destination airports with a traffic flow, which prohibits all of the arrivals being "bunched together". These "flow restrictions" often begin in the middle of the route, as controllers will position aircraft landing in the same destination so that when the aircraft are close to their destination they are sequenced.

As an aircraft reaches the boundary of a Center's control area it is "handed off" or "handed over" to the next Area Control Center. In some cases this "hand-off" process involves a transfer of identification and details between controllers so that air traffic control services can be provided in a seamless manner; in other cases local agreements may allow "silent handovers" such that the receiving center does not require any co-ordination if traffic is presented in an agreed manner. After the hand-off, the aircraft is given a frequency change and begins talking to the next controller. This process continues until the aircraft is handed off to a terminal controller ("approach").

Radar Coverage

Since centers control a large airspace area, they will typically use long range radar that has the capability, at higher altitudes, to see aircraft within 200 nautical miles (370 km) of the radar antenna. They may also use TRACON radar data to control when it provides a better "picture" of the traffic or when it can fill in a portion of the area not covered by the long range radar.

In the U.S. system, at higher altitudes, over 90% of the U.S. airspace is covered by radar and often by multiple radar systems; however, coverage may be inconsistent at lower altitudes used by unpressurized aircraft due to high terrain or distance from radar facilities. A center may require numerous radar systems to cover the airspace assigned to them, and may also rely on pilot position reports from aircraft flying below the floor of radar coverage. This results in a large amount of data being available to the controller. To address this, automation systems have been designed that consolidate the radar data for the controller. This consolidation includes eliminating duplicate radar returns, ensuring the best radar for each geographical area is providing the data, and displaying the data in an effective format.

Centers also exercise control over traffic travelling over the world's ocean areas. These areas are also FIRs. Because there are no radar systems available for oceanic control, oceanic controllers provide ATC services using procedural control. These procedures use aircraft position reports, time, altitude, distance, and speed to ensure separation. Controllers record information on flight progress strips and in specially developed oceanic computer systems as aircraft report positions. This process requires that aircraft be separated by greater distances, which reduces the overall capacity for any given route.

Some Air Navigation Service Providers (e.g. Airservices Australia, The Federal Aviation Administration, NAVCANADA, etc.) have implemented Automatic Dependent Surveillance-Broadcast (ADS-B) as part of their surveillance capability. This new technology reverses the radar concept. Instead of radar "finding" a target by interrogating the transponder, the ADS-equipped aircraft sends a position report as determined by the navigation equipment on board the aircraft. Normally, ADS operates in the "contract" mode where the aircraft reports a position, automatically or initiated by the pilot, based on a predetermined time interval. It is also possible for controllers to request more frequent reports to more quickly establish aircraft position for specific reasons. However, since the cost for each report is charged by the ADS service providers to the company operating the aircraft, more frequent reports are not commonly requested except in emergency situations. ADS is significant because it can be used where it is not possible to locate the infrastructure for a radar system (e.g. over water). Computerized radar displays are now being designed to accept ADS inputs as part of the display. This technology is currently used in portions of the North Atlantic and the Pacific by a variety of states who share responsibility for the control of this airspace.

Precision approach radars are commonly used by military controllers of airforces of several countries, to assist the Pilot in final phases of landing in places where Instrument Landing System and other sophisticated air borne equipements are unavaiable to assist the pilots in marginal or *near zero visibility* conditions. This procedure is also called Talkdowns.

Flight Traffic Mapping

The mapping of flights in real-time is based on the air traffic control system. In 1991, data on the location of aircraft was made available by the Federal Aviation Administration to the airline industry. The National Business Aviation Association (NBAA), the General Aviation Manufacturers Association, the Aircraft Owners & Pilots Association, the Helicopter Association International, and the National Air Transportation Association petitioned the FAA to make ASDI information available on a "need-to-know" basis. Subsequently, NBAA advocated the broad-scale dissemination of air traffic data. The Aircraft Situational Display to Industry (ASDI) system now conveys up-to-date flight information to the airline industry and the public. Some companies that distribute ASDI information are FlightExplorer, FlightView, and FlyteComm. Each company maintains a website that provides free updated information to the public on flight status. Stand-alone programs are also available for displaying the geographic location of airborne IFR (Instrument Flight Rules) air traffic anywhere in the FAA air traffic system. Positions are reported for both commercial and general aviation traffic. The programs can overlay air traffic with a wide selection of maps such as, geo-political boundaries, air traffic control center boundaries, high altitude jet routes, satellite cloud and radar imagery.

Problems

Traffic

The day-to-day problems faced by the air traffic control system are primarily related to the volume of air traffic demand placed on the system and weather. Several factors dictate the amount of traffic that can land at an airport in a given amount of time. Each landing aircraft must touch down, slow, and exit the runway before the next crosses the beginning of the runway. This process requires at least one and up to four minutes for each aircraft. Allowing for departures between arrivals, each runway can thus handle about 30 arrivals per hour. A large airport with two arrival runways can handle about 60 arrivals per hour in good weather. Problems begin when airlines schedule more arrivals into an airport than can be physically handled, or when delays elsewhere cause groups of aircraft that would otherwise be separated in time to arrive simultaneously. Aircraft must then be delayed in the air by holding over specified locations until they may be safely sequenced to the runway. Up until the 1990s, holding, which has significant environmental and cost implications, was a routine occurrence at many airports. Advances in computers now allow the sequencing of planes hours in advance. Thus, planes may be delayed before they even take off (by being given a "slot"), or may reduce speed in flight and proceed more slowly thus significantly reducing the amount of holding.

Weather

Beyond runway capacity issues, weather is a major factor in traffic capacity. Rain or ice and snow on the runway cause landing aircraft to take longer to slow and exit, thus reducing the safe arrival rate and requiring more space between landing aircraft. Fog also requires a decrease in the landing rate. These, in turn, increase airborne delay for holding aircraft. If more aircraft are scheduled than can be safely and efficiently held in the air, a ground delay program may be established, delaying aircraft on the ground before departure due to conditions at the arrival airport.

In Area Control Centers, a major weather problem is thunderstorms, which present a variety of hazards to aircraft. Aircraft will deviate around storms, reducing the capacity of the en-route system by requiring more space per aircraft, or causing congestion as many aircraft try to move through a single hole in a line of thunderstorms. Occasionally weather considerations cause delays to aircraft prior to their departure as routes are closed by thunderstorms.

Much money has been spent on creating software to streamline this process. However, at some ACCs, air traffic controllers still record data for each flight on strips of paper and personally coordinate their paths. In newer sites, these flight progress strips have been replaced by electronic data presented on computer screens. As new equipment is brought in, more and more sites are upgrading away from paper flight strips.

Call Signs

A prerequisite to safe air traffic separation is the assignment and use of distinctive call signs. These are permanently allocated by ICAO (pronounced "ai-kay-oh") on request usually to scheduled flights and some air forces for military flights. They are written callsigns with 3-letter combination like KLM, AAL, SWA, BAW, DLH followed by the flight number, like AAL872, BAW018. As such they appear on flight plans and ATC radar labels. There are also the *audio* or *Radio-telephony* callsigns used on the radio contact between pilots and Air Traffic Control not always identical with the written ones. For example BAW stands for British Airways but on the radio you will only hear the word *Speedbird* instead. By default, the callsign for any other flight is the registration number (tail number) of the aircraft, such as "N12345" or "C-GABC". The term *tail number* is because a registration number is usually painted somewhere on the tail of a plane, yet this is not a rule. Registration numbers may appear on the engines, anywhere on the fuselage, and often on the wings. The short *Radio-telephony* callsigns for these tail numbers is the first letter followed by the last two, like C-BC spoken as Charlie-Bravo-Charlie for C-GABC or the last 3 letters only like ABC spoken Alpha-Bravo-Charlie for C-GABC or the last 3 numbers like 345 spoken as three-four-five for N12345. In the United States the abbreviation of callsigns is required to be a prefix (such as aircraft type, aircraft manufacturer, or first letter of registration) followed by the last three characters of the callsign. This abbreviation is only allowed after communications has been established in each sector.

The flight number part is decided by the aircraft operator. In this arrangement, an identical call sign might well be used for the same scheduled journey each day it is operated, even if the departure time varies a little across different days of the week. The call sign of the return flight often differs only by the final digit from the outbound flight. Generally, airline flight numbers are even if eastbound, and odd if westbound. In order to reduce the possibility of two callsigns on one frequency at any time sounding too similar, a number of airlines, particularly in Europe, have started using alphanumeric callsigns that are not based on flight numbers. For example DLH23LG, spoken as lufthansa-two-tree-lima-golf. Additionally it is the right of the air traffic controller to change the 'audio' callsign for the period the flight is in his sector if there is a risk of confusion, usually choosing the tail number instead.

Before around 1980 International Air Transport Association (IATA) and ICAO were using the same 2-letter callsigns. Due to the larger number of new airlines after deregulation ICAO established the 3-letter callsigns as mentioned above. The IATA callsigns are currently used in aerodromes on the announcement tables but never used any longer in Air Traffic Control. For example, AA is the IATA callsign for American Airlines — ATC equivalent AAL. Other examples include LY/ELY for El Al, DL/DAL for Delta Air Lines, LH/DLH for Lufthansa etc.

Technology

Many technologies are used in air traffic control systems. Primary and secondary radar are used to enhance a controller's "situational awareness" within his assigned airspace — all types of aircraft send back primary echoes of varying sizes to controllers' screens as radar energy is bounced off their skins, and transponder-equipped aircraft reply to secondary radar interrogations by giving an ID (Mode A), an altitude (Mode C) and/or a unique callsign (Mode S). Certain types of weather may also register on the radar screen.

These inputs, added to data from other radars, are correlated to build the air situation. Some basic processing occurs on the radar tracks, such as calculating ground speed and magnetic headings.

Usually, a Flight Data Processing System manages all the flight plan related data, incorporating-in a low or high degree-the information of the track once the correlation between them (flight plan and track) is established. All this information is distributed to modern operational display systems, making it available to controllers.

The FAA has spent over USD$3 billion on software, but a fully-automated system is still over the horizon. In 2002 the UK brought a new area control centre into service at Swanwick, in Hampshire, relieving a busy suburban centre at West Drayton in Middlesex, north of London Heathrow Airport. Software from Lockheed-Martin predominates at Swanwick. However, Swanwick was initially troubled by software and communications problems causing delays and occasional shutdowns.

Some tools are available in different domains to help the controller further:

- Flight Data Processing Systems: this is the system (usually one per Center) that processes all the information related to the Flight (the Flight Plan), typically in the time horizon from Gate to gate (airport departure/arrival gates). It uses such processed information to invoke other Flight Plan related tools (such as e.g. MTCD), and distributes such processed information to all the stakeholders (Air Traffic Controllers, collateral Centers, Airports, etc.).
- STCA (Short Term Conflict Alert) that checks possible conflicting trajectories in a time horizon of about 2 or 3 minutes (or even less in approach context-35 seconds in the French Roissy & Orly approach centres) and alerts the controller prior the loss of separation. The algorithms used may also provide in some systems a possible vectoring solution, that is, the manner in which to turn, descend, or climb the aircraft in order to avoid infringing the minimum safety distance or altitude clearance.
- Minimum Safe Altitude Warning (MSAW): a tool that alerts the controller if an aircraft appears to be flying too low to the ground or will impact terrain based on its current altitude and heading.
- System Coordination (SYSCO) to enable controller to negotiate the release of flights from one sector to another.

- Area Penetration Warning (APW) to inform a controller that a flight will penetrate a restricted area.
- Arrival and Departure Manager to help sequence the takeoff and landing of aircraft.
  - o The Departure Manager (DMAN): A system aid for the ATC at airports, that calculates a planned departure flow with the goal to maintain an optimal throughput at the runway, reduce queuing at holding point and distribute the information to various stakeholders at the airport (i.e. the airline, ground handling and Air Traffic Control (ATC)).
  - o The Arrival Manager (AMAN): A system aid for the ATC at airports, that calculates a planned Arrival flow with the goal to maintain an optimal throughput at the runway, reduce arrival queuing and distribute the information to various stakeholders.
  - o passive Final Approach Spacing Tool (pFAST), a CTAS tool, provides runway assignment and sequence number advisories to terminal controllers to improve the arrival rate at congested airports. pFAST was deployed and operational at five US TRACONs before being cancelled. NASA research included an Active FAST capability that also provided vector and speed advisories to implement the runway and sequence advisories.
- Converging Runway Display Aid (CRDA) enables Approach controllers to run two final approaches that intersect and make sure that go arounds are minimized
- Center TRACON Automation System (CTAS) is a suite of human centred decision support tools developed by NASA Ames Research Center. Several of the CTAS tools have been field tested and transitioned to the FAA for operational evaluation and use. Some of the CTAS tools are: Traffic Management Advisor (TMA), passive Final Approach Spacing Tool (pFAST), Collaborative Arrival Planning (CAP), Direct-To (D2), En Route Descent Advisor (EDA) and Multi Center TMA.

- Traffic Management Advisor (TMA), a CTAS tool, is an en route decision support tool that automates time based metering solutions to provide an upper limit of aircraft to a TRACON from the Center over a set period of time. Schedules are determined that will not exceed the specified arrival rate and controllers use the scheduled times to provide the appropriate delay to arrivals while in the en route domain. This results in an overall reduction in en route delays and also moves the delays to more efficient airspace (higher altitudes) than occur if holding near the TRACON boundary is required to not overload the TRACON controllers. TMA is operational at most en route air route traffic control centers (ARTCCs) and continues to be enhanced to address more complex traffic situations (e.g. Adjacent Center Metering (ACM) and En Route Departure Capability (EDC))
- MTCD & URET
    - o In the US, User Request Evaluation Tool (URET) takes paper strips out of the equation for En Route controllers at ARTCCs by providing a display that shows all aircraft that are either in or currently routed into the sector.
    - o In Europe, several MTCD tools are available: iFACTS (NATS), ERATO (DSNA), VAFORIT (DFS), New FDPS (MASUAC). The SESAR Programme should soon launch new MTCD concepts.

URET and MTCD provide conflict advisories up to 30 minutes in advance and have a suite of assistance tools that assist in evaluating resolution options and pilot requests.

- Mode S: provides a data downlink of flight parameters via Secondary Surveillance Radars allowing radar processing systems and therefore controllers to see various data on a flight, including airframe unique id (24-bits encoded), indicated airspeed and flight director selected level, amongst others.
- CPDLC: Controller Pilot Data Link Communications — allows digital messages to be sent between controllers and

pilots, avoiding the need to use radiotelephony. It is especially useful in areas where difficult-to-use HF radiotelephony was previously used for communication with aircraft, e.g. oceans. This is currently in use in various parts of the world including the Atlantic and Pacific oceans.

- ADS-B: Automatic Dependent Surveillance Broadcast — provides a data downlink of various flight parameters to air traffic control systems via the Transponder (1090 MHz) and reception of those data by other aircraft in the vicinity. The most important is the aircraft's latitude, longitude and level: such data can be utilized to create a radar-like display of aircraft for controllers and thus allows a form of pseudo-radar control to be done in areas where the installation of radar is either prohibitive on the grounds of low traffic levels, or technically not feasible (e.g. oceans). This is currently in use in Australia, Canada and parts of the Pacific Ocean and Alaska.
- The Electronic Flight Strip system (e-strip): A system of electronic flight strips replacing the old paper strips is being used by several Service Providers, such as NAV CANADA, MASUAC, DFS, being produced by several industries, such as Indra Sistemas, Thales Group, Frequentis, Avibit, SAAB etc. E-strips allows controllers to manage electronic flight data online without Paper Strips, reducing the need for manual functions.
- SkyRec: Hardware based video recording tool that records and replays all information captured on ATCO screens. Used for legal recording (coupled with voice recording), training and post event analysis.

AIR NAVIGATION SERVICE PROVIDERS (ANSPS) AND TRAFFIC SERVICE PROVIDERS (ATSPS)

The regulatory function remains the responsibility of the State and can be exercised by Government and/or independent Safety, Airspace and Economic Regulators depending on the national institutional arrangements. Often you will see a division between the Civil Aviation Authority (CAA) (the Regulator) and the ANSP (the Air Navigation Service Provider). An Air Navigation Service

Provider — The air navigation service provider is the authority directly responsible for providing both visual and non-visual aids to navigation within a specific airspace in compliance with, but not limited to, International Civil Aviation Organization (ICAO) Annexes 2, 6, 10 and 11; ICAO Documents 4444 and 9426; and, other international, multi-national, and national policy, agreements or regulations.

An Air Traffic Service Provider is the relevant authority designated by the State responsible for providing air traffic services in the airspace concerned — where airspace is classified as Type A through G airspace. Air traffic service is a generic term meaning variously, flight information service, alerting service, air traffic advisory service, air traffic control service (area control service, approach control service or aerodrome control service). Both ANSPs and ATSPs can be public, private or corporatized organisations and examples of the different legal models exist throughout the world today. The world's ANSPs are united in and represented by the Civil Air Navigation Services Organisation (CANSO) based at Amsterdam Airport Schiphol in the Netherlands.

In the United States, the Federal Aviation Administration (FAA) provides this service to all aircraft in the National Airspace System (NAS). With the exception of facilities operated by the Department of Defence (DoD), the FAA is responsible for all aspects of U.S. Air Traffic Control including hiring and training controllers, although there are contract towers located in many parts of the country. A contract tower is an Airport Traffic Control Tower (ATCT) that performs the same function as an FAA-run ATCT but is staffed by employees of a private company (Martin State Airport in Maryland is an example). DoD facilities are generally staffed by military personnel and operate separately but concurrently with FAA facilities, under similar rules and procedures. In Canada, Air Traffic Control is provided by NAV CANADA, a private, non-share capital corporation that operates Canada's civil air navigation service.

8

Commando

The term commando, in English, means a specific kind of individual soldier or military unit. In contemporary usage, commando usually means élite light infantry and/or special forces units, specialised in amphibious landings, parachuting, rappelling and similar techniques, to conduct and effect attacks. Originally "a commando" was a type of combat *unit*, as opposed to an individual in that unit. In other languages, *commando* and *kommando* denote a "command", in the sense of a military unit.

In the militaries of most countries, commandos are distinctive in that they specialise in assault on conventional military targets. This is in contrast to other special forces units, which specialise in counter-terrorism, reconnaissance, and sabotage. However, the term commando is sometimes used in relation to units carrying out the latter tasks (including some civilian police units).

History

The word *commando* originated in the Portuguese language (*Comando* in Portuguese), in which it means simply "command". The modern sense of the word stems from the Dutch/Afrikaans *kommando,* which was derived from the Portuguese word, as a result of contact between Afrikaners and Portuguese settlers in Africa (and in Dutch and Afrikaans *kommando* still also means "command" including e.g. instructions given to computers).

After the Dutch Cape Colony was established in 1652, a system known as Commando Law was created. This compelled settlers, known as Free Burgers, who had been released from their indentures with the Dutch East India Company, to equip themselves with a horse and a firearm, in exchange for the right to a piece of agricultural land. When required, a mounted militia force known as a *kommando* would be formed, to defend the colony. As the European population at the Cape increased it was no longer practical to make every Burger comply with the Commando Law and a voluntary militia system was introduced.

In conflicts with southern African peoples (such as the Xhosa and the Zulu during and after the Great Trek), Boer communities and farmsteads formed self-equipped, mounted commandos among themselves.

In the final phase of the Second Boer War, 75,000 Boers occupied the attention of the 450,000-strong British Empire forces. Because of the numerical imbalance, the commandos (militias) adopted guerrilla or raiding tactics, to minimise their casualties and prolong the war. These tactics gave *commando* its modern sense of specialised raiding forces.

During and after WWII in Britain, unexplained newspaper and radio news references to the deeds of "the commandos" led to public misunderstanding about what the singular meant and thus to the modern common habit of using "a commando" to mean one member of such a unit, or one man engaged on a raiding-type operation.

World War II

Germany

In December 1939, following the success of German infiltration and sabotage operations in the Polish campaign, the German Office for Foreign and Counter-Intelligence (OKW Amt Ausland/ Abwehr) formed the Brandenburger Regiment (known officially as the 800th Special Purpose Training and Construction Company). The Brandenburgers conducted a mixture of covert and conventional operations but became increasingly involved in ordinary infantry actions and were eventually converted to a Panzer-Grenadier Division, suffering heavy losses in Russia. Otto Skorzeny (most famed for his rescue of Benito Mussolini) conducted many special operations for Adolf Hitler. Skorzeny commanded Sonderlehrgang z.b.V. Oranienburg, Sonderverband z.b.V. Friedenthal, and SS-Jäger-Bataillon 502, all SS commando units. A report written by Major-General Robert Laycock in 1947 said there was a German raid on a radar station on the Isle of Wight in 1941.

Italy

Italy employed specialist trench raiding teams to break the stalemate of static fighting against Austria-Hungary, in the Alpine battles of World War I.

These teams were called "Arditi" (meaning "daring, brave ones"); they were almost always men under 25 in top physical condition and, possibly at first, bachelors (due to the fear of very high casualty rates). Actually the Arditi (who were led to the lines just a few hours prior to the assault, having been familiarised with the terrain via photo-reconaissance and trained on trench systems re-created ad hoc for them) suffered "fewer" casualties than regular line infantry and were highly successful in their tasks. Many of them volunteered for extreme right formations in the turbulent years after the war (the Fascist Party took pride in this and adopted the style and the mannerism of Arditi), but some of different political persuasions created the "Arditi del Popolo" (People's Arditi) and for some years held the fascist raids in check, defending Socialist and Communist Party sections, buildings, rallies and meeting points.

During the Liberation of Rome in 1944, US troops broke into the Italian Ministry of Defence building in the Italian capital and seized all the WWI materials and documents pertaining to Arditi units in the archives.

Italy's most renowned commando unit of World War II was *Decima Flottiglia MAS* ("10th Assault Vehicle Flotilla") which, from mid-1940, was responsible for the sinking and damage of a considerable tonnage of Allied ships in the Mediterranean.

After Italy surrendered in 1943, some of the Decima Flottiglia MAS were on the Allied side of the battle line and fought with the Allies, renaming themselves the *Mariassalto*. The others fought on the German side and kept their original name but did not operate at sea after 1943, being mostly employed against Italian partisans; some of its men were involved in atrocities against civilians.

In post-war years the Italian marine commandos were re-organised as the "Comsubin" (an abbreviation of 'Comando Subacqueo Incursori', or Underwater Raiders Command).

United Kingdom

In 1940, the British Army also formed "independent companies", later reformed as battalion sized "commandos", thereby reviving the word. It was intended that the British Army Commandos would be small, highly mobile surprise raiding and reconnaissance forces. They were not intended to remain in field operations for more than 36 hours and carried all they needed. Army Commandos were all volunteers selected from existing soldiers still in Britain.

During the war the British Army Commandos spawned several other famous British units such as the Special Air Service, the Special Boat Service and the Parachute Regiment. The British Army Commandos themselves were never regimented and were disbanded at the end of the war.

The British Special Operations Executive (SOE) also formed commando units from British and displaced European personnel eg. Cichociemni for the purpose of conducting raiding operations in occupied Europe. One example is Norwegian Independent Company 1, which was responsible for the destruction of heavy water facilities in Norway during 1941.

The Royal Navy also controlled Royal Navy Beach Parties, based on teams formed to control the evacuation of Dunkirk in 1940. These were later known simply as RN Commandos, and they did not see action until they successfully fought for control of the landing beaches (as in the disastrous Dieppe Raid of 19 August 1942). The RN Commandos, including Commando "W" from the Royal Canadian Navy, saw action on D-Day.

In 1942, the Royal Navy's nine Royal Marines infantry battalions were reorganized as Commandos, numbered from 40 to 48, joining the British Army Commandos in combined Commando Brigades. After the war the Army Commandos were disbanded. The Royal Marines form an enduring Brigade-strength capability as 3 Commando Brigade.

The Royal Air Force also formed 15 commando units in 1942, each of which was 150 strong. These units consisted of trained technicians, armourers and maintainers who had volunteered to undertake the commando course. These RAF commandos accompanied the Allied invasion forces in all theatres; their main role was to to allow the forward operation of friendly fighters by servicing and arming them from captured air fields. However due to the forward position of these airfields, the RAF commandos were also trained to secure and make safe these airfields and to help defend them from enemy counter attack.

United States

In mid-1942, the United States Army formed its Army Rangers in Northern Ireland under William O. (Bill) Darby. The Rangers were designed along the similar lines to the British Army commandos, who supervised their training. The first sizable Ranger action took place in August 1942 at the Dieppe Raid, where 50 Rangers were dispersed among the British Commandos. The first full Ranger action took place during the invasion of North West Africa in (Operation Torch) in November 1942.

During 1941, the United States Marine Corps formed commando battalions, inspired by both the British commandos and the tactics used by Chinese Communist forces, from whom they acquired the war cry "gung-ho". The USMC commandos were known collectively as Marine Raiders. On orders from President Franklin D. Roosevelt through a proposal from OSS Director Colonel William J. Donovan and the former Commander of the United States Marine Detachment Major Evans F Carlson, directed the formation of what would become The Marine Raiders. Initially this unit was to be called Marine Commandos and they were to be the counterpart to the British Commandos. The name Marine Commandos met with much controversy within the Marine Corps leading Commandant Thomas J. Holcomb to state, "the term 'Marine' is sufficient to indicate a man ready for duty at any time, and the injection of a special name, such as 'Commando,' would be undesirable and superfluous." President Roosevelt's son James Roosevelt served with The Marine Raiders. The Raiders initially saw action at the Battle of Tulagi and the Battle of Makin, as well as the Battle of Guadalcanal, the Battle of Empress Augusta Bay, and other parts of the Pacific Ocean Areas. In February 1944 the four Raider battalions were converted to regular marine units.

Canada

A joint Canadian-American Commando unit, the 1st Special Service Force, nicknamed the Devil's Brigade, was formed in 1942 under the command of Colonel Robert Frederick. The unit initially saw service in the Pacific, in August 1943 at Kiska in the Aleutians campaign. However most of its operations occurred during the Italian campaign and in southern France. Its most famous raid, which was documented in the film *Devil's Brigade*, was the battle of Monte la Difensa. In 1945, the unit was disbanded; the Canadian members were sent to the 1st Canadian Parachute Battalion as replacements, and the American members were sent to either the 101st Airborne Division or the 82nd Airborne Division as replacements.

Australia

Following the British example, the Australian Army formed commando units, known as Australian independent companies in the early stages of World War II. They first saw action in early 1942 during the Japanese assault on New Ireland, and in the Battle of Timor. Part of the 2/1st Independent Company was wiped out on New Ireland, but on Timor, the 2/2nd Independent Company formed the heart of an Allied force which engaged Japanese forces in a guerrilla campaign. The Japanese commander on the island drew parallels with the Boer War, and decided that it would take a numerical advantage of 10:1 in order to defeat the Allies. The campaign occupied the attention of an entire Japanese division for almost a year. The independent companies were later renamed commando squadrons, and they saw widespread action in the South West Pacific Area, especially in New Guinea and Borneo. In 1943, all the commando squadrons except the 2/2nd and 2/8th were grouped into the 2/6th, 2/7th and 2/9th Cavalry Commando Regiments.

Later in the war the Royal Australian Navy also formed commando units along the lines of the Royal Navy Commandos to go ashore with the first waves of major amphibious assaults, to signpost the beaches and carry out other naval tasks. These were known as RAN Commandos. Four were formed — lettered A, B, C and D like their British counterparts — and they took part in the Borneo campaign. Z Force, an Australian-British-New Zealand military intelligence commando unit, formed by the Australian Services Reconnaissance Department, also carried out many raiding and reconnaissance operations in the South West Pacific theatre, most notably Operation Jaywick, in which they destroyed tonnes of Japanese shipping at Singapore Harbour. An attempt to replicate this success, with Operation Rimau, resulted in the death of almost all those involved. However, Z Force and other SRD units continued operations until the war's end.

Greece

The Sacred band was a Greek special forces unit formed in 1942 in the Middle East, composed entirely of Greek officers and officer cadets under the command of Col. Christodoulos Tsigantes. It fought alongside the SAS in the Libyan desert and with the SBS in the Aegean, as well as with General Leclerc's *Free French Forces* in Tunisia. It was disbanded in August 1945.

Japan

In 1944-45, Japanese *Teishin Shudan* ("Raiding Group") and *Giretsu* ("heroic") detachments made airborne assaults on Allied airfields in the Philippines, Marianas and Okinawa. The attacking forces varied in size from a few paratroopers to operations involving several companies. Due to the balance of forces concerned, these raids achieved little in the way of damage or casualties, and resulted in the destruction of the Japanese units concerned. Considering that there were no plans to extract these forces, and the reluctance to surrender by Japanese personnel during that era, they are often seen in the same light as *kamikaze* pilots of 1944-45.

After 1945

Australia

In Australia, the Army's commando squadrons were disbanded at the end of the war. However, in 1954, two Citizens Military Force (reserve) units, 1 and 2 Commando Companies, were raised. 1st Commando Regiment (1 Cdo Regt), a regimental structure for the reserve commando companies – and 126 Signal Squadron (Special Forces) – was formed during the 1980s. It adopted the green berets worn by its World War II predecessors.

In 1997, the Australian government ordered the conversion of 4th Battalion, Royal Australian Regiment (4RAR) into a permanent, non-reserve commando battalion, with instructors from 1st Commando Regiment and Australian Special Air Service Regiment (SASR). 126 Signal Squadron was reassigned to 4RAR and 301 Signal Squadron re-raised to join 1 Cdo Regt. In 2009, 4RAR was renamed 2nd Commando Regiment (2 Cdo Regt).

1 Cdo and 2 Cdo utilise identical selection and training courses. One company of 2 Cdo is responsible for counter-terrorism operations and response in eastern Australia and is officially known as Tactical Assault Group-East (TAG-E). This company mirrors its sister unit (the original Tactical Assault Group) in the West (TAG-W), which is part of the SASR.

Commandos from 1CDO and 2CDO have been deployed on peacekeeping and combat missions in several countries, including East Timor, the Solomon Islands, Iraq and Afghanistan.

Brazil

Brazil created its special operations forces in the 1950s. There are commando units in the Brazilian Army and in the navy. In Brazilian Army the main unit is the Brazilian Special Operations Brigade.Brazilian Navy have the COMANF Amphibious Commandos of Brazilian Marine Corps

Canada

Canadian commando forces were disbanded and recreated at various times in the post-war years, and in 1968 the Canadian Airborne Regiment was formed. It was divided into three Airborne Commandos each of company strength. This resulted in a ceiling of about 750 members in all ranks, organized into three smaller company-sized commandos. The three airborne commandos took shape around the three regimental affiliations: 1 Commando with the Royal 22 Régiment, 2 Commando with Princess Patricia's Canadian Light Infantry, and 3 Commando with The Royal

Canadian Regiment. The Canadian Airborne Regiment was disbanded after the torture and murder of Shidane Arone, a Somalia civilian, in 1993, and other allegations of wrongdoing within the Regiment. Later, parliamentary investigations would question why such an elite commando unit was sent on a peacekeeping mission. (The Canadian Joint Task Force Two, or JTF2, is also sometimes referred to as a "commando" unit, but it is technically a specialist counter-terrorist unit.)

GERMANY

The German Army currently operates the Fernspähkompanie (Germany's elite long range reconnaissance company), and the Kommando Spezialkräfte (KSK). The KSK is stationed in Calw, in the Black forest area in southern Germany. It consists of about 1,100 soldiers, but only a nucleus of these are in fighting units. Exact numbers are not available, as this information is considered to be secret. The KSK is a part of the Special Operations Division (Div. Spezielle Operationen-DSO).

The fighting units are divided into four commando companies of about 100 men each and the *special commando company* with veteran members, taking supporting tasks. Each of the four commando companies has five specialised platoons:

- 1st platoon: land insertions
- 2nd platoon: airborne operations
- 3rd platoon: amphibious operations
- 4th platoon: operations in special geographic or meteorologic surroundings (e.g. mountains or polar-regions)
- 5th platoon: reconnaissance, sniper and counter-sniper operations
- Command Platoon

There are four commando squads in every platoon. Each of these groups consists of about four equally skilled soldiers. One of each group is specially trained as weapons expert, medic, combat engineer or communications expert respectively. Additionally a group can contain other specialists, e.g. heavy weapons or language experts.

Another special unit, the Kampfschwimmer (comparable to the U.S.N. SEALS) are operated by the German Navy.

INDIA

In India, the term Commando is used liberally for almost any unit that has more training than their peers. This is especially true in the police forces. However, there are certain units that are trained to internationally acceptable standards. These units are some of the best trained in the world, with rich operational experience in various environments.

The Para Commandos are a special forces unit of the Indian Army. Formed in 1966, the Para Commandos are the largest and most important part of the Special Forces of India. They are highly-trained units of the Indian Army, meant to operate behind enemy lines.

The Garud Commando Force is the Special Forces unit of the Indian Air Force. The unit derives its name from *Garuda*, a divine bird-like creature of Hindu Mythology, but more commonly the word for eagle in Sanskrit. Garud is tasked with acting as quick response teams during attacks on critical Air Force bases and installations, search and rescue of downed pilots, forward air control and carry out strikes againsts enemy air defences and radar installations.

MARCOS (marine commandos) is a commando unit of the Indian Navy designed to carry out operation on air, sea and land.

National Security Guard (NSG) personnel are popularly known as Black Cat Commandos. Their task is two fold. The Special Protection Group provides protection to the political elite of the nation. The NSG carries out hostage rescue and anti-terrorist operations. Ghatak Force is a battalion level special unit in the Indian Army, with one in each battalion. They are used as elite infantry to spearhead attacks, carry out reconnaissance and further the objectives on the battalion in the battlefield.

The Force One is an elite commando force, which is a specialised counter terrorism unit to guard the Mumbai metropolitan area, one of the largest metropolitan areas in the world, formed by Government of Maharashtra on the lines of National Security Guards (NSG)..

Pakistan

Special Service Group (SSG) is an independent commando division of the Pakistan Army. It is an elite special operations force. Official numbers are put at 2,100 men, in 3 Battalions; however the actual strength is classified. Based out of Cherat and Attock, the SSG was created in 1956 with active support from U.S. Special Operations Forces. That year the 19th Battalion of the Baloch Regiment (19 Baloch) was selected for conversion to a Special Operation Force. The SSG also has a unit in the Pakistan Navy known as SSGN. The SSGN currently maintains headquarters in Karachi headed by Pakistan Navy Commander. The SSG in 2001 created a special forces unit for the Pakistan Air Force called the Special Service Wing otherwise known as SSW. This new component to the Special Forces of Pakistan is still being trained and built up.

Portugal

The Portuguese Army created the *Comandos,* during the Portuguese Colonial War to conduct special actions in Portuguese territory or abroad, to fight as assault infantry / shock troops and to provide the high political and military commands with a force able to conduct irregular operations. The first units were created in Northern Angola in 1962. Beyond the *Comandos,* the Portuguese Armed and Security Forces used several other commando type forces in the Colonial War in Angola, Mozambique and Guinea, like the *Caçadores Especiais* (Special Hunters) of the Portuguese Army, the *Caçadores Paraquedistas* (Parachute Hunters) of the Portuguese Air Force, the *Fuzileiros Especiais* (Special Marines) of the Portuguese Navy, the *Flechas* (Arrows) of the International and State Defence Police and the *Grupos Especiais* (Special Groups) of the Government of Mozambique. Presently, the Portuguese Armed Forces have the following commando type forces: the Special Operation Troops, the *Comando* Troops, the Parachute Troops, the Marines Special Actions Detachment and the Force Protection Force of the Air Force.

Rhodesia

During the Rhodesian Bush War of 1965-1980, the Rhodesian military increased its usage of commando type of operations in fighting a counter-insurgent war againt freedom-fighters (political dissidents seeking majority rule)until the formation of Zimbabwe.

- Rhodesian Light Infantry
- Rhodesian SAS
- Selous Scouts

United Kingdom

3 Commando Brigade, Royal Marines is under the command of the Royal Navy's Commander in Chief Fleet. All Royal Marines (other than the Royal Marines Band Service) are commando trained on entry to the Corps, with supporting units and individuals from the other services undertaking the All Arms Commando Course as required.

The Brigade is made up of the UK Landing Force Support Group (Headquarters Battalion), 40 Commando (home base: Taunton), 42 Commando (Bickleigh, Plymouth) and 45 Commando (Arbroath, Scotland), the Commando Logistic Regiment, 539 Assault Squadron Royal Marines, 29 Commando Regiment Royal Artillery, 24 Commando Regiment Royal Engineers and 1st battalion, The Rifles.

Vietnam

The North Vietnamese produced some of the most effective commando units of the post WWII era. Called sappers, these units represented a force economy measure for the NVA (North Vietnamese Army) and the Viet Cong. With large scale conventional attacks increasingly untenable, small commando operations came into their own, particularly after the Tet Offensive, and at times inflicted severe damage to US and ARVN troops and bases.

Sappers were originally supporting adjuncts to regular formations prior to 1967, but in time, independent formations were created throughout the Vietnam arena. Sappers could operate in support of a larger regular infantry formation, or as the main spearhead themselves, with regulars as backup. In the spearhead mode, they represented their most potent threat. A typical raiding operation was divided into 4 elements: Assault, Fire-Support, Security and Reserves. Assault teams were generally broken down into three-five man cells. Fire-support was critical, as it forced defenders to keep their heads down, while infiltrating assault elements made their final penetrations. One of the most devastating attacks was against the US Firebase, FSB Maryann in 1971.

While small in terms of total men deployed throughout the Vietnam theatre, sapper attacks had a significant impact for the NLF/PAVN effort. As one US Army history puts it:

From the beginning of 1968 until mid-1969, sappers were essential to the enemy's effort. Although they participated in only 4 percent of all assaults, these made up 12 percent of all significant assaults—those which inflicted serious damage. In 1969, the average raid inflicted more than $1,000,000 damage and accounted for more allied casualties.

PARA COMMANDOS (INDIA)

The Para Commandos are a special forces unit of the Indian Army. Formed in 1966, the Para Commandos are the largest and most important part of the Special Forces of India. They form the highly-trained Corps of the Indian Army and, generally, all the Indian Special Forces (SF) personnel are selected from it.

History

The parachute units of the Indian Army are among the oldest airborne units in the world. The first unit was authorized on 15 May 1941 and on 27 October 1941, the 50th Indian Parachute Brigade had been formed, comprising the 151st British Parachute Battalion, 152nd Indian Parachute Battalion & 153rd Gurkha Parachute Battalion.

During the Indo-Pakistani War of 1965, an ad hoc unit, named Meghdoot Force, consisting of volunteers from various infantry units was organized by Maj Megh Singh of the Brigade of the Guards. The unit performed well in combat and the Government authorized the raising of a commando unit. Lt Col Megh Singh was selected to raise the unit which was to be part of the Brigade of the Guards, but parachute qualification being an integral part of all special operations, the unit was transferred to the Parachute Regiment and raised as its 9th Battalion (Commando) on 1 July 1966. The erstwhile members of the Meghdoot Force formed the nucleus and the new unit based in Gwalior. In June 1967 the unit was split equally into two to form a second commando unit, designated as 10th Battalion, both with three Companies each. 10th Battalion was mandated to operate in the Western Desert and 9th Battalion in the northern mountains. In 1969, these battalions were redesignated as 9 and 10 Para (Commando) battalions.

In 1978, the 1st Battalion of the Parachute Regiment, as an experiment, was converted to become the third commando battalion and kept as the tactical reserve. Already a recipient of the Chief of Army Staff Unit Citation twice and GOC-in-C Eastern Command Unit Citation once, the unit is all set to celebrate its 250th Raising Day in 2011.

1995 saw the formation of the fourth commando battalion when the 21st Battalion, the Maratha Light Infantry was selected to convert to special forces and slated for the Eastern Command. After stringent selection and training process that spanned more that a year, on 1 February 1996, the unit under Col VB Shinde, was formally inducted into the Parachute Regiment as the 21st Battalion (Special Forces), The Parachute Regiment.

The unit has done well in its short lifespan and is the proud recipient of the Chief of Army Staff Unit Citation twice (1997 and 2006) and GOC-in-C Eastern Command Unit Citation once (2008) among a host of individual gallantry awards.

With the changing scenario in military operations and the need for more special forces units, 2 Para Battalion began the conversion process from parachute to para-commando role, followed closely by the 3rd and the 4th battalions, raising the strength of the special forces to seven battalions. The Parachute Regiment presently has seven special forces, three parachute, two Territorial Army and one Counter-Insurgency (Rashtriya Rifles) battalions in its fold.

Functions

- Intelligence collection.
- Subversion and sabotage of vital enemy infrastructure and communications through deep penetration and surgical strikes behind enemy lines.

- Covert and overt special operations as part of the Indian Army's counter-terrorist operations.
- Hostage rescue operations within and beyond Indian territory.

Organization

The Parachute Regiment presently has seven special forces, three parachute, two Territorial Army and one Counter-Insurgency (Rashtriya Rifles) battalions in its fold.

Para (SF) operate in assault teams which work individually or in coordination with other teams or units. Previously, each Para (SF) battalion had a geographical specialization and remained assigned to that sector. 1 Para Commandos, with deep sea divers in its ranks, specialized in anti-hijacking and hostage crises; 9 Para, with experienced mountaineers, was dedicated to mountainous and high-altitude warfare, 10 Para for desert warfare and the 21 Para for jungle warfare. However, these specializations have been dispensed with, and all special forces units are equally capable of operating in all conditions.

Personnel

Selection

All Indian paratroopers are volunteers. Some enter the Para regiments directly from civilian life, while others transfer in from regular army units.

Selection and Training

All members of the special forces are volunteers, either fresh from recruitment or after having served in other units. They are put through a probationary period of three months where they undergo various physical, mental and psychological tests, the majority being rejected with the rejection rate averaging 70–80 percent.

Those selected are awarded the maroon beret, the qualification badge (balidaan), and the shoulder titles of Special Forces. They are further sent to the Paratroopers' Training School (PTS) at Agra, Uttar Pradesh for their Basic Course in Paratrooping, which includes ground and air training. Those who are successful are made to do five static line jumps from varying altitudes which include one night jump and one with full battle equipment. On completion of the five jumps, the individual is awarded the coveted parachute wings which is worn on the right chest

As training is an ongoing process in the army, more so in the special forces, the members are further trained in specialised mode of infiltration and exfiltration, either by air (Combat Freefall) or sea (scuba diving). Some return to PTS to undergo the free-fall course, which in order to successfully pass requires at least 50 jumps from altitudes up to 22,500 feet. Both HALO (High Altitude Low Opening) and HAHO (High Altitude High Opening) techniques are learned. The ability to use the HAHO method and specially designed maneuverable parachutes called HAPPS (High Altitude Parachute Penetration System) to conduct stealth insertions over distances up to 50 km is also perfected..

For combat diving training, the commandos are sent to the Naval Diving School.

Daily routine begins with a 5 km morning run. Infiltration, assault and ambush tactics are refined and perfected. Special attention is given to CQB, urban warfare, counter-terror warfare and unarmed combat.

Off and on, night and weapons training and field craft involving 20 km treks with 60 kg (132 lb.) loads and live ammunition. Monthly forced marches with 65 kg combat loads over 30 km and quarterly night drops with full combat loads are also conducted. In addition to this in-house training, the commandos also attend a number of schools run by the Army that specialize in unconventional warfare.

These include the Junior Leaders' Commando Training Camp in Belgaum, Karnataka, the Parvat Ghatak School (for high altitude mountain warfare) in Tawang, Arunachal Pradesh, the High Altitude Warfare School (HAWS) in Sonamarg, Kashmir and the Counterinsurgency and Jungle Warfare School (CIJWS) in Vairengte, Mizoram. These schools are among the finest of their kind anywhere and routinely host students from other countries.

Recently the Indian government has allowed USSOCOM (United States Special Operations Command) personnel to attend courses held by CIJWS and may grant access to HAWS as part for further military cooperation between the two countries. In reciprocation, many operators are sent to the US to train with the Army Rangers and other units.

U.S. Army Special Forces have conducted joint HAHO training with the Para Commandos in 1992, underwater training in 1995 and anti-terrorism training in 1997. It is thought that the French Foreign Legion also has approached CIJWS regarding the courses taught by them. Para Commandos can also undergo a complete Combat Divers course, in which they earn a combat diver badge.

They are also experienced in conducting SHBO (special heli-borne operations) and typically employ Cheetahs, MI-8/MI-17, ALH (Dhruv)helicopters for this purpose.

Combat History

1971 Indo-Pakistan War

Para Commandos were first deployed in combat in the 1971 Indo-Pak War where they performed gallantly. The 9 Para saw action through a daring raid on a Pakistani Artillery positions at Mandhol. This raid resulted in the destruction of six 122mm guns belonging to the Pakistan Army's 172 Independent Battery.

Apart from the destruction of guns, ammunition and other vital equipment, the Pakistanis suffered 37 killed, 41 wounded and a great loss of face. This raid, launched at a crucial time to enable India's 25th Infantry Division to continue their operations on Daruchian (a Pakistani occupied post), won the 9 Para the Battle Honour for action in Mandhol.

10 Para was baptized in combat with successful raids on enemy posts at Chachro and Virawah, under Sawai Bhawani Singh Bahadur who won a Maha Vir Chakra for these daring raids.

By the late 1970s, Indian paratroopers were using High-Altitude, Low-Opening (HALO jump) techniques.

Operation Bluestar 1984

In 1984 the Para Commandos were involved in Operation Bluestar. They were charged with the eviction of Sikh militants from the Golden Temple in Punjab. 80 members of 1 Para Cdo were given the task of assaulting two areas of the temple, of which one area required divers. However there were a number of setbacks as a result of poor intelligence on the strength of the militants who were trained by Gen. Shabeg Singh himself, operating low light, the conventional manner of the raid and the lack of high precision CQB (close quarter battle) skills; all of which resulted in a mission failure. The diver mission was aborted after the first team got bogged down. The commandos never achieved their aims as a result of which tanks were brought in to finish the job.This action directly resulted in the establishment of the Anti-Terror National Security Guards, with specialized skills in close-quarter, urban combat.

Sri Lanka 1987

The late 1980s saw the Para Commandos in action in Sri Lanka, as part of Operation Pawan. However, lack of proper planning by the Indian Peace Keeping Force (IPKF) and insufficient intelligence on the LTTE's whereabouts, led the initial heli-borne assault on Jaffna University on 11 October 1987 to be a tragic failure.

Six soldiers lost their lives in that ill-fated mission, but unlike the Sikh Light Infantry who lost their lives gallantly fighting to the last, the Para commandos due to their superior training, took refuge under a house, after they got misguided by a youth who offered his service to help the commandos track Prabhakaran by taking them for a wild goose chase. They engaged the enemy for a full 24 hours and picked up all their dead with their weapons after reinforcements arrived next morning.

After the failed assault on Jaffna City, the 10 Para Cdo participated in November 1987 for a heli-borne assault in the town of Moolai, 14 miles to the north-west. 25 LTTE guerrillas were killed and an arms depot seized. In order to give the commandos battle experience, 1 Para Cdo was rotated home in early 1988 and replaced by 9 Para Cdo.

This battalion was scheduled to return home in June 1988, but the tour of duty was extended due to a planned air assault into the coastal swamps around Mullaittivu. The mission was a great success, in that it located several arms caches. The 9 Para Cdo also provided 12 men for the security of the Indian High Commission in Sri Lanka.

Operation Cactus 1988

With the capture of Maldives, an island nation off the south western coast of India on 3 November 1988 by PLOTE mercenaries, the army turned to the elite 6 Para. 6 Para flew in on 4 November 1988 in a fleet of Il-76, An-32 and An-12 transport aircraft. One team rescued the president, another took over the airfield and a third rescued Maldivian security personnel besieged in their NSS HQ. Later 3 Para was also deployed to the Maldives. When mercenaries tried to escape by sea along with hostages, they were intercepted by the Indian navy. Thus, 6 Para conducted the first ever international intervention by the Indian army without any loss of life.

1990 to the Present

Since the mid-90s the role of Para Commandos as a counter terrorist force has increased substantially. They are now actively involved in counter terrorist operations in Kashmir as an essential part of the Home Ministry's decision to conduct pro-active raids against militants in the countryside and mountains. The practice of take-the-fight-to-them involves extensive aerial reconnaissance followed by para-dropping operators into the target area. These missions continue for weeks at a stretch and include raids on terrorist camps and ambushes along infiltration routes.

Personnel include Para Commandos, NSG and special units of the Rashtriya Rifles-a paramilitary unit created to deal with the Kashmir insurgency. They may also include MARCOS personnel, many of whom are seconded to the Army for CT operations. Despite the Army's insistence, the government has not sanctioned cross border raids on terrorist camps in Pakistan.

There have been reports in the press of Para Commandos taking part in hostage rescue missions in Kashmir but details remain Classified. The 9 Para (SF) saw action in the 1999 Kargil War, where they conducted a number of raids to remove a combined force of Pakistani special forces (SSG), light infantry and militants who had infiltrated across the border and had dug in on the mountaintops.

They typically operated in 6 man teams (5 men and 1 officer) for Reconnaissance on mountaintop bunkers primarily involving high-altitude scaling at night, with night vision as help. They also took part in the follow up raids.

The Vishesh Bal were recently involved in Operation Khukri, in Sierra Leone in June 2000 where Indian troops were part of a multinational UN peacekeeping force. About 120 operators commanded by Major Harinder Sood were airlifted from New Delhi to spearhead the mission to rescue 223 men of the 5/8 Gorkha Rifles who were surrounded and held captive by the Revolutionary United Front (RUF) rebels for over 75 days.

The operation, involving Mi-25/35 helicopter gun ships of the Indian Air Force and other infantry battalions, was a complete success with no Indian casualties other than a few shrapnel wounds. The Special Air Service who were present as part of the British force, loaned the Para Commandos their Chinook transport helicopters for the initial assault.

Equipment

Para Commandos have access to all types of infantry weapons required for a particular mission.

9

Wing (Military Aviation Unit)

Wing is a term used by different Military aviation forces for a unit of command. The terms wing and group are used for different-sized units from one country or service to another. In some military aviation services, a wing is a relatively large formation of two or more groups, which in turn control two or more squadrons. In other contexts a wing is a smaller unit, comprising two to four squadrons, with several wings forming a group. For example, In the United States Air Force, a wing is equivalent to a British Royal Air Force group, both are equivalent to an army regiment, and a USAF group is equivalent to a British RAF wing.

British pattern	American pattern
Group	Wing
Wing	Group
Squadron	Squadron

British Usage

Origins

On its establishment in 1912, the British Royal Flying Corps (RFC) was intended to be an inter-service, combined force of the British Army and Royal Navy. Given the rivalry that existed between the army and navy, new terminology was used, in order to avoid marking the corps out as having an army or navy ethos. Accordingly, the word "wing", with its allusion of flight, was chosen as the term of subdivision and the corps was split into a "Military Wing" (i.e. an army wing) and a "Naval Wing". Each wing consisted of a number of squadrons (the term "squadron" already being used by both the Army and the Navy).

By 1914, the naval wing had become the Royal Naval Air Service, and gained its independence from the Royal Flying Corps. In 1915, the Royal Flying Corps had significantly expanded and it was felt necessary to create organizational units which would control two or more squadrons; the term "wing" was re-used for these new organizational units.

The Royal Flying Corps was amalgamated with the Royal Naval Air Service in 1918, creating the Royal Air Force. The RFC usage of wing was maintained in the new service.

Current use

Unit type	Commanding Officer
Operational flying wings	Group Captain
Ground-based wings	Wing Commander

In most Commonwealth air forces, as well as some others, a wing is usually made up of three or four squadrons. In these air forces a wing is inferior to a group. Originally all wings were usually commanded by a wing commander (equivalent to a lieutenant colonel). From World War II onwards, operational flying wings have usually been commanded by group captains (equivalent to colonels), whereas ground-based wings have continued to be commanded by wing commanders.

A wing may also be used for non-flying units, such as the infantry forces of the RAF Regiment, (in which a wing equates to a battalion). Additionally, RAF stations are administratively divided into wings. In 2006, expeditionary air wings were established at the RAF's main operating bases. These expeditionary air wings consist of the deployable elements of the main operating base and other supplementary forces. Expeditionary air wings may be subordinated to an expeditionary air group.

In the British Air Training Corps, a wing consists of a number of squadrons within a designated geographical area, usually named after the county in which it is based. In this regard, a wing is inferior to a "region" which is made up of six wings. In all, there are 36 Air Training Corps wings in six regions within the United

Kingdom, each of which is commanded by a RAFVR(T) wing commander.

Canadian Usage

While the original Royal Canadian Air Force followed the British pattern, the modern Canadian Forces Air Command is an example of a Commonwealth air force which does not follow British usage. The size of a wing (base) follows US usage; it varies greatly and may comprise personnel numbering in the thousands.

In the 1990s, the Canadian Forces Air Command (the post-1968 RCAF) altered the structure of those bases under its control, declaring them to be Wings under the overall control of 1 Canadian Air Division in Winnipeg. For instance, CFB Trenton in Ontario was redesignated 8 Wing Trenton. The base commander of these bases (as well as other wings whose headquarters were stood up on bases not controlled by Air Command, such as 16 Wing at CFB Borden and 1 Wing at CFB Kingston) were re-designated Wing Commanders (or Wg Comd). As well as continuing their functions as the commanding officers of the bases they were assigned to, they also serve as formation commanders to all squadrons and units duly assigned to them by 1 CDN AIR DIV HQ and AIRCOM HQ (regardless if they are physically located on the base in question or elsewhere; as witness 12 Wing in Nova Scotia, which has one unit, 443 Maritime Helicopter Squadron, based at Patricia Bay near CFB Esquimalt in British Columbia, on the other side of the country from Shearwater).

United States Usage

By comparison, in the United States Air Force, a wing is normally the organizational tier below a Numbered Air Force. Most USAF wings are commanded by a Colonel, but some are commanded by Brigadier Generals. USAF wings structured to fulfill a mission from a specific base, and contain a headquarters and four groups: an operations group, a maintenance group, a medical group and a mission support group. Such a wing is referred to as a Combat Wing Organization, which is comparable to a brigade in the US Army. Other wings, such as Air Expeditionary Wings, exist for various other purposes, and their scope may extend to one base, one theatre or worldwide. In the

United States Navy, a wing is a group of two or more squadrons of aircraft that are based on land rather than on an aircraft carrier. A Carrier air wing (or Carrier Air Group) consists of seven squadrons, four of which are of fighters or fighter-bombers.

In the United States Marine Corps, a wing is an overall command consisting of at least two Marine Aircraft Groups and their subordinate squadrons and support units. Its commander is usually a Major General. In the Civil Air Patrol, there are 52 wings (each of the 50 states plus Washington, D.C. and Puerto Rico). Each wing supervises the individual groups and squadrons, which are the basic operational unit of the organization. Some wings, for example Delaware Wing have only one group due to the small size of the wing.

Equivalents in other Countries

Most other Western air forces tend to follow the US nomenclature, insofar as having squadrons coming directly under groups. Immediately above this however, some air forces have foreign terms which are equivalent to a US "wing". For example: *Geschwader* in Germany; *Polk* in Russia; *Stormo* in Italy; and *escadre* in pre-World War II French Air Force, which is also the official French translation of a wing in modern-day Canadian Forces.

AREA CONTROL CENTER

In air traffic control, an Area Control Center (ACC), also known as a Center, is a facility responsible for controlling instrument flight rules aircraft en route in a particular volume of airspace (a Flight Information Region) at high altitudes between airport approaches and departures. In the United States, such a Center is referred to as an Air Route Traffic Control Center (ARTCC).

A Center typically accepts traffic from, and ultimately passes traffic to, the control of a Terminal Control Center or of another Center. Most Centers are operated by the national governments of the countries in which they are located. The general operations of Centers worldwide, and the boundaries of the airspace each Center controls, are governed by the ICAO. In some cases, the function of an Area Control Center and a Terminal Control Center are combined in a single facility. For example, NATS combines the London Terminal Control Centre (LTCC) and London Area Control Centre (LACC) in Swanwick in the UK.

FAA Definition

The United States Federal Aviation Administration defines an ARTCC as [a] facility established to provide air traffic control service to aircraft operating on IFR flight plans within controlled airspace, principally during the en route phase of flight. When equipment capabilities and controller workload permit, certain advisory/assistance services may be provided to VFR aircraft. An ARTCC is the U.S. equivalent of an Area Control Center (ACC).

Subdivision of Airspace into Sectors

The Flight Information Region controlled by a Center may be further administratively subdivided into Areas comprising two to seven sectors. Each Area is staffed by a set of controllers trained on all the sectors in that area.

Sectors use a distinct radio frequencies for communication with aircraft. Each sector also has secure landline communications with adjacent sectors, approach controls, areas, ARTCCs, flight service centers, and military aviation control facilities. These landline communications are shared among all sectors who need them and are available on a first-come, first-serve basis. Aircraft passing from one sector to another shall be handed off and requested to change frequencies to contact the next sector controller. Sector boundaries are specified by an aeronautical chart.

Center Operations

Air traffic controllers working within a Center communicate via radio with pilots of instrument flight rules aircraft passing through the Center's airspace. A Center's communication frequencies (typically in the very high frequency amplitude modulation aviation bands, 118 MHz to 137 MHz, for overland control) are published in aeronautical charts and manuals, and will also be announced to a pilot by the previous controller during a hand-off.

In addition to radios to communicate with aircraft, Center

controllers have access to communication links with other Centers and TRACONs. In the United States, Centers are electronically linked through the National Airspace System, which allows nationwide coordination of traffic flow to manage congestion. Centers in the United States also have electronic access to nationwide radar data.

Controllers use radar to monitor the progress of flights and instruct aircraft to perform course adjustments as needed to maintain separation from other aircraft. Aircraft with Center contact can be readily distinguished by their transponders. Pilots may request altitude adjustments or course changes for reasons including avoidance of turbulence or adverse weather conditions. Controllers can assign routing relative to location fixes derived from latitude and longitude, or from radionavigation beacons such as VORs. Typically, Centers have advance notice of a plane's arrival and intentions from its pre-filed flight plan.

Oceanic Air Traffic Control

Some Centers have ICAO-designated responsibility for airspace located over an ocean such as ZOA, the majority of which is international airspace. Because substantial volumes of oceanic airspace lie beyond the range of ground-based radars, oceanic airspace controllers have to estimate the position of an airplane from pilot reports and computer models (procedural control), rather than observing the position directly (radar control, also known as positive control). Pilots flying over an ocean can determine their own positions accurately using the Global Positioning System and can supply periodic updates to a Center. A Center's control service for an oceanic FIR may be operationally distinct from its service for a domestic overland FIR over land, employing different communications frequencies, controllers, and a different ICAO code. Pilots typically use high frequency radio instead of very high frequency radio to communicate with a Center when flying over the ocean, because of HF's relatively greater propagation over long distances.

Aviation Light Signals

In the case of a radio failure or aircraft not equipped with a radio, air traffic control may use a signal lamp to direct the aircraft.

The signal lamp has a focused bright beam and is capable of emitting three different colors: red, white and green. These colors may be flashed or steady, and have different meanings to aircraft in flight or on the ground. Planes can acknowledge the instruction by wiggling their wings, moving the ailerons if on the ground, or by flashing their landing or navigation lights during hours of darkness.

GLOBAL AIR TRAFFIC MANAGEMENT

Global Air Traffic Management (GATM) is a concept for satellite-based communication, navigation, surveillance and air traffic management. The Federal Aviation Administration and the International Civil Aviation Organization, a special agency of the United Nations, established GATM standards in order to keep air travel safe and effective in increasingly crowded worldwide air space. Efforts are being made worldwide to test and implement new technologies that will allow GATM to efficiently support Air Traffic Control.

Airservices Australia ADS-B initiative is one of the major implementation programs in this field. This initiative will facilitate the certification of this new technology allowing further implementation.

The two core satellite constellations are the Global Positioning System (GPS) of the USA and the Global Navigation Satellite System (GLONASS) of Russia. The third largest constellations would be Europe's GALILEO when it becomes fully operational. These systems provide independent capabilities and can be used in combination with future core constellations and augmentation systems.

Signals from core satellite are received by ground reference stations and any errors in the signals are identified. Each station in the network relays the data to area-wide master stations where correction information for specific geographical areas is computed. The correction message is prepared and uplinked to a geostationary communication satellite (GEO) via a ground uplink station. This message is broadcast to receivers on board aircraft flying within the broadcast coverage area of the System. The system is known in the USA as WAAS (Wide Area Augmentation System), in

Europe as EGNOS (European Geostationary Navigation Overlay System), in Japan as MSAS (MTSAT Satellite Based Augmentation System) and in India as GAGAN (GPS Aided Geo Augmented Navigation).

The system employs various techniques to correct equatorial anomalies. The advantage of the system is, it is Global in scope and it has the potential to support all phases of flight providing a seamless global navigation guidance.

This could eliminate the need for a variety of ground and airborne systems that were designed to meet specific requirements for certain phases of flight. Standard and Recommended Practices for the air traffic management based on a global navigation satellite system are developed by ICAO (International Civil Aviation Organization). Thus the system has to meet ICAO standards to become operational.

INTERNATIONAL CIVIL AVIATION ORGANIZATION

The International Civil Aviation Organization (ICAO), a major agency of the United Nations, codifies the principles and techniques of international air navigation and fosters the planning and development of international air transport to ensure safe and orderly growth. Its headquarters are located in the *Quartier International* of Montreal, Canada.

The ICAO Council adopts standards and recommended practices concerning air navigation, its infrastructure, Flight inspection, prevention of unlawful interference, and facilitation of border-crossing procedures for international civil aviation. In addition, the ICAO defines the protocols for air accident investigation followed by transport safety authorities in countries signatory to the Convention on International Civil Aviation, commonly known as the *Chicago Convention*.

The ICAO should not be confused with the International Air Transport Association (IATA), a trade organization for airlines also headquartered in Montreal, or with the Civil Air Navigation Services Organisation (CANSO), an organization for Air Navigation Service Providers (ANSP's) with its headquarters at Amsterdam Airport Schiphol in the Netherlands.

Statute

The 9th edition of the Convention on International Civil Aviation includes modifications from 1948 up to year 2006. The ICAO refers to its current edition of the Convention as the *statute,* and designates it as ICAO Doc 7300/9. The Convention has 18 Annexes. These Annexes are listed by title in the article Convention on International Civil Aviation.

Standards

The ICAO also standardizes certain functions for use in the airline industry, such as the Aeronautical Message Handling System AMHS; this probably makes it a standards organization.

The ICAO defines an International Standard Atmosphere (also known as ICAO Standard Atmosphere), a model of the standard variation of pressure, temperature, density, and viscosity with altitude in the Earth's atmosphere. This is useful in calibrating instruments and designing aircraft.

The ICAO standardizes machine-readable passports worldwide. Such passports have an area where some of the information otherwise written in textual form is written as strings of alphanumeric characters, printed in a manner suitable for optical character recognition. This enables border controllers and other law enforcement agents to process such passports quickly, without having to input the information manually into a computer. ICAO publishes Doc 9303, Machine Readable Travel Documents, the technical standard for machine-readable passports. A more recent standard is for biometric passports. These contain biometrics to authenticate the identity of travellers. The passport's critical information is stored on a tiny RFID computer chip, much like information stored on smartcards. Like some smartcards, the passport book design calls for an embedded contactless chip that is able to hold digital signature data to ensure the integrity of the passport and the biometric data.

Codes registered with ICAO

Both ICAO and IATA have their own airport and airline code systems. ICAO uses 4-letter airport codes and 3-letter airline codes. In the continental United States, the ICAO codes are usually the same as the IATA code, with a prefix of "K" — LAX is KLAX. Canada follows a similar pattern, where a prefix of "C" is usually added to an IATA code to find the ICAO code — YEG is CYEG. In the rest of the world, the codes are unrelated, as the IATA code is phonic and the ICAO code is location-based; for example, Charles de Gaulle Airport has an ICAO code of LFPG, and an IATA code of CDG.

ICAO is also responsible for issuing alphanumeric aircraft type codes that contain 2-4 characters. These codes provide the identification that is typically used in flight plans. An example of this is the Boeing 747 that would use (depending on the variant) B741, B742, B743, etc.

ICAO provides telephony designators to aircraft operators worldwide. These consist of the three-letter airline identifier and a one-or two-word designator. They are usually, but not always, similar to the aircraft operator name.

For example, the identifier for Aer Lingus is EIN and the designator is Shamrock, while Japan Airlines International is JAL and Japan Air. Thus, a flight by Aer Lingus numbered 111 would be written as "EIN111" and pronounced "Shamrock One Eleven" on the radio, while a similarly numbered Japan Airlines flight would be written as "JAL111" and pronounced "Japan Air One Eleven".

ICAO maintains the standards for aircraft registration ("tail numbers"), including the alphanumeric codes that identify the country of registration.

Regions and Regional Offices

The ICAO has seven regional offices serving nine regions:

1. Asia and Pacific, Bangkok, Thailand
2. Middle East, Cairo, Egypt
3. Western and Central Africa, Dakar, Senegal
4. South America, Lima, Peru
5. North America, Central America and Caribbean, Mexico City, Mexico
6. Eastern and Southern Africa, Nairobi, Kenya
7. Europe and North Atlantic, Paris, France

ICAO and Climate Change

Emissions from international aviation are specifically excluded from the targets agreed under the Kyoto Protocol. Instead, the Protocol invites developed countries to pursue the limitation or reduction of emissions through the International Civil Aviation Organisation (ICAO). ICAO's environmental committee continues to consider the potential for using market-based measures such as trading and charging, but this work is unlikely to lead to global action. It is currently developing guidance for states who wish to include aviation in an emissions trading scheme (ETS) to meet their Kyoto commitments, and for airlines who wish to participate voluntarily in a trading scheme.

Emissions from domestic aviation are included within the Kyoto targets agreed by countries. This has led to some national policies such as fuel and emission taxes for domestic air travel in the Netherlands and Norway respectively. Although some countries tax the fuel used by domestic aviation, there is no duty on kerosene used on international flights. (Aviation Environment Federation)

ICAO is currently against the inclusion of aviation in the European Union Emissions Trading Scheme (EU ETS). However, the EU is pressing ahead with its plans to include aviation from 2011.

Investigations of Air Disasters

ICAO has conducted just two investigations involving air disasters. Both incidents involved passenger airliners shot down while in international flight over hostile territory. The first incident occurred on February 21, 1973, during a period of tension which would lead to the Israeli-Arab "October war", when a Libyan Arab Airlines Flight 114 was shot down by Israeli F-4 jets over the Sinai Peninsula. The second incident occurred on Sept. 1, 1983, during a period of heightened Cold War tension, when a Soviet Su-15 interceptor shot down a straying Korean Air Lines Flight 007 just west of Sakhalin Island. KAL 007 was carrying 269 people..

10

India Defence Consultants

INTRODUCTION

Mozambique's decades long civil war ended, the economy improved, and the crime rate went down. President Joaquim Alberto Chissano attributes the war's demise and these other positive trends largely to the Transcendental Meditation (TM) and TM-Sidhi programmes. He and other Mozambique governmental leaders are convinced that these changes occurred because members of the Mozambique Armed Forces and police school students practiced the TM programme. The core of the TM programme is a simple meditation technique. Physicist and Vedic scholar Maharishi Mahesh Yogi founded the organization that teaches this practice. Today even more members of the Mozambique military are learning to practice this non-religious technique for about twenty minutes twice a day. Worldwide, over five million people have learned the technique.

After the General Peace Agreement was signed in 1992, Maharishi Vedic University presented the TM programme to the Mozambique government as a scientifically validated means of creating order and quelling further conflict. To maintain its fragile peace, the Joint Chiefs of Staff of Mozambique implemented the TM programme in different military units of Ground, Naval and Air Forces.

In all, more than 16,000 people learned the TM programme, and practiced it daily in large groups. Additionally, more than 3,000 went on to learn the more powerful TM-Sidhi programme, including Yogic Flying. The goal was to achieve the *Maharishi*

Effect, a phenomenon in which the number of people practicing the programme reaches a critical mass, creating coherence, peace and harmony throughout the nation. After the programme was underway in 1993, positive trends were noticed. Peace was maintained. Crime, which is normally expected to increase at the end of a war, actually decreased, as predicted by Maharishi Effect scientists. The next year, the military began to be demobilized. Lt. General Tobias Dai, then Commander of the Armed Forces (now the Defence Minister), noticed a sudden change. "What is very clear is that once the positive effect is created, if group practice is stopped, the previous tendencies of higher collective stress, as determined from the crime indexes and the tense situations in the country, began to rise again. In 1994, there was a remarkable decrease in coherence in the country as a result of decreased participation in the group practice of the Transcendental Meditation and TM-Sidhi Programmes..."

Dai attributed the dip in coherence to the demobilization of the troops and anticipated ending of TM courses for future police officers. Dai also said in 1994 that "until now, although with several difficulties, the maintenance of peace has been possible during these 2 years, and free and just elections have been carried out..." Coherence-creating groups of meditators were re-created. A year later, the U.S. National Defence Council Foundation dropped Mozambique from the list of conflicts in the world, and stability has since been sustained.

In the beginning, conventional military strategists scoffed at Mozambique's novel strategy. However, today, due to success on many fronts, other militaries may be attracted to the new technology. After all, many of today's "tried and proven" military technologies were yesterday's pipe dreams. For instance, although the breech-loading rifle was far superior to muzzle loaders, it took years for armies to adopt them. Few leaders thought that Billy Mitchell could sink battleships with flying machines made of wood, cloth, and baling wire. Military history has shown that new scientific technologies can give a strategic advantage, even at a distance. For instance, the radar "shield" deployed in England during World War II maximized the fighting power of the under-sized Royal Air Force. These examples show why the Italian airpower advocate General Giulio Douhet's strategy still applies today: *"Victory smiles upon those who anticipate the change in the character of war, not upon those who wait to adapt themselves after the changes occur"* The quest to develop superior weapons technology has been fueling an arms race for centuries. Now another revolutionary change in the character of war could be on the horizon. In the tradition of military pioneers, military leaders might be well advised to anticipate the changes that could occur after widespread implementation of this promising human resource-based technology.

There are three important components to any discipline: the observer, the process of observation, and the observed. Unlike conventional military science, Maharishi's Supreme Military Science places emphasis on the observer. Its goal is to develop the full potential of each individual military professional. This emphasis is unique. Although conventional military training involves physical conditioning to increase performance, it does not train military personnel to develop their full potential. Instead of striving to increase human performance, militaries devote their attention largely to increasing destructive power, accuracy, and delivery speed of weaponry. This oversight presents today's warriors with extra challenges.

High-technology weaponry demands that military personnel perform at their optimum. All ranks must be in top mental as well as physical condition. Experience has shown that victory depends on taking the right action with appropriate speed and accuracy. Their minds need to remain strong and clear even when duty requires strenuous and protracted hours. Frequently, decisions must be made instantly, on an intuitive level. If these decisions and actions are incorrect, the consequences can be tragic whether in a fighting or deployed in operations other than war. For all these reasons, today all members of the armed forces are stretched in the limits of human performance.

The challenge to maintain broad comprehension, perfect mind-body coordination, and lively intelligence under difficult circumstances has increased for modern military professionals. Stress is likely to be the most significant underlying factor. Stress is increasing for many reasons. For instance, "[t]he nature of warfare is changing. Lengthy military commitments designed to win conflicts are being replaced by short-term deployments intended to prevent them." The military particularly in the United States is being called upon to maintain effectiveness despite cutbacks. Therefore, it will be necessary in such cases for already-stressed, overworked personnel to continue to do more with less. The demand for back-to-back deployments and station tenures leads to increased divorce and marital discord, and the use of tobacco, alcohol and drugs. Such manifestations of stress reduce the fitness, effectiveness and operational readiness of individuals. Increased stress in the military may take its toll in other ways. For instance, a U.S. Army survey suggests that spousal abuse is occurring in one of every three Army families each year—double the civilian rate. The Pentagon's Readiness Task Force admits that stress is taking a heavy toll on service members and has contributed to a jump in suicides in the military. Obviously, reducing or even eliminating stress and the associated performance-limiting behaviors contributes to greater individual performance and to successful military campaigns. Most hardened combat veterans as well as inexperienced troops realize that if they could be free from stress and strain they would perform more dynamically.

Published research suggests that stress can be reduced through the practical components of Maharishi's Supreme Military Science. These components involve application of simple, mental procedures known as the Transcendental Meditation (TM) and TM-Sidhi programme. The TM technique originates from the Vedic tradition. More than four million people worldwide have learned the TM technique. The goal of practicing the TM programme is not to become a passive individual but to eliminate stress and its performance limiting consequences, in part through providing a unique deep state of rest. Rest is the basis for more successful dynamic activity.

INDIVIDUAL BENEFITS PROVIDED BY MAHARISHI'S SUPREME MILITARY SCIENCE

The TM programme has been adopted to reduce stress in military, governmental and other institutional settings. For example, over 26,000 military police in a number of Brazilian states learned the TM technique between 1987 and 1988. In a study involving 6,300 military police in the State of Bahia, Brazil disciplinary measures decreased 69% for officers and 35% for cadets after learning the technique. Doctor's visits also decreased—26% for officers and 55% for cadets. Also, community relations improved. For instance, the number of positive reports received by the military police department from the citizens of Salvador, Brazil increased 1,206% after officers were instructed in the TM programme. A study conducted on 289 cadets at the Police Academy of Piauí, Brazil showed significant improvements in behavior, attitude, health, and academic performance after learning the TM technique.

In a more direct test of the effects of the programme on performance, Sandahl, of the National Defence Research Institute in Karlstad, Sweden, conducted a study on 15 applicants who were rejected for pilot training with the Royal Swedish Air Force (RSAF). The potential pilots were rejected by the RSAF drafting committee because of inadequate performance on the *Defence Mechanism Test* (DMT) but were considered suitable otherwise. Subsequently, eight of the applicants practiced the TM programme for 18 months and showed a significant improvement in DMT scores compared to a non-meditating control group. Sandahl proposed that the reduced neuroticism resulting from regular practice of the programme reflected a decrease in *hidden mental turbulence*, leading to better performance.

Tests on other stress-related problems have been equally promising. For instance, American Vietnam War veterans suffering from post-traumatic stress disorder were randomly assigned either the TM technique or psychotherapy alone. The veterans who practiced the technique showed significant improvement on eight measures: alcohol problems, emotional numbness, insomnia, anxiety, post-Vietnam Stress disorder, family problems, depression, and employment record. The veterans who participated in psychotherapy alone did not show significant improvement. The practitioners of the TM technique also showed a more rapid physiological recovery from a stressful stimulus, as gauged by habituation of the skin resistance response. A number of other studies have found beneficial effects of the TM program on stress-induced neuroendocrine dysfunctions that contribute to cardiovascular and other chronic diseases. Also, over 24 studies have shown that the TM program fosters significant reductions in substance abuse, such as tobacco, alcohol, and all types of illegal and prescribed drugs.

Aside from these studies of stress-related change, there are other studies documenting benefits of the TM programme that could give military personnel the edge in battle. For example, a study by Reddy, Bai, and Rao showed that speed, agility, reactions, coordination, endurance, and perception improved after learning the TM programme. In other studies, three months of practicing the TM technique resulted in subjects showing significantly increased field independence (i.e., increased ability to focus, increased stability of spatial orientation, broader comprehension, increased resistance to distraction) compared to controls. Other research has measured a greater ability to assimilate and structure experience improved memory and learning ability, increased creativity, and greater autonomic stability. Other effects include enhanced neurological efficiency, faster choice reaction time, improved self-confidence, increased self-reliance, and greater inner control. Holistic growth has been indicated by psychophysiological means such as increases in global EEG coherence, and through psychological tests of intelligence, moral reasoning, and personality.

The aforementioned research suggests a military that adopts this proven human resource technology would be at an advantage on the battlefield. However, this strategic advantage over an adversary would not in itself intimidate the opponent. The next section will explain how combat could be reduced through this consciousness-based technology.

BENEFITS TO SOCIETY PROVIDED BY MAHARISHI'S SUPREME MILITARY SCIENCE

"Peace through strength" has been a popular military strategy Unfortunately, a strong military projects a threatening image even when deployed for humanitarian missions. This was eviden during the peacekeeping operation in Somalia. The military wa invited in as a friendly force to restore order. Later, the outside military forces were reviled and persecuted by many civilians who had earlier pleaded for their help delivering and safeguarding their lives, food, and supplies.

There is a Need for New Strategies of Prevention

The survival and progress of a nation depend on the effectiveness of its national defence. However, it is clear today that even with the world's best military equipment and preparedness, the current defence paradigm is unable to totally protect any nation. Regardless of military strength, no nation today enjoys total freedom from the fear of politically motivated violence. Fighting in the family of nations influences every nation. Even if it is not directly a participant in hostilities, a response of fear and hatred is generated. This leads to military budget increases, stockpiling of armaments, and arousal of suspicions. In theory, since World War II, deterrence or fear-based strategies have been used to protect and promote peace. Apparently, this strategy has not worked.

According to figures produced by the Hamburg University Research Unit on Wars, Armament, and Development (AKUF), over 186 wars have occurred since 1945. In 1994 there were thirty-one major armed conflicts in twenty-seven locations around the world. The Stockholm International Peace Research Institute (SIPRI) also claims that there were thirty major-armed conflicts in 1995. That same year the U.S. National Defence Council Foundation conservatively counted a record seventy-one conflicts world-wide. In 1996, SIPRI counted twenty-seven major armed conflicts world-wide. It documented twenty-five major armed conflicts in 1997, and twenty-seven major armed conflicts in 1998 as well as in 1999.

Although most of these conflicts were civil wars or ethnic hostilities, thousands of lives have been lost. However, a new strategic paradigm may be emerging. Prevention-oriented strategies are influencing military strategists. This trend parallels the increasing emphasis on prevention-oriented medicine by American Health Maintenance Organizations because it is wiser, and it costs less, to prevent illness from arising in the first place than to cure it after it occurs. This prevention orientation is beginning to affect the thinking of government and military leaders. Former U.S. Secretary of Defence William Perry spearheaded this movement when he said to a gathering at Harvard University:

Preventive medicine creates the conditions which support health, making disease less likely and surgery unnecessary. Preventive defence creates the conditions which support peace, making war less likely and deterrence unnecessary.

Perry also emphasized that preventive defence is forward looking, not passive or philanthropic. He is quoted as saying: "It's about hard work and ingenuity today, so that we don't have to expend blood and treasure tomorrow" The research being reviewed here suggests the preventive approach need not be "hard work" if the *right tool* is used. Studies by over 50 investigators from 17 universities and research institutes support the idea that the military could utilize the technologies available in Maharishi's Supreme Military Science to prevent an enemy from arising. In order to comprehend how this could be done requires understanding the apparent source of war—stress in collective consciousness of society.

Concept of Collective Consciousness

To understand the concept of collective consciousness a military example may be useful. Military units such as battalions, divisions, squadrons, wings, fleets, battlegroups, etc. are social structures. Each unit exhibits its own varying degree of orderliness and harmony that produces its own collective spirit or morale. Throughout history high morale has been a powerful strategic asset. This is especially true concerning the society the military protects.

For example, contrast the morale of the U.S.A. during World War II with the lack of it during the Vietnam conflict. Similarly, Maharishi's Supreme Military Science views society's "morale" as an aspect or manifestation of collective consciousness, a potential strategic asset. The collective consciousness of society is proposed to be the sum of the influences created by its individual members. This collective consciousness, in turn, affects the thoughts and feelings of those same individuals.

Stress in Collective Consciousness Starts Wars

Maharishi's Supreme Military Science propounds that the outbreak of collective violence or warfare is due to the build-up of stress and tension in society's collective consciousness. If the collective consciousness is full of tension and fear, then disorder is more liable to erupt than if the prevailing mood is one of contentment. Social injustice and unfavorable economic conditions thrive in as well as contribute to chaotic environments. Unresolved religious, territorial, political, and cultural differences further contribute to unrest. Thus, the frustrated and dissatisfied population of any country contributes to its instability. The build up of this sort of friction in the nation becomes dangerous to its sovereignty, producing an unstable government that is more prone to war. The social unrest and political instability contributed to the coming to power of Adolf Hitler. Disorder can take the form of civil strife or of conflict with neighboring countries. If a war between nations, a civil war, or even a *coup d'état*, occurs, the possibilities of escalation may increase because, frequently, other groups or nations are tempted to take advantage of the situation. For instance, after war had broken out in Europe, Japan sought to gain new footholds in other territories besides China during World War II. Unmitigated crises before, and the reign of terror during, both World Wars are among many historical examples of collective stress driving social disorder and spilling out into nearby nations.

The Maharishi Effect

Over the years, many published, peer-reviewed studies have presented evidence that the practical components of Maharishi's Supreme Military Science—the practice of the Transcendental Meditation and TM-Sidhi programme singly or in groups creates an upsurge of harmony and orderliness in society. These changes have been theorized to occur through raising the coherence in collective consciousness. The societal changes such as reductions in war deaths, improvements in economic conditions, and reductions in crime, violence, accidents, and illness that the studies have shown occurred when the number of practitioners of the TM programme reached about *1%* of the population in the area under study (usually a city). Studies involving participants in the more advanced TM-Sidhi programme show similar results when approximately the *square root of 1%* of the population practiced the technique in a group. These coherence-creating effects were predicted by Maharishi over thirty years ago. His prediction was based partly on the description of a strategic shield of "national armor" called *"rashtriya kavach"* described in the Vedic literature. Later, scientists who validated his prediction named the phenomenon the Maharishi Effect in his honour. Today a growing number of physicists support the validity of the Maharishi Effect. The basic principle underlying this effect is often observed in physical energy systems.

Physics has identified certain internally coherent systems, such as superconductors that have the ability to *shield themselves from disruptive influences*. While the more usual, *incoherent systems are easily penetrated by disorder from outside*. One example of such an invisible or "invincible" shield is called the Meissner Effect. It takes place at the quantum level of superconductivity. In a superconductor, the coherent collective functioning of the electrons spontaneously excludes an external magnetic field. This system maintains its impenetrable status because no random or chaotic activity can take place within it. On the other hand, this phenomenon of invincibility does not occur in ordinary electrical conductors because the random activity of the incoherent and disordered electrons allows penetration by an external magnetic field.

PHYSICS DESCRIBES THE UNIFIED FIELD

Historically, the most effective means to counter a potential enemy's military technology is to make that technology obsolete. The state-of-the-art weaponry of any age invariably harnesses more powerful and profound laws of nature. Maharishi Effect technology appears to operate from what modern physicists describe as the ultimate source of power—the unified field of all the laws of nature. Theoretical physics during the past decade has evolved to a progressively more unified understanding of the basic laws of nature, culminating in the recent discovery of completely unified field theories. These theories locate a single field of intelligence at the basis of all matter and force fields in the universe. In this field, all the known fundamental forces of nature: the weak force, the strong force, the electromagnetic force, and gravitation are unified.

Could the Unified Field be Harnessed as a Military Technology?

Could this field of intelligence be tapped? Most modern scientists are puzzled by the concept of consciousness and the mind's relationship to physics. In ancient cultures from time immemorial there was no puzzle: a coherent human mind contacts deeper levels of creation. Today, world-renowned physicists and others theorize that consciousness sprouts from the quantum mechanical level the most abstract level, the unified field. If this is correct, then the mind inherently operates at these subtle and powerful levels of nature. The results of tests of the Maharishi Effect discussed below are too far-reaching to be explained by field effects associated with any of the four basic forces of nature. For this reason, scientists involved in these studies are convinced the Maharishi Effect must operate on the most profound and powerful level—the unified field of all the laws of nature.

Selected Maharishi Effect research

Over 50 studies suggest that by taking full advantage of the Maharishi Effect militaries could quickly create more peaceful collective consciousness in society and reducing warfare, crime, violence, and other forms of negative social behavior. In the following paragraphs, several of these studies are reviewed.

A study that was conducted in the town of Baskinta, Lebanon found that when 1% of the people were taught the Transcendental Meditation technique the number of war casualties and crises decreased significantly as compared to four towns near Baskinta with comparable demographics. There had been an average of two incoming artillery shells per day in Baskinta during the previous two years. After becoming a 1% city, the shelling stopped for the following two years even though the rate continued to climb in the five control cities with comparable demographics. Differences between Baskinta and the control villages reached a significance of $p<.005$. The results of this study were predicted in advance, strongly suggesting a causal influence for the Maharishi Effect in reducing conflict.

In other studies, Davies and later Davies & Alexander looked at how the war in Lebanon was affected by seven large assemblies that had reached the theoretically sufficient number of TM-Sidhi practitioners. The results of applying Maharishi Effect technology were striking (i.e., a 71% reduction in war deaths, a 68% reduction in war injuries, and a 48% reduction in the overall level of conflict) and cooperation among antagonists increased 66% [$p<.00001$ for each variable]. These data were obtained by a trained Lebanese rater, blind to the purpose of the experiment, who reviewed reports from eight international news sources and the regional Foreign Broadcast Information Service. These figures were found to be uninfluenced by controlling for holidays, announced events, seasonality, or other trends using a dependent time series analysis. Also, combined analysis of the data from these seven assemblies would normally be expected to show a statistical effect of diminishing the demonstrated results. Combining the results of all seven assemblies gave an extraordinary probability outcome ($p<10$), consistent with the assumption that substantive and replicable variations were being assessed. Therefore, this study presents strong evidence that Maharishi Effect technology is a reliable means to reduce enmity, instability and violence on a national scale.

In this study, a Maharishi Effect group was established in Israel in the summer 1983. The number of participants varied daily from a low of 65 to a high of 241. Time series analysis and transfer function analyses were simultaneously used. The results were compared on six variables, and three composite quality of life indicators. Specific predictions of study outcomes were made in advance and lodged with an independent review board of experts. The board also approved the statistical methods in advance of the study. Results indicated that War intensity dropped 45% ($p<.0045$), War deaths dropped 76% ($p<.02$) from a mean of 40 deaths per day to 9.7 per day. Crime in Israel dropped 12% ($p<.0016$) from a mean of 608 per day to 535 per day. Crime in Jerusalem dropped 8.8% ($p<.023$) from a mean of 46.7 per day to 42.6 per day. Fires dropped 30% ($p<.045$) from a mean of 8 per day to 5.6 per day. Auto accident fatalities fell 34% ($p<.024$) from a mean of 3.9 per day to 2.5 per day. Taken together, quality of life improved by 1.3 standard deviation units in Israel ($p<.0001$), by.75 in Lebanon ($p<.02$) and by.94 in Jerusalem ($p<.003$).

Evidence indicates that the technology of the Maharishi Effect generates cooperation and friendliness rather than suspicion and hatred. A study by Orme-Johnson, Dillbeck, Bousquet & Alexander revealed that when TM-Sidhi groups went to 5 world trouble spots—Lebanon, Iran, Rhodesia (Zimbabwe), Kampuchea, and Nicaragua—where they did nothing other than to practiced the TM-Sidhi programme together in groups for 10 weeks, violence and disorder rapidly decreased in each country. During the stay there was significant local progress towards peace. After their departure, situations worsened. For the entire year (1978) 14,567 events were recorded in the Conflict and Peace Data Bank (COPDAB), the world's largest such resource. Contingency table analysis of COPDAB data compared to a 10-week control period, a 1-year baseline, and a 10-year baseline showed significant improvement in each case. Time series analysis showed the project had a strong and statistically significant effect world-wide. Compared to a ten-week baseline, world-wide trends improved. Hostile acts between countries as well as between factions within the trouble spots decreased 16.7% ($p<.002$). Cooperative events, as a proportion, rose nationally by 13.2% ($p<.007$). Also, the type of events reported shifted significantly, from military (i.e., wars, guerrilla raids, troop deployment, security pacts, defence treaties, etc.), to non-military issues (i.e., culture, economy, political order, law, environment, etc.), with an increase of 21.8 percentage points in non-military issues. This finding could be interpreted as a shift in the society's collective consciousness from an emphasis on destruction to an emphasis on more societal cooperation.

Other evidence suggests it may not be necessary to send military coherence creating groups to the "hot spots" around the world, if the TM-Sidhi groups are sufficiently large. Orme-Johnson, Dillbeck, Alexander, Chandler & Cranson, found that three large assemblies (approaching 7,000, roughly the square root of 1% of world's population) of practitioners of the Transcendental Meditation and TM-Sidhi programme decreased international conflicts ($p<.025$, $p<.005$ and $p<.01$ for each of the three assemblies) and international terrorism ($p<.025$) on three occasions during 1983-85. Time-series analysis using objective data on terrorism obtained from the Rand Corporation ruled out the possibility of spurious correlations due to trends and cycles in the data. Other known variables that might affect the process were also controlled for.

Coherence of Brain Function a Probable Mechanism?

The complete understanding of how meditating individuals or groups can create such "effects at a distance" requires more study. However, preliminary research has utilized neurophysiological and biochemical approaches to gain some insights into possible mechanisms involved. For example, increased brain wave (EEG) coherence during meditation has been correlated with higher IQ and moral reasoning. These changes in the levels of coherence occur when different parts of the brain work together in synchrony. When large groups collectively practice the more advanced TM-Sidhi programme, increases in EEG coherence are produced in subjects far removed from the group. One experiment showed an increase in "intersubject" EEG coherence (the coherence of brain waves between different individuals) one thousand miles from the group. A biochemical study has shown that on days when large numbers of people practiced these techniques, both practitioners and non-practitioners in the local area exhibited higher availability of serotonin, a neurochemical associated with well-being or happiness. Low serotonin is known to play a role in human aggression and hostility.

COHERENT PHYSICAL SYSTEMS

Maharishi also predicted the coherence-creating effects of the Transcendental Meditation and TM-Sidhi programme on social systems before scientific studies supported his prediction. He based his prediction not only on ancient knowledge, as mentioned earlier, but also on discussions with physicists about coherent physical systems such as the laser.

Laser light is more powerful than conventional light because it is more orderly and coherent. Apollo astronauts on the moon could see laser light shone from the earth at levels as low as 15 watts. Fifteen watts is about the energy output of a night-light! However, these astronauts could not see the millions of watts of conventional light illuminating New York City at night. What made the difference?

The intensity of normal light is emitted in direct proportion to the number of atoms involved. Excited atoms emit photons as they return to the ground state. Light is emitted in different directions at various frequencies creating what physicists call "incoherent light," all mixed up. In a laser, however, a type of collective behavior emerges that is distinguished by its orderliness. The atoms are perfectly correlated with each other and no longer act independently. They operate together as one coherent and complete system. The result is that the intensity of the light emitted by a number of atoms, N, is increased tremendously, actually in proportion to N squared. If 100 atoms are perfectly in phase with one another in the laser, they will radiate with an intensity of 100, or 10,000 times that of a single atom.

Defensive Defence System

The Maharishi Effect appears to strike at the most fundamental strategic point—the level where enemies arise—stress in collective consciousness. If enemies are not born there are no battles. Warfare and violence become obsolete. For this reason, Maharishi's consciousness-based strategy may be the first truly *defensive* system for maintaining peace. At least militarily speaking, if a nation has no enemies it is invincible. It remains "friends" with everyone, ensuring security. History shows national invincibility is not possible through weapons or material defences alone because newer and better weapons can always be developed. Invincibility is gained, however, if all other nations are our allies. If a Maharishi Effect shield really works, as studies so far suggest it does, "Prevention Wings" of experts in this technology deployed in every nation could create a permanent shield of friendliness that would surround and protect the nation. For these simple but profound reasons, the strategic advantage that might be gained by implementing such a consciousness-based technology as an addition to existing defence systems is much greater than it might at first appear. As with any other technological breakthrough, concepts change only as the practical benefits become clearly manifest.

Character of War

The concept of using a military's collective consciousness to radiate coherence and eliminate stress is hardly a widely accepted military strategy in today's arena of military might. Defensive radar systems routinely radiate electromagnetic waves over a hundred miles, but the idea that human minds might radiate a peaceful influence which might be used to create a defence system is novel. Most people today view the human mind or consciousness as being trapped inside the head. It will take a leap of understanding for most leaders to adopt the strategy of improving collective consciousness as an effective way of preventing conflict before it has arisen.

Military Science Technology

In a time of increased responsibility, increased costs of military hardware and declining military budgets in most countries, the technology discussed here is unique in its promise for meeting multiple laudable goals. First, a Prevention Wing is cost-effective. Considering the hundreds of billions of dollars spent worldwide on defence the cost of implementing this technology is minor. Once convinced, militaries adopt the latest technologies to accomplish their missions. Research suggests that this human resource technology is the most advanced and practical means to defend a nation. It is simple to implement and produces immediate results. The research suggests that any nation's military can cheaply and quickly create global defence and a lasting peace. Furthermore, the technology is completely humane—it promotes progress and positive evolutionary trends both within the nation and in surrounding nations.

Avert the Danger Before it Comes

The post-USSR world has proven to be a more dangerous place than one might have imagined. There are no well-defined opponents. Wars will be less predictable. Nuclear weapons from the former Soviet arsenal are allegedly available on the world black market. Biological weapons popularly called "poor man's nukes" are even easier to acquire. Current military strategies are not well designed for the possibility of even one of these winding up in the hands of rogue elements such as terrorists. New defence technologies must be evaluated and implemented to deal with such threats. Further field-testing the potential of a military prevention wing to avert dangers that have not yet come could be accomplished quickly, inexpensively, and conclusively. Such tests of coherence-creating effects of the TM and TM-Sidhi programme, and its ability to reduce collective societal stress, could be replicated in countries large and small throughout the world. History indicates the effect of introducing such "coherent systems" could prevent hostilities.

Warriors since Sun Tzu have championed the idea that the supreme art of war is to win without fighting. If such prevention wings of the military continue to be successful, as they appear to have been in Mozambique, they could drastically change the character of military intervention even beyond the dreams of Douhet and Sun Tzu. In the tradition of military pioneers, today's military leaders might consider creating their own coherence-creating groups.

President Chissano of Mozambique has expressed his willingness to endorse his experiences to any government or head of state who inquires. He relates his and his countrymen's experiences as follows, "First I started the practice of Transcendental Meditation myself, then introduced the practice to my close family, my cabinet of ministers, my government officers, and my military. The result has been political peace and balance in Nature in my country…People ask me if this is a religion. I have explained to them that I may keep my religion but I should take advantage of this science and make maximum use of it....We will not stop praying in our churches, we will not stop praying in our mosques, we will not stop praying in our synagogues, but we will make an appeal to the support of Nature through the application of this technology (of consciousness)."

11

Defence Administration: Its Planning and Program

The first detailed Clinton defence plan was presented to the Congress in the fiscal year 1995 budget submission. Congressional debate this year revolves around the issues of whether the forces in the plan will be sufficient to fight potential threats and whether they are folly funded in the plan.

This memorandum addresses these issues. It analyzes the capability of the forces the Clinton Administration expects to have by the late 1990s and their affordability in both the near and longer term. The memorandum also evaluates alternatives, but in keeping with the Congressional Budget Office's (CBO's) mandate to provide objective analysis, it makes no recommendations. It is provided as background for testimony by Robert D. Reischauer, Director of CBO, before the House Committee on Armed Services.

Lane Pierrot of CBO's National Security Division prepared the analysis, drawing on the work of a number of other CBO analysts. Neil M. Singer, R. William Thomas, and Michael A. Miller provided direction during the analysis. Geoff Cohen developed the analysis of capability for two regional wars and assisted with the overall project Karen Ann Watkins also provided extensive assistance during the analysis. The discussion of the costs of operating weapons builds on analysis done by William P. Myers and Lisa Siegel. William P. Myers also estimated detailed weapons costs. Frances Lussier, Ivan Eland, and Lane Pierrot provided analysis of long-term funding for the services, while David Mosher and Raymond J. Hall, Wayne Glass, Rachel Schmidt, and Ellen Breslin Davidson and Amy Plapp did the same for ballistic missile defence, environmental cleanup, defence conversion, and DoD health costs, respectively. Rachel Schmidt compiled that analysis. Debbie Clay-Mendez and Amy Belasco contributed freely from their analysis on issues relating to operations and maintenance, military personnel, and readiness. David Mosher, Michael O'Hanlon, and James Homey made useful suggestions during review. Ellen Breslin Davidson reviewed the memorandum for accuracy. Paul L. Houts edited it, with assistance from Christian Spoor, and Cynthia Cleveland prepared it for publication.

INTRODUCTION

The fiscal year 1995 budget request is the first budget to contain the Clinton Administration's detailed plans for defence. The plans are based on analysis done over the past year as part of the Administration's bottom-up review (BUR). The review proposes cuts in conventional forces in all services to meet the Administration's targets for defence spending. As a result of the planned cuts in dollars and force structure, two major questions have surfaced that lie at the heart of this year's defence debate:

- Are the dollars the Administration plans to devote to defence spending sufficient to support the forces that it expects to have?
- Are the forces in the Administration's plans sufficient for its defence strategy, defined by this Administration as well as its predecessor as the ability to engage in two nearly simultaneous regional conflicts?

Clinton defence targets provide about $104 billion less funding for defence during the 1995-1999 period than the Bush Administration would have provided. But the BUR analysis suggests a number of forces could be cut while still maintaining the capability to fight two regional wars.

The analysis also recommended canceling or scaling back a number of programs. As a result of these reductions, the $1.2 trillion the Administration expects to spend on defence during the 1995-1999 period should be roughly sufficient to meet requirements.

The Clinton plan cuts operating funding less than it cuts forces. Operating funding would decline by 27 percent from 1990 levels, while major types of forces would be cut from about one-third (Army divisions and Navy ships) to almost one-half (Air Force wings). Thus, the planned operating funding should be sufficient to support the programmed forces. Procurement should also be roughly sufficient, although the Administration expects to buy considerably fewer ships, planes, and tanks than were bought in 1990. CBO's estimates suggest that Department of Defence (DoD) stocks of most major weapons should suffice at least through the 1990s.

The Administration's plan is subject to several risks, though they are small as a percentage of the plan's total funding. They raise concerns nonetheless because the budget fits snugly under the discretionary caps set out in the Omnibus Budget Reconciliation Act of 1993 (OBRA-93), and because the risks could arise after defence has experienced a number of years of declining budgets and thus the flexibility to address them might be lessened.

The risks include the shortages the Administration has identified in its plan; additional costs if savings from infrastructure reductions are delayed; and the possibility that costs will increase because of factors such as growth in weapons costs or requirements for environmental cleanup. Conversely, the Clinton Administration might make several further spending reductions if funding shortages arise.

The question of the affordability of the Administration's forces is more problematic in the long term. Over the 2000-2010 period, DoD would need an average of $12 billion to $25 billion more per year than the funding it would have if its budget only grew enough to offset inflation beyond 1999. (The range in these estimates relates to whether the Congressional Budget Office (CBO) assumes that the costs of future weapons grow.) The necessity for additional funding arises because future administrations would have to buy more major weapons on average during this period than are needed in the near term. Modest annual real growth in defence spending-about 1.5 percent annually from 2000 to 2010-would provide enough money even for the higher of these two budget paths. Should additional funding for defence not be forthcoming, further force cuts could be necessary to balance operations and acquisition funding.

However, further cuts to forces might be acceptable. The threats facing the United States are lower than they were during the Cold War. Instead of planning to fight a major conventional power such as the former Soviet Union, defence guidance calls for the capability to fight two smaller regional powers, though at the same time. CBO's analysis suggests that the forces the BUR provides would bring substantial capability to bear in two regional wars.

Ratios of the capability of friendly to hostile forces in Southwest Asia would grow from about 0.6:1 at the beginning of conflict to about 2.8:1 after about three months of deliveries of U.S. troops and equipment. A nearly simultaneous conflict in Korea would start out with a ratio of about 1:1 and grow to about 2.6:1 after about two months of deliveries. These force ratios would provide sufficient capability to mount offensive operations in part of each theatre while retaining enough forces to prevent further gains by the opposition.

These results suggest that DoD may be able to withstand further force reductions and still be able to bring significant forces to bear in two regional wars. CBO's analysis considers an alternative that would operate fewer forces. The Congress might wish to consider such a step if DoD encounters funding problems in the future. Alternatively, the Congress may wish to consider cutting acquisition programs or making changes in the ways DoD operates its forces.

CBO's analysis also includes an alternative that keeps forces at 1994 levels, rather that cutting them to the levels in the BUR. According to CBO's analysis of the forces the United States might field in two regional wars, this alternative provides additional capability, but the increased capability would require about $70 billion more for DoD than the Administration plans to provide during the 1995*1999 period. Although concerns about a more uncertain world might lead to desires for additional defence spending, this spending might not be readily available in the face of overall budget constraints.

BUDGETARY DECISIONS FOR DEFENCE

Budgetary decisions for defence are not made in a vacuum; the overall outlook for the federal budget and the deficit may dictate future defence budgets as much as requirements for defence spending derived from DoD planning scenarios. As long as the Administration and the Congress remain concerned about the impact of continuing deficits on the economy, prospects for the deficit will constrain future federal spending. In particular, the Omnibus Budget Reconciliation Act of 1993 extended caps through 1998 on total discretionary spending-the portion of the budget that includes the bulk of defence funding.

The Deficit

CBO's March 1994 projections for future deficits are lower this year than last CBO projects that the deficit will decline from the 1993 level of $255 billion to $228 billion in 1994, then drop sharply to about $180 billion in 1995 and 1996. After that, deficits will begin to rise again, and by 1999 they are projected to be at $213 billion, or about 80 percent of the 1993 level. Expressed as a percentage of the gross domestic product (GDP), the deficit remains at about 2.5 percent of GDP over the 1995-1999 period after dropping sharply in 1994. The ambitious deficit reduction package contained in OBRA-93 contributes enormously to the cuts in deficit levels in 1994 and beyond.

Discretionary Caps

Caps on discretionary spending-established by the Budget Enforcement Act of 1990 and extended by OBRA-93-detennine the amount of spending available to defence. Discretionary spending encompasses programs controlled by annual appropriation bills and is divided into three categories: defence, international, and domestic. In 1991,1992, and 1993, separate caps applied to the defence budget. From 1994 through 1998-the last year of the OBRA-93 caps-defence spending will be constrained by annual limits on total discretionary spending. OBRA-93 caps both the spending authority the Congress creates in these bills (budget authority) and the expenditures that result from that authority (outlays).

The caps for discretionary budget authority provide modest growth in nominal budget authority, rising from $518 billion in 1995 to $533 billion in 1998. This increase, however, falls short of increases needed by component programs for projected inflation. Hence, the programs under the caps must make reductions in real-inflation-adjusted-terms. The caps on total outlays increase only slightly-from $545 billion in 1995 to $550 billion in 1998-and are even more restrictive than the budget authority caps given the current mix of spending.

How will these caps affect defence spending? Since defence must now compete with other discretionary programs for funds under the overall caps, this question is difficult to answer with certainty. The Administration's plan for discretionary spending represents one possible path. Under that plan, all elements of discretionary spending would experience real reductions over the 1995-1998 period. The Administration's plan falls short of the amount needed to keep pace with inflation by about $120 billion. The Administration plans for defence to absorb the bulk of this difference-almost 80 percent.

ADMINISTRATION'S REDUCTIONS IN DEFENCE SPENDING

If the Administration's reductions in defence spending are realized, defence's share of GDP will decline from 4.2 percent in 1994 to 2.9 percent in 1999. After the reductions are made, defence spending will reach its lowest share of GDP since World War H.

Some proponents of altering the priorities in the Administration's plan might argue that, based on this trend, defence should receive more funding. Others will feel that a better way to address this question is to look at the components of the Administration's defence program in comparison with the threats faced by the United States, which clearly are less severe than at any time during the Cold War, despite the uncertain progress toward democracy in some of the former Warsaw Pact nations and the outbreak of ethnic hostilities in many countries.

Trends in the threat to the United States can and do affect the size of the defence establishment The Department of Defence expects to spend $1.2 trillion over the next five years to maintain forces, buy existing weapons, and develop new ones. Although the Clinton Administration's plan provides much less spending than previous administrations had planned, cuts in the numbers of forces and in weapons modernization programs suggest that the Clinton Administration's reduced program is broadly consistent with its funding plan.

Force Reductions and the Operating Accounts

The United States will be able to field considerably fewer major forces than it could during the Cold War. Most of the cuts will have been made by 1995. Active Army divisions and Navy ships will be cut by about a third from 1990 to 1995. The number of tactical fighter wings in the Air Force will fall by an even larger percentage, to only about half the 1990 level. The number of active Army divisions will shrink by about 17 percent beyond 1995, and the Navy will lose 12 percent more ships. (The Army expects, however, to make most of the personnel cuts associated with these force reductions by 1995.) The Marine Corps will retain the same number of major units as in 1990, though Marine Corps personnel will decline by 12 percent over that period. Reserve forces generally will undergo smaller reductions than active forces-perhaps reflecting their lower operating costs-though tactical air reserves, protected in earlier budgets, are slated for cuts in this plan.

Funds to support these forces appear in the military personnel title, which provides pay and benefits for DoD's service members, and in the operation and maintenance title that pays for a number of different items, many of which relate to readiness. Both categories of funding will decline less than the forces they support. Compared with fiscal year 1990's funding level, military personnel funding will decline in real terms by about 23 percent by 1995, and by about 33 percent by 1999.

The number of active military personnel will decline from 1990 by about 26 percent by 1995 and about 30 percent by 1999. This decline suggests that the number of active personnel will also be cut less than the forces they operate.

Operation and maintenance (O&M) funding, too, declines by lower percentages than major forces. O&M spending will be down by only 10 percent in 1995 compared with 1990, and will decrease by only 21 percent by the end of the Future Years Defence Program in 1999. Funding in the accounts that make up this title is often perceived-along with military pay-to relate to what DoD terms "readiness"—that is, the ability of U.S. forces to go to war quickly and perform well. What determines readiness is not always well understood. But having well-trained, intelligent troops and functioning equipment-which are paid for largely out of O&M-are certainly important components of readiness. Thus, the smaller reduction in O&M spending, as compared with forces, may reflect the priority the Administration and the services place on maintaining readiness.

These priorities are also reflected in indicators of current readiness, according to a CBO analysis conducted at the request of the House Budget Committee. DoD uses a number of indicators to measure readiness-most with limitations. But some of the more objective measures suggest that DoD has been able to preserve the readiness of its forces despite overall funding cuts. For example, the quality of recruits in 1993 remained at very high levels, and the percentage of DoD's stock of equipment that is ready to fight ("mission capable") has changed little, if at all, from levels in place since the mid-1980s.

Even measures that appear to portend trouble-such as large backlogs in repair of equipment-may be misleading. The Army's maintenance backlog, for example, includes equipment made available from demobilized active units that has been sent to depots for reconditioning before being distributed to reserve units. The principal impact of that backlog will be to delay improvements in reserve readiness and capability rather than to lower the current readiness levels of active forces.

Cuts to Procurement

Procurement accounts have taken the brunt of DoD's budget cuts. Cuts to procurement accounts make up about 60 percent of the $87 billion real reduction between 1990 and 1995 in the annual DoD budget. Procurement appropriations pay for the aircraft, ships, tanks, and missiles that DoD uses to equip its forces, as well as a number of other systems. Fewer new weapons need to be bought to support a smaller force size. But annual procurement of major weapons has shrunk considerably more than forces. For example, in 1995, the Administration requests funds for six new ships, about a third of the 1990 level of 20. Aircraft procurement drops to a tenth of its 1990 level DoD plans to buy no new tanks for the Army in 1995, compared with 448 in 1990-though it requests funds for modernizing older Ml tanks.

This procurement ^holiday" should be acceptable hi the near term. According to CBO estimates, DoD will not run short of ships, fighter aircraft, or tanks through the planning period, despite the planned low levels of procurement Indeed, the military services will have excess numbers of many types of equipment well into the first decade of the next century. DoD bought major weapons in large quantities during the 1980s, and the stock acquired then will suffice for a number of years. In addition, the cuts in forces will delay the need for replacing many types of weapons, since they permit DoD to equip the smaller number of units with the newest equipment

The procurement holiday, however, cannot last indefinitely. Under the Administration's plans, the procurement accounts would grow modestly in real terms by 1999 to a level that is almost 60 percent of 1990 funding, compared with less than 50 percent in 1995. Funding for procurement will be almost $10 billion higher in 1998 and 1999 than in 1995, as several new weapons enter production. But even with the increased funding, the number of weapons bought will be at low levels and eventually DoD will need to increase procurement quantities. More ships, planes, and tanks than are included in the Administration's procurement plan would be needed to sustain its forces in the steady state. (To calculate steady-state procurement, CBO simply divided the number of weapons DoD needs in its inventory by the length of service of each system. This yields a rough calculation of the number of weapons DoD would need to buy each year if past purchases had been made evenly. Eventually DoD may need to buy even more than steadystate quantities, since the majority of weapons bought in the 1980s would normally be retired toward the end of the next decade.)

Research, Development Test, and Evaluation. RDT&E accounts will receive small reductions through 1995 relative to 1990 levels, being cut by 14 percent compared with a 54 percent reduction for procurement funding. This difference may reflect a deliberate policy of protecting funding for development Developing weapons and getting them into the hands of service personnel takes longer than buying new equipment and fielding larger forces. This policy also reflects the premium die military services place on technological superiority. But RDT&E alsc reflect increases in some nontraditional costs. For example, mos. of the funds that the Administration expects to spend to help the defence industrial base convert to commercial activities are appropriated in the RDT&E accounts.

The Administration plans to cut RDT&E during the Future Years Defence Program period more than it has been cut recently. The Administration plans for RDT&E funding to fall to about 64 percent of its 1990 level during the period that funding for procurement is growing. Cutting funding for development may not be a problem for a number of years. The regional powers that the United States might face in conflict typically have much less sophisticated equipment than U.S. forces. Arms sales of top-oftheline Russian equipment could somewhat improve the military capability of potential U.S. adversaries, but they may not be financially capable of largescale arms purchases.

The United States may also have less to fear from technological breakthroughs by potentially hostile nations. For many years, the major innovator hostile to U.S. interests was the former Soviet Union. Russia may seek to continue some Soviet development programs, but cash shortages and changed priorities are likely to curtail many of the efforts.

ADMINISTRATIONS PLANS FOR DEFENCE SPENDING

Several possible problem areas affect the affordability of the Administration's defence plan. Although each of the these potential problems is important when budget resources are tightly capped, they do not amount to much as a percentage of funding included in DoD's plans; Perhaps the most reasonable concern about these issues is that they illustrate the size of the problems DoD might face, after several years of budget cuts that could limit the department's flexibility.

Added Costs in the Administration's Plan

According to Secretary of Defence William Perry, the Administration's defence plan is some $20 billion short of funding the forces it calls for. That amount apparently is the result of three factors: underfunding of the forces the Clinton Administration found in place under the Bush Administration's plan; additional costs for military and civilian pay as the result of Congressional action; and assumptions about inflation that have changed since enactment of OBRA-93. Some of the costs were offset by additional funding added by the Administration to its original DoD spending plan.

The Bush Administration's plan for defence funding totaled $1,325 billion over the 1995-1999 period (according to the Clinton Administration's reestimate). The Clinton Administration's 1994 budget for defence, however, provided only $1,221 billion for that period, a difference of $104 billion. The bottom-up review, by cutting forces, canceling or deferring modernization programs, and achieving additional infrastructure savings, managed to reduce defence costs by $91 billion, according to DoD estimates. The remaining $13 billion was to be found in savings during the normal program and budget review that followed the completion of the BUR.

Meanwhile, the Congress included in the 1994 DoD appropriations bill a pay raise for military personnel and locality pay adjustments for civilian employees (the Administration's request provided for neither in 1994). The higher rates of pay added some $11 billion to estimates of DoD costs for the 1995-1999 period Pay was not the only higher price DoD faced: the Administration's estimates of purchase price inflation for 1995 and beyond also increased future defence costs. Together, these three factors-the BUR shortfall, higher pay rates, and purchase price inflation-created a budget shortfall that former Secretary of Defence Les Aspin estimated at $47 billion. Two events subsequently reduced the shortfall. First, DoD's program and budget review cut an additional $16 billion from the 1995-1999 estimates.

Second, the Clinton Administration agreed to adjust upward the fiscal year 1995 budget request and out-year budget projections to fund the higher rates of pay. Together these actions reduced the shortfall from $47 billion to Secretary Perry's reported $20 billion.

The Administration, however, did not adjust its out-year defence topline projections for the higher inflation rates in the 1995 economic outlook. Since the problem is in the out-years, not in fiscal year 1995, the decision taken was to defer acting on the $20 billion shortfall until the 1996 budget request is prepared. At that point, several options may present themselves. If inflation projections are lowered next year, much of the problem might evaporate. If inflation is as projected (or higher still), the Administration could either agree to adjust the defence top line to reflect it, or, perhaps more likely, make additional reductions reflecting changes in programs or delays in execution to align DoD spending with the overall resource constraint. Another possibility is that DoD could identify savings from management efficiencies or acquisition reform that could offset the difference-certainly possible since $20 billion is only about 2 percent of DoD's $12 trillion plan.

Cuts to Infrastructure

The Administration plans to make aggressive efforts to reduce DoD's infrastructure. About 20 percent of the savings the Administration expects from the bottom-up review relate to cuts in infrastructure. The Administration may experience budget pressure if it is unable to alter the balance between major combat forces and the forces and infrastructure that support them. These numbers illustrate the magnitude of the shortfall that could occur if the Administration found it difficult to cut operating spending as much as it plans during the five-year period. In the aggregate, however, the additional funding needed is quite small as a percentage of the Administration's request.

Historically, roughly half of DoD operating costs have varied with force levels, and the other half have been relatively fixed. Thus, a 10 percent reduction in forces could be expected to yield a 5 percent savings in support costs, defined here as training, logistics, medical costs, headquarters, and costs to operate bases. This formula suggests that it might be difficult to realize large savings on infrastructure. But the usefulness of historical data to project future infrastructure savings may be limited. The history reflects a period when DoD kept roughly the same number of facilities. As the base structure shrinks in parallel with declines in force levels, this fixed element of support costs will diminish.

If there is a problem, failure might cause a repetition of the Army's actions in 1993. At that time, the Army was forced to cut its operating tempo-summarized in the average number of miles Army personnel drive tanks per year-when assumptions about infrastructure savings proved optimistic. To save money, the Army dropped its actual tank miles to 600 from the budgeted level of 800. Since the number of miles driven is an indicator of training that directly relates to how well Army personnel can perform in battle, such a large cut in miles driven could affect readiness.

Added Costs for Environmental Cleanup

Increasing costs for environmental cleanup could also heighten the need for defence funds. These additional costs might total about $20 billion, about $4 billion on average for each of the next five years. The Administration plans to spend about $12 billion on environmental restoration costs during the 1995-1999 period. But actual costs have been two to three times DoD's original estimates on cleanup projects DoD has undertaken.

Finally, weapons costs could grow. For example, DoD will begin buying the F-22, a new fighter for the Air Force, during the next five years. The F-22's unit cost is likely to rise above current assumptions, since the Administration plans to cut the number of planes bought. Cost increases stemming from reductions in total quantities result from buying fewer weapons at the end of the program when producers are more experienced. Thus, they might not affect funding in the early years of the program, but the F-22 still could cost more in the near term if the transition from development to production turns up costly problems, as some press reports are suggesting. CBO has not done an exhaustive analysis of all of the programs in the 1995-1999 period because of a lack of detailed data, but the F-22 does not appear to be alone as a candidate for cost growth. Among the other programs that might increase in cost are the V-22, the C-17, a joint trainer for the Air Force and Navy, a number of tactical missile systems, and the Seawolf submarine.

PROSPECTS FOR DECREASES IN DEFENCE SPENDING

Several factors might counterbalance potential cost increases. One is the prospect that the Administration may further reduce strategic and ballistic missile defence programs. The Administration focused on conventional weapons in the bottom-up review, but it promised that a detailed study of strategic forces is under way. It is difficult, of course, to estimate how much might be saved from alternatives that have not yet been specified.

Although costs for environmental cleanup may rise significantly during the next five years, the Congress and DoD could reduce spending for cleanup or at least moderate its growth. Savings could come from using more efficient methods of characterizing contaminated sites, applying less costly methods of cleanup, and negotiating less stringent cleanup standards for contaminated facilities. Alternatively, DoD could delay remediating costly contamination in cases where there is no immediate threat to public health and safety. The Army reduced the costs of cleaning Fort Meade by more than 60 percent by converting an artillery practice range into a game preserve with restrictions on public use.

In addition, according to Administration officials, DoD is planning a number of procurement reforms that could produce savings that have not been incorporated in the DoD budget. These reforms include making greater use of commercial products and exchanges of electronic data and reducing the overhead cost of government suppliers. Making more use of computer-aided design might also reduce costs.

Several analyses have tried to estimate savings associated with these types of reforms, though results range widely. CBO has no basis for estimating the portion of DoD's acquisition budget that would be affected, nor the magnitude of that effect. But it does seem clear that some savings can be achieved. If savings are realized-and history is replete with examples of overly optimistic assumptions about savings from reform-they probably would not be significant until after the year 2000. This timing could improve the long-run affordability of the Administration's plan. It is also useful to consider prospects for defence budgets over a longer period than just the next five years, to assess whether current policies might lead to future problems. The projection period of this portion of CBO's analysis is from the year 2000 to 2010. This extended a look is necessary since many weapons have long service lives and development efforts do not reach fruition for many years.

Future defence spending is heavily influenced by whether costs of weapons grow. CBO has made two estimates of long-term budgets. One estimate assumes that future administrations successfully constrain the growth of costs for future weapons. The other assumes that costs grow at rates that are consistent with historical experience. Both estimates assume that operating costs remain at 1999 levels, since DoD will have made its planned force cuts by then. The estimates also incorporate Administration or service plans for long-term procurement where they are available. In several cases where there is considerable uncertainty about what the Administration will do, CBO has made a best guess about what plans might materialize.

LONG-TERM TRENDS ASSUMING NO COST GROWTH

Even if the costs of weapons do not grow above current estimates, DoD's budgets will need to grow in real terms from the funding level the Administration expects in 1999, the last year of the current plan. Growth occurs largely because CBO assumes that future administrations will need to buy more weapons during this period than it plans to buy during 1995 through 1999. For example, CBO assumed that DoD would buy an average of 48 fighters for the Air Force in each year from 2000 through 2010. This estimate compares with about five fighters bought annually, on average, during the 1995-1999 period.

Even without additional increases in costs, projections of needed funding exceed the 1999 level from 2000 to 2010, though costs are lower than the funding requested in this year's budget. On average, DoD would need to receive about $12 billion annually above what the Administration plans for in 1999, or about 5 percent more.

Growth occurs fairly early in the extended projection period. From the Administration's planned 1999 budget of $241 billion, funding climbs rapidly to a peak of $262 billion in 2002, when CBO assumes that an aircraft carrier, F-22 fighters, and C-17 transports will be procured simultaneously. Projections move downward after the early 2000s as C-17 production is completed, but it edges up near 2010 when CBO assumes that the planes to be developed under the Administration's Joint Advanced Strike Technology (JAST) program will enter procurement.

Long-Term Trends Assuming Costs Grow

If histoiy is a guide, weapon costs will be higher for new generations of weapons. Each new generation of tactical fighters has cost more than the preceding design, as much as two or three times more in some cases. The Navy's ships have grown in cost by 3 percent a year in real terms. And the Army's Ml tank costs more than twice its predecessor, the M60. If, as CBO assumes in its second estimate, these trends continue into the future, pressure for higher funding levels will be greater.

Since CBO did not alter the quantities and phasing of the weapons procured, peaks in the projection occur in the same years as in the no-growth case, but they are higher. Funding would total $278 billion in 2002, for example, almost $40 billion more than the Administration's plan for 1999 and $14 billion more than the Administration's request for fiscal year 1995. On average over the 2000-2010 period, DoD would need annual budgets that are higher than 1999 levels by almost $25 billion, or about 10 percent Modest real growth in the defence budget beyond 1999 would provide DoD with ample funding even if the cost of weapons grows. About *15* percent annual real growth from 2000 to 2010 would provide sufficient funding, though higher real growth early in the period, offset by lower growth toward the end of the projection period, would be needed to match peaks and valleys in the estimate.

Some may argue that it is reasonable to assume that DoD will receive some real increases over the long tenn. Real increases of 1.5 percent a year are about 1 percentage point less than the rate of growth of gross domestic product through 1999. If GDP continued to grow at that rate through and beyond 1999, but defence spending rose only enough to cover growth in the cost of weapons, DoD's share of GDP would continue to fall from levels that are already historically low.

Conversely, some students of defence issues may argue that measuring DoD's share of GDP ignores an important point: the threat the United States faces is much smaller than it was during earlier periods. It is reasonable, they believe, for national priorities to accord much lower funding levels to DoD if the United States faces smaller threats. Thus, the affordability of the Administration's plan is closely linked to whether the forces the Administration plans to field are sufficient to meet the requirements it has set forth for them.

PLANNING SCENARIOS SEVERAL ADMINISTRATIONS

The United States faces a much less formidable array of threats today than during the Cold War. But the need to fight in two wars simultaneously-based on the planning scenarios several administrations have laid out-would keep forces at higher levels than would be required simply to match the capabilities of potential adversaries individually.

Smaller Threats

During the Cold War, the United States expected the former Soviet Union to be able to field the equivalent of more than 90 armored divisions. The massive power of the former Soviet Union exceeded the capability of U.S. forces even at Cold War levels. This comparison, however, may overstate relative Soviet superiority for several reasons. The former Soviet Union would not have been able to devote all of these forces to a war on its western flank, since it would probably have withheld forces to protect itself against attack from the east. Non-U.S. NATO allies would have brought more capability to a European war than the non-Soviet nations of the former Warsaw Pact. Finally, the overwhelming Soviet superiority on the ground might have been at least partially offset by superior U.S. air assets, also shown in Figure 4. U.S. naval forces were also superior, and communications and readiness were probably at higher levels, although this is not reflected in these measures.

Few analysts foresee a return to Cold War tensions between the United States and Russia, despite current uncertainties and concerns. But even if Russia were to return to a more combative posture, the capability it can field is considerably diminished from estimates of Soviet capability. As with the Soviet Union, Russian scores may be somewhat misleading since Russia would probably not be able to devote all of these forces to a western war. In addition, geopolitical changes may mean that some of its former allies would be adversaries in such a war.

GBO's analysis uses an evaluation system called TASCFORM that was developed by The Analytic Sciences Corporation (TASC) for DoD. TASCFORM assigns a quantitative score-derived from assessments by military experts—!or types of weapons, based on the characteristics of those weapons. The scores are best viewed as a measure of the combat potential of weapons in various forces, since they do not account for a number of factors, many of which might favor the United States in conflict. These omitted factors include personnel quality and training, the capabilities of communications equipment, appropriate warfightmg strategy and tactics, and the ability of logistics forces to support personnel and maintain weapons. The measures also do not account for luck, leadership, and morale. Russian ground forces will retain less than half of the capability of the former Soviet Union, though Russia may keep about 75 percent of the former Soviet Union's air capability. Even these estimates may accord too much capability to Russian weapons, since a number of reports-including testimony by the Director for Combat Support at the Defence Intelligence Agency-indicate that the readiness of Russian forces is declining for a number of reasons, including lack of funds for supplies, spare parts, and training.

The Administration argues that it has sized future forces to be able to win virtually simultaneous conflicts against two regional powers. The Administration's analysis in the bottom-up review assumes-for planning purposes-that the two hostile countries would be Iraq and North Korea. As the figure shows, both Iraq and North Korea have much more modest capability than either the Russian Republic or the former Soviet Union. However, the Administration wishes to have the capacity to fight two wars-one in Southwest Asia and one on the Korean peninsula~at almost the same time. So perhaps a better measure of the capability of the forces the Administration expects to have would be an estimate of scores for the forces the United States could field to each theatre, assuming both contingencies occur together.

The Administration's Planned Forces and Two Regional Conflicts CBO estimated the buildup of U.S. forces in each of two theaters based on a number of assumptions. CBO's major assumptions were:

- o The war with Iraq would start first, and about a month later war would break out on the Korean Peninsula;
- o DoD would have the forces and equipment the Administration expects to have in 2000, including combat forces, lift, and prepositioned equipment;
- o The United States would fight with only indigenous forces as allies-Saudi and Kuwaiti forces in Southwest Asia and South Korean forces on the Korean peninsula;
- o Forces are counted once they arrive in theatre. Thus, United States, allied, and hostile forces are measured as theaterwide buildups rather than as units deployed in a combat scenario;
- o Army Guard combat units would not be deployed to the regional conflicts, though guard and reserve support units would participate, as would air combat units; and finally,
- o One of two Army divisions in Europe would remain in place.

CBO's results reflect a number of actions this Administration, the previous administration, and the Congress have taken or are taking to improve U.S. airlift and sealift Those actions include buying a number of sealift ships, improving the capability of the Ready Reserve fleet, and procuring 40 C-17s.

In all, improvements in mobility will cost about $33 billion. The Administration also plans to preposition equipment for three brigades of Army forces in Southwest Asia and aboard ships that could be at ports in Saudi Arabia soon after a war begins.

The Department of Defence has also taken a number of administrative actions that should facilitate mobilization. CBO assumed that the United States would act to begin full mobilization upon the outbreak of conflict. In Operation Desert Storm, although the United States did deploy a number of air and ground units quickly, a second wave of forces was deployed considerably later when the United States decided to engage in an offensive operation. Without these improvements, certain of the unified commanders question whether today's airlift and sealift forces could cope with even one major regional contingency, let alone two. "Strategic lift in this country is broken right now," General Joseph P. Hoar, the Commander of Central Command, which encompasses the Middle East, has said in testimony before the Senate Armed Services Committee. General Hoar based his statement on several factors, including the recent limitation on the use of C-141 aircraft while cracks in wing supporting members were being repaired, uncertainty about the fate of the new C-17 airlifter, and possible limitations on the Maritime Administration's ability to secure crews for sealift ships it draws from the Ready Reserve Force.

CBO has not assessed the airlift and sealift problems that the services are experiencing today, though it appears that the problems that exist are being addressed. Most C-141s, for example, will have been inspected and repaired and returned to full service by the end of 1994. Also, in response to General Hoar's comments, Secretary of the Air Force Sheila Widnall said the United States would use all of its airlift aircraft, including the reserves, in war. More aircraft would thus be available than are for the peacetime fleets to which General Hoar was apparently referring. And the Administration has proposed assistance for the merchant marine fleet that might address concerns about the availability of crews for sealift ships. In any case, the analysis presented here is premised on the implementation of actions to improve airlift and sealift and to increase dramatically the prepositioning of equipment.

Results

The results of CBO's analysis, the United States and its allies could build forces to have substantial superiority in both theaters over the three-month period CBO examined in its analysis. Results for Southwest Asia. In the Southwest Asia conflict, Iraq would start out with about double the capability of the indigenous forces of Saudi Arabia and Kuwait. By CBO estimates, the United States would be able to land enough forces to attain modest superiority within several weeks, and by the end of the period of CBO's analysis, allied forces would attain a ratio of 2.8:1. Results for Korea. A conflict on the Korean peninsula would find friendly forces in a better starting position than in Southwest Asia, largely because of the strength of South Korean forces-augmented by forward-deployed U.S. forces-compared with North Korean capability. Because CBO assumes the United States would devote to the Korean contingency fewer heavy Army forces and more air and naval forces that can be deployed more rapidly, the ratio of friendly forces to enemy forces would rise to more than 2:1 by about one month after mobilization for the Korean war began. The ratio would build to about 2.6:1 within about two months.

What Measure of Superiority Is Required? Based on highly aggregated planning factors, the capability of the forces in both scenarios should be enough to assure a successful campaign, even if U.S. and allied forces take the offensive. A rough rule of thumb is that an attacker needs a local force ratio of at least 3:1 to win. Local balances of 3:1 in areas of offensive operations would need to be matched by sufficient forces in areas where no attack is planned to keep the enemy from achieving similar concentrations. For example, if the United States and its allies had an overall ratio of 2.7:1, then they could build to a local ratio of at least 3:1 over 20 percent of the area of engagement, while retaining a defensive ratio of 1:1 or higher throughout. Some analysts viewed defensive theaterwide balances from about 0.8:1 down to 0.5:1 as high enough to prevent a successful attack by the Warsaw Pact against NATO during the Cold War.

These conclusions about force ratios certainly do not apply in every instance. History is replete with examples of campaigns won by outnumbered forces, in some cases with inferior equipment. Since leadership, luck, and morale are difficult to quantify, even the most complex models have failed to solve this problem. Military tacticians would agree, though, that more is better, and that the outcome of underestimating the forces needed is likely to be higher U.S. casualties.

GBO asked the services and the Joint Chiefs of Staff (JCS) to review the analysis underlying these results. The most commonly raised criticism was that CBO's modeling efforts are too simplistic and do not forecast war outcomes. Another concern was that the forces CBO allocates to each conflict are not the specific forces the JCS would allocate in their own planning scenarios, nor does CBO's assumption of a month-long separation between the outbreak of the two wars match details in JCS planning scenarios. The Marine Corps argued that it would take several days longer to unpack equipment and test it before forces would be available to fight. The Navy raised the issue that enemy mining of port facilities could slow the arrival of U.S. forces. Finally, constraints on the capacity of port facilities and airfields could also limit the pace of the buildup.

These reservations suggest that CBO's analysis should be used with caution. Factors that could be incorporated in more detailed wargaming might suggest that higher levels of forces or lift could be needed. If, as the JCS suggested, enemy forces were to overrun friendly ports or airfields (as they did in Korea in 1950), a prolonged struggle could ensue to retake ports via amphibious assault. Or friendly forces might need to travel from greater distances to the engagement and fight for longer periods to regain territory. Deployment times could also be longer if the Navy had to engage in a prolonged minesweeping campaign before transport ships could land their equipment.

The JCS's detailed deployment schedules are classified, and CBO deliberately elected not to use them. But the forces described in the bottomup review should be common to both analyses: the only issues are where they would go and in what order. Shifting forces that CBO assumed would be deployed later to earlier deployment, or shifting forces from one region to the other, ought not to change the overall outcome substantially.

Finally, estimates of airfield and seaport limitations indicate that under most assumptions, there would be little or no long-term delay in deployment because of crowding. A report by the Military Traffic Management Command-a part of Transportation Command that works out the details of U.S. mobility plans-concludes that seaports are largely capable of supporting a full deployment; similarly, Air Mobility Command noted that normally, the Continental United States "does not represent a system constraint" The total capacity of Saudi airports and seaports is well above requirements, as is South Korea's seaport capacity. Assuming the host nations were willing to allow deployment to displace commercial traffic, no delays would be incurred. A possible limitation is the lack of availability of the South Korean airports because of conflict; in such a case, Japanese airbases would be large enough to absorb the excess. In-theatre assets (such as the C-130 aircraft) could then deliver assets to forward bases, as could the new C-17 airlifter.

Despite their limitations, the force ratios that result from CBO's model should serve as a rough guide for assessing how much capability the Administration's forces might provide in two wars. CBO's admittedly simple deployment model suggests that the Administration's planned force levels would bring substantial capability to two regional wars and that improvements in mobility should accelerate the buildup of that capability.

Of course, the United States has never had to face the actuality of two regional powers engaging in aggression against their neighbors within the same month-at least not where U.S. interests were sufficiently involved to cause it to go to war. DoD's planning process, which is understandably pessimistic on these matters, produces a "worst-case" scenario. If one were more optimistic, then perhaps one could plan for forces that are sufficient to fight in one regional conflict. Under this scenario the United States might be able to make further force reductions if, as the earlier analysis of long-term budgets suggests, more cuts need to be made in the defence budget.

SEVERAL ALTERNATIVES TO THE ADMINISTRATION'S PLANS

CBO conducted an analysis of several alternatives to the Administration's plans, looking at the cost and capability of:

- o Larger and smaller forces;
- o Cuts in operating costs for planned force levels; and
- o Further procurement and development cuts.

Increased Forces

A number of participants in the defence debate have argued

that the Administration's plan cuts forces too deeply. Concerned about tensions in Eastern Europe, perceived difficulties in fighting two wars at once, and the sharp decline in forces, they argue that cutting forces below today's levels is unwise. If the United States forces were to remain at today's levels, the Army would retain 12 active divisions-about 20 percent more than the Administration plans. The Navy would keep 387 ships, about IS percent more than planned. The Air Force would be about 10 percent bigger, with 22 tactical fighter wings.

Increased Capability. Retaining 1994 force levels would increase the capability of U.S. forces to fight two regional wars. Because of lift constraints, however, most of the additional capability would not arrive until the end of the period CBO used in its analysis. An exception to this might be tactical aircraft: Navy tactical aircraft could arrive aboard carriers. Air Force tactical aircraft could probably fly to the theatre quickly but would not be able to fight until their squadron equipment had arrived. Eventually, regional balances might rise to 3.2:1 in Southwest Asia compared with 2.8:1 for the Administration's forces. Korean balances would remain at 2.6:1.

Increased Costs. Costs for this alternative would increase both in the near term and in the longer term. The relatively large near-term increase would necessitate either substantially reallocating funds from other discretionary spending to defence compared with the Administration's plan, or relaxing the OBRA-93 caps.

Near Term. Assuming that the funding in the 1994 operating accounts would be sufficient to maintain 1994 force levels, operating costs would be almost $70 billion higher over the five-year period. Procurement funding would probably not need to rise appreciably for most systems since, as indicated earlier, DoD has surpluses of most major weapon systems. One exception to this finding is in the arena of naval carrier aircraft, where DoD will experience shortages even under the Administration's plan. Indeed, the Navy plans to take a number of measures including placing Marine Corps aircraft in Navy wings and reducing the number of aircraft per carrier to deal with its shortages. If the Navy retained two extra air wings, as this option assumes, it would need to buy about 48 more F/A-18s—roughly the number of planes for two wings-during the five-year period, and it would need several billion dollars more in procurement funds.

If these near-term increases were not offset by other reductions in the defence budget, it would mean that DoD would experience much smaller reductions in spending. If discretionary caps remain in place, defence would absorb only about 20 percent of the real reduction taken by discretionary programs to meet the caps, and domestic discretionary spending might have to absorb more than 70 percent of the reduction. This outcome compares with that of defence absorbing about 80 percent of the reduction in the Administration's plan.

Longer Term, Over the longer term, larger forces raise even more concerns about affordability. CBO has not done a detailed analysis of the added costs. But the addition to annual operating costs would be joined by substantially higher requirements for procurement funding, since more equipment would be needed for the larger number of forces.

Though there is some support for adding to the defence budget, there may be just as much or more pressure to save additional amounts from defence. Pressure for large budget reductions may have eased somewhat because of concerns about world events. But pressure for decreases may result simply as budget forecasts become reality. The following options discuss ways of making modest cuts to defence spending.

Smaller Forces. If the United States were to cut two additional tactical air wings, two more carriers, and three of the Army's four light divisions from the Administration's force levels, the defence budget might be about $23 billion lower than the Administration plans during the five-year period through 1999.

After such force reductions, military capability would of course be lower. The ratios of forces in Southwest Asia would fall to about 2.6:1 after all active forces were deployed from the 2.8:1 for the BUR forces. The Korean ratio would fall from 2.6:1 for the BUR forces to about 2.5:1. The United States might be able to make up shortfalls with reserve ground forces, though they would not be ready early in either war. In the preceding analysis, CBO did not assume that units in the Army National Guard would be deployed, since this presentation of analysis discusses only three months and even the readiest of the Guard's units might take about that long to become ready to be deployed, according to Army estimates. It also seemed reasonable that the United States would withhold some forces even when engaged in two conflicts. Mobilized Guard units might fill this role. But if more forces were cut, as this option assumes, at least some of the Guard units might also be deployed eventually, thus offsetting the reductions in active capability.

Reduce Operating Costs for Planned Forces. Another way to save operating dollars might be to reduce the funds spent per unit. This reduction could be made by flying planes less, keeping ships in port, and cutting down on the number of days tanks are driven (so-called operating or "op" tempo.) It might also be done by relying more on reserve forces.

Reduce the Operating Tempo of Forces. CBO lacks the data to estimate the total decrease in funding that results from reductions in operating tempo, but it may be relatively small compared with reducing the number of forces. For example, a SO percent reduction in the number of hours flown by an Air Force F-16 squadron would produce a cut of only about 20 percent of the squadron's direct operating costs. It might produce even more modest reductions in indirect costs, and none at all in overhead. (About $8 million would be cut out of an annual squadron operating cost of about $40 million in 1995 dollars.)

Perhaps more important, keeping up training depends heavily on operating tempo, and a number of military leaders have emphasized the priority they give to avoiding decreasing training and creating "hollow forces." But DoD has made some cuts to the operating tempo of some forces, particularly those that had to be available immediately for strategic deterrence purposes during the Cold War. For example, strategic bombers that remained on 24-hour alert no longer do so. There may be other areas-for example, the fleet of Trident submarines-where operating tempo could be cut, thus producing savings.

Relv More on Reserves. DoD could also rely more on reserve forces. Reserve forces typically cost less to operate than active forces. For example, divisions in the Army National Guard cost only about 25 percent as much as active divisions. Air and naval reserve forces also cost less than their active counterparts, though they save less than ground forces. These lower costs probably had a good deal to do with the total-force policy originally articulated by then Secretary of Defence Melvin Laird in the early 1970s. Defence planners, confronted with the formidable threat of the former Soviet Union and a public disillusioned by defence spending as U.S. participation in the war in Vietnam drew to a close, proposed relying on cheaper reserve forces. The United States could do this again and reduce the average costs of the forces it keeps.

Heavier reliance on reserve forces, however, would raise concerns about readiness, particularly for the Army, where savings are greatest. Such concerns probably arise from a perception that Guard forces were not available quickly enough in the war with Iraq. The active Army now expects to fill out its divisions with three active brigades, rather than keeping two active brigades and counting on Guard brigades to round out the division on mobilization. Reversing this policy and also looking for opportunities in the other services to make more use of reserve forces could save substantial amounts of money, though, once again, probably less than would outright force cuts. At least for Army forces, concerns would then be raised about whether Guard forces can be available quickly enough to be useful in rapidly arising regional wars.

A number of reductions to procurement funds might also be considered, especially in the near term. Development funding might also be cut. Reduce Procurement Funding, Although DoD's budgets will buy considerably fewer weapons during the next five years than they have in past periods, some weapons might not be needed to counter the smaller and less capable threats the United States might face. In its annual publication on possible deficit reductions, CBO provides a number of options that would cancel systems. The Congress might consider eliminating some of these systems, perhaps replacing them with less costly ones.

DoD expects to buy several weapons-particularly ships-not because of current shortfalls in inventory, but rather to preserve the industrial capability needed for potential future procurement. In contrast, DoD has been willing to forgo producing new equipment to maintain the industrial base for tanks, though it does plan on substantial modifications to the existing tank fleet that should sustain much of the capability for tank production. To meet budget targets, the Army once was willing to cancel all tank production. At that time, it argued that the cost of continuing tank production exceeds the cost of storing plant stock and facilities until the next time a tank is needed for inventory purposes (around 2009, though the Array may wait longer since it has not yet started development of a new tank).

The Navy and the Air Force might be able to tolerate similar gaps in new procurement. As with Army tanks, the Navy has excess stocks of ships and the Air Force of planes, compared with the stocks they would need for the smaller planned forces. Both services, however, seem to be at least contemplating the possibility of accelerating retirement schedules of less desirable equipment to bring inventories more in line with requirements. In view of this surplus, further cuts to procurement might be taken, especially if there are other ways to hedge against lost production facilities. CBO has not performed a detailed analysis to determine if problems exist that make the Army's willingness to "mothball" its industrial base less appropriate for the other services.

The Congress or the Administration could also reduce development funding further. The Administration plans to reduce funding for development by 1999 to about 12 percent of the budget. This share is lower than the 14 percent share that development was given in 1994, but it remains higher than its historical share of about 11 percent from 1950 to 1993. Given reduced worries about innovation by potential adversaries, further cuts to development might be acceptable. Cutting development's share of DoD funding by 1 percentage point per year, while keeping other titles at their requested levels, would save about $12 billion over the five-year period starting in 1995. Ultimately, such reductions may be difficult to realize. In particular, under the RDT&E title it may not be easy to cut those portions of spending that reflect nontraditional spending with high priority, such as funds for defence conversion and environmental cleanup. In addition, the United States may want to keep a fairly high level of basic research even in a fairly safe world because research is a relatively inexpensive hedge against uncertainty.

12

The Department of Defence

The Department of Defence (DOD) is the executive department in the federal government that is responsible for providing the military forces needed to deter war and to protect the security of the United States. The major elements of the military forces under its control are the Army, Navy, Air Force, and Marine Corps, consisting of about 1.5 million men and women on active duty. They are backed, in case of emergency, by 1 million members of reserve units. In addition, the DOD employs approximately nine hundred thousand civilians.

Although every state has some defence activities, the central headquarters of the DOD is in northern Virginia at the Pentagon, the "world's largest office building."

The National Security Act of 1947 (50 U.S.C.A. § 401) created the National Military Establishment, which replaced the War Department and was later renamed the Department of Defence. It was established as an executive department of the government by the National Security Act Amendments of 1949, with the secretary of defence as its head (5 U.S.C.A. § 101). Since 1949, many legislative and administrative changes have occurred, evolving the department into the structure under which it currently operates.

Structure of Department

The DOD includes the Office of the Secretary of Defence, the military departments and the military services within those departments, the chair of the Joint Chiefs of Staff and the Joint Staff, the unified combatant commands, the DOD agencies, the

DOD field activities, and such other offices, agencies, activities, and commands as may be established or designated by law or by the president or the secretary of defence.

Office of the Secretary

The secretary of defence is the principal adviser on defence policy to the president. The secretary is responsible for the formulation of general defence policy and DOD policy and for the execution of approved policy. Under the direction of the president, the secretary exercises authority, direction, and control over the DOD. The deputy secretary of defence has full power and authority to act for the secretary of defence. Three positions are designated as undersecretary of defence. The undersecretary of defence for acquisition and technology chairs the Defence Acquisition Board and advises the secretary of defence on all matters relating to the acquisition system, research and development, test and evaluation, production, logistics, military construction, procurement, and economic affairs.

The undersecretary of defence for policy advises the secretary of defence on policy matters relating to overall international security and political-military affairs, including North Atlantic Treaty Organization affairs, arms limitations agreements, and international trade and technology. The undersecretary of defence for personnel and readiness develops policies and administrative processes to ensure that the military forces have sufficient readiness to execute the National Military Strategy; develops civilian and military personnel policies including health and drug policies, equal opportunity programs, and family issues and support; and oversees matters concerning the reserve components.

The comptroller and chief financial officer of the DOD is the principal adviser and assistant to the secretary of defence for budgetary and fiscal matters, including financial management, accounting policy, and systems and budget formulation and execution. The director of operational test and evaluation serves as a staff assistant and adviser to the secretary of defence, prescribing policies and procedures for the conduct of operational test and evaluation within the department, including assessments of operational effectiveness and of the suitability of major defence acquisition programs. The assistant secretary of defence for command, control, communications, and intelligence agence (C3I) is the principal staff assistant and adviser to the secretary of defence for C3I, information management, counterintelligence, and security countermeasures. The assistant secretary of defence for legislative affairs is responsible for maintaining a direct liaison with Congress, coordinating departmental actions relating to congressional consideration of the legislative program of the department, coordinating responses to requests for information by members of Congress, and arranging for witnesses from the DOD and the various military departments at congressional hearings on defence matters.

The general counsel is the chief legal officer of the DOD and is responsible for the preparation and processing of legislation, executive orders, and proclamations, and reports and comments thereon. The general counsel also serves as director of the Defence Legal Services Agency, providing legal advice and services for the Office of the Secretary of Defence, its field activities, and the defence agencies. The general counsel also administers the Defence Industrial Security Clearance Review Program and the Standards of Conduct Ethics Program. The inspector general serves as an independent and objective official in the DOD. The inspector general is responsible for conducting, supervising, monitoring, and initiating audits, investigations, and inspections relating to programs and operations of the department. The inspector general coordinates activities designed to promote economy, efficiency, and effectiveness in the administration of such programs and operations, and to prevent and detect Fraud and abuse in them.

The assistant secretary of defence for public affairs is responsible for the functional areas of the DOD, which include public and internal information, audiovisual activities, community relations, and security clearance. The assistant secretary also reviews information intended for public release, and implements programs under the Freedom of Information Act (5 U.S.C.A. § 552) and Federal Privacy Act (5 U.S.C.A. § 552a) within the DOD. The assistant secretary of defence for intelligence oversight conducts independent oversight inspections of DOD intelligence and counterintelligence operations to ensure compliance with legal requirements, and reviews all allegations that raise questions of legality or propriety involving intelligence and counterintelligence activities.

The director of administration and management serves as the principal staff assistant to the secretary and deputy secretary of defence on matters concerning department-wide organizational and administrative management, and also serves as the director of the Washington Headquarters Service.

Joint Chiefs of Staff

The Joint Chiefs of Staff consists of a chair and vice chair, the chief of staff of the U.S. Army, the chief of naval operations, the chief of staff of the U.S. Air Force, and the commandant of the Marine Corps. The chair of the Joint Chiefs of Staff is the principal military adviser to the president, the National Security Council, and the secretary of defence. While serving, the chair holds the grade of general or admiral and outranks all other officers of the armed forces.

The chair of the Joint Chiefs of Staff helps the president and the secretary of defence to provide for the strategic direction and planning of the armed forces, including resource allocation, the assessment of the military strength of potential adversaries, and the preparation of both contingency plans and joint logistic and mobility plans. In addition, the chair coordinates military education and training, represents the United States on the Military Staff Committee of the United Nations, and convenes and presides over regular meetings of the Joint Chiefs of Staff.

Response to Terrorism

Recent acts of Terrorism have required the Department of Defence to reconsider some of its methods for protecting the United States from foreign threats. The September 11th Attacks perpetrated by the terrorist organization al Qaeda not only destroyed the World Trade Center towers in New York City but also severely damaged the Pentagon building in Virginia. In the months following these attacks, the U.S. military engaged in operations in Afghanistan, which had harbored suspected al Qaeda leader Osama bin Laden. Since the campaign against Afghanistan, the secretary of defence under President GEORGE W. BUSH, Donald Rumsfeld, has become a central figure in the American media.

The War on Terrorism, dubbed Operation Enduring Freedom by President Bush, has required the Department of Defence to work closely with other nations. The department has assisted in rebuilding Afghanistan after the former regime, known as the Taliban, was toppled. Since that time, the department has focused much of its attention on nations that have been suspected of assisting and harboring terrorist organizations—especially Iraq. In 2002 and 2003, the United States maintained a campaign calling for the disarmament of Iraq, a campaign that led to the second armed conflict between the two countries in twelve years when the United States attacked Iraq on March 19, 2003.

The Department of Defence also restructured other operations and developed new defence strategies in light of new threats against the United States. In 2002, the department redrafted the Unified Command Plan as part the largest restructuring of the military since World War II. The revised structure places more emphasis on terrorism and other threats, with considerable focus on the development of technologies to assist in fighting these threats. Homeland security has also been a primary focus for the department. In 2002, more than 10,000 members of the National Guard provided security at the nation's airports and borders.

Field Activities

The American Forces Information Service, established in 1977 under the supervision of the assistant secretary of defence for public affairs, is responsible for the department's internal information program and visual information policy. The Armed Forces Radio and Television Service and Broadcast Center and the American Forces Press and Publications Service (which includes among its many products the *Current News Early Bird*) function under the director of the American Forces Information Service. *Current News Early Bird* is a Pentagon-produced newspaper that contains clippings and analysis of defence-related articles from newspapers around the country. The American Forces Information Service provides policy guidance and oversight for departmental periodicals and pamphlets, the *Stars and Stripes* newspapers, military command newspapers, and the Defence Information School, among other projects.

The Department of Defence Civilian Personnel Management Service was established on August 30, 1993, and functions under the authority, direction, and control of the under-secretary of defence for personnel and readiness. It provides services in civilian personnel policy, support, functional information management, and civilian personnel administration to DOD components and their activities.

The Department of Defence Education Activity (DODEA) was established in 1992, and also functions under the authority, direction, and control of the undersecretary of defence for personnel and readiness. It consists of three sub-ordinate entities: the DOD dependents schools, the DOD section 6 schools, and the Continuing Adult and Post-Secondary Education Office. The DODEA formulates, develops, and implements policies, technical guidance plans, and standards for the effective management of defence activities and programs both stateside and overseas.

The Office of Civilian Health and Medical Program of the Uniformed Services (OCHAMPUS) was established as a field activity in 1974. The office administers a civilian health and medical care program for retired service members and the spouses and dependent children of active duty, retired, disabled, and deceased service members, and also administers a program for payment of emergency medical and dental services provided to active duty service members by civilian medical personnel. The Defence Medical Programs Activity develops and maintains the department's Unified Medical Program to provide resources for all medical activities, including planning, programming, and budgeting construction projects for medical facilities. It also provides information systems and related communications and automated systems in support of the activities of the DOD Military Health Services System (MHSS), the Defence Enrollment Eligibility and Reporting System, the Tri-Service Medical Information System, the Reportable Disease Database, and other department-wide automated MHSS information systems.

The Defence Prisoner of War/Missing in Action Office was established on July 16, 1993, under the authority, direction, and control of the assistant secretary of defence for international security affairs. It provides centralized management of prisoner of war–missing in action (POW-MIA) affairs with the DOD. The office provides DOD personnel to negotiate with officials of foreign governments to achieve the fullest possible accounting of missing U.S. military personnel and also assembles and administrates information and databases on U.S. military and civilian personnel who are, or were, prisoners of war or missing in action. The office declassifies DOD documents and maintains open channels of communication between the department and Congress, POW-MIA families, and veterans' organizations.

The Defence Technology Security Administration was established on May 10, 1985 and functions under the control, direction, and authority of the undersecretary of defence for policy. This office is responsible for reviewing the international transfer of defence technology, goods, services, and munitions, consistent with U.S. foreign policy and national security objectives. The Office of Economic Adjustment is responsible for planning and managing the DOD's economic adjustment programs and for assisting federal, state, and local officials in cooperative efforts to alleviate any serious social and economic side effects resulting from major departmental realignments or other actions. The office supports the secretary of defence in his or her capacity as chair of the Economic Adjustment Committee, an interagency group established to coordinate federal economic adjustment activities.

The Washington Headquarters Service is headed by the director of administration and management. It provides administrative anu perational support to certain DOD activities in the Washington, D.C., area. This support includes budgeting and accounting, personnel management, office services, security, travel aid, information and data systems, and other services as required.

13

Indian Army and Frontier Warfare 1914-1939

Between 1849 and 1947 the inhabitants of the mountainous no-man's-land located between the administered areas of the North-West Frontier Province (NWFP) and Afghanistan posed an insistent threat to the security of British India. In many respects this local and immediate problem of tribal control overshadowed the more distant threat of war with Afghanistan or the USSR on this most sensitive strategic frontier of the British Empire, tying down large numbers of British and Indian troops in a long series of inconclusive skirmishes and major campaigns. What was known to generations of imperial soldiers as alternatively hill warfare, tribal warfare, mountain warfare or most commonly frontier warfare had distinctive characteristics and was the most prevalent form of actual fighting carried out by British and Indian troops.

This article will chart the changing nature of military operations on the Frontier between 1914-1939, which were altered by improvements in tribal military effectiveness and changes in the organisation, equipment and training of imperial troops. In particular, this article will demonstrate how the lessons learnt by the British armed forces during these operations were passed on to successive generations of officers and men in the form of official specialised training manuals and systems of instruction.

THE ARMY IN INDIA

The basic characteristics of Frontier fighting had long been known to imperial troops. Following the annexation of the Punjab in 1849 they were first brought into direct contact with the heavily-armed trans-border Pathan tribes, who repeatedly raided areas now under direct British administration, and attacked trading caravans. The localised armed forces raised specifically to protect the trans-Indus areas-the Punjab Irregular Force (PIF)-quickly learnt, during a long series of 'butcher and bolt' punitive military expeditions, that fighting in mountainous terrain against tribal lashkars (war parties) posed a range of difficulties very different from those encountered in conventional warfare. When operating in tribal territory Indian troops were tied to protecting of long, vulnerable and cumbersome columns of pack transport, carrying food, water and ammunition, on which they depended in the barren hills. Freedom of movement was restricted to the valley floors while lightly-equipped opposing tribesmen operated with comparative freedom on the hill sides. A lack of reliable intelligence and maps made it difficult to select suitable objectives, while the difficult climate and endemic diseases in tribal territory often inflicted heavier casualties than the opposing tribesmen. On the other hand tribesmen were well acquainted with fighting in their native mountains, matching their relative strengths of mobility, flexibility and superior marksmanship, in elusive guerrilla warfare against cumbrous British columns.

By trial and error the PIF evolved a series of specialised principles and minor tactics tailored to local conditions in tribal territory. To meet the tribesmen on the equal terms, its infantry regiments developed light infantry skills-skirmishing, skill-at-arms, marksmanship, self-reliance and fieldcraft-modeled on those of their opponents. Mountain artillery batteries were also raised equipped with light ordnance capable of being transported in the hills on pack mules.

When operating in tribal territory the heart of the tactical problem for the British and Indian troops lay in successfully bringing the tribesmen to battle and preventing their harassment of the cumbrous self-contained main body of imperial columns. Offensive tactics were emphasised at all stages of a campaign to bring the enemy to battle and to demoralise tribal opposition. Yet this often proved impossible forcing recourse to the destruction of villages and crops.

It was quickly discovered that the key to success lay in controlling the flanking high ground and dominating the surrounding terrain by fire. Outlying piquets would shield vulnerable British columns as they moved by 'crowning the heights' on either side of the route of march, withdrawing to rejoin the main body only when it had passed by. Initially, the short range of Pathan firearms (300 yards) meant that piquets were seldom overlooked by other positions within effective range and were secure except from direct assault. The evacuation of a piquet was often, however, the point of greatest danger when tribesmen normally seized the vacant position and attacked its retreating garrison. To prevent successful tribal attacks the posting and withdrawal of piquets involved considerable skill and led to the development of elaborate codes and drills by the PIF.

At night, encampments located on the valley floors would be surrounded in a similar manner by piquets intended to keep the tribesmen at arms length. Elaborate field defences, consisting of a perimeter wall constructed from rocks, stores or bales of fodder, encompassed each camp to stop rushes by swordsmen, provide cover from sniping, shelter for sleeping troops and to prevent infiltration by rifle thieves.

The withdrawal of the British and Indian columns represented the biggest tactical difficulty for any expedition. Tribal attacks on rearguards normally intensified making their extraction under fire the greatest problem for commanders and which necessitated the development of further tactical drills. The brutal treatment frequently meted out to British or Hindu dead and wounded by tribesmen exerted a powerful influence on hill warfare, necessitating rapid counter-attacks to recover them as they could not be allowed to fall into enemy hands.

Those principles and minor tactics developed by the PIF (renamed the Punjab Frontier Force (PFF) in 1865) were a comparatively simple and pragmatic response to hill warfare. A combination of repeated practical experience and specialised training directed solely towards hill warfare made its units highly effective as guardians of the administrative border of the Punjab (later the NWFP) which they monopolised. Yet as the PFF was a localised force retained under the control of the Punjab Government rather than the military authorities until 1886, these methods were not passed on to the regular army in a coherent manner. Until regular troops were deployed in the Punjab for the first time in large numbers during the 1880s and 1890s mountain warfare remained the prerogative of the frontier regiments and batteries. Following the 1897-98 Tirah campaign, when British and Indian regulars suffered comparatively heavy casualties at tribal hands, a range of official specialised manuals for frontier warfare were produced and appropriate training introduced during the early 1900s. This was of particular importance when the PFF was finally de-localised in 1903 (greatly simplifying organisational problems caused by maintaining a specialised force) and made liable for service throughout India.

In 1908 this new approach to training for colonial warfare on the frontiers of India was thoroughly vindicated during the Zakka Khel and Mohmand punitive expeditions, when small, lightly equipped and highly trained columns of regular troops inflicted heavy casualties on the opposing tribesmen. Nevertheless, in 1909 the specialised manuals promulgated following the 1897-98 campaigns were abandoned by the Indian military authorities when, in accordance with a decision made at the Imperial Defence Conference, it was decided to adopt Field Service Regulations (FSR) as the basis of training for all the imperial armies. Henceforth British and Indian troops relied for guidance in frontier fighting on the general principles of war and six condensed paragraphs that only provided a bare outline of the specialised tactics required in tribal territory. This important change in providing guidance, however, had no significant impact on the efficiency of the Army in India which, by 1914, contained large numbers of officers and men who had considerable experience and a long tradition of frontier fighting.

FIRST WORLD WAR 1914-1918

The First World War quickly exposed the shortcomings of this approach to training for frontier fighting when most highly experienced pre-war regular regiments were sent overseas. Their under-officered and poorly equipped replacements had far less training and experience in mountain warfare, and this caused serious concern to the military authorities as unrest spread in the hills during 1915. When British Territorial Army (TA) regiments were deployed in the NWFP, whose officers lacked any real military knowledge or training, the inherent limitations of relying solely on the principles of war and limited information contained in *FSR* to govern training were exposed.

As a stop-gap measure, a Mountain Warfare School was opened in May 1916 using innovative teaching methods specifically to train cadres of TA officers and NCOs in frontier fighting, who in turn would instruct their own units. Despite this development a serious lack of uniformity was evident in applying the principles and minor tactics of mountain warfare during operations conducted by 1st (Peshawar) and 2nd (Rawalpindi) divisions in November 1916. This was highlighted at a conference at Dehli between 22nd-24th February 1917 when Major-General William Bunbury called for definite rules to be laid down as he believed lack of uniformity was a source of serious danger in the field. Other senior officers, however, openly opposed publication of a special manual or any additions to FSR.

A series of disastrous skirmishes in Waziristan during the Spring further underlined the need for specialised training. On 2nd May 1917 the GOC Northern Command warned: 'If we employ troops inexperienced in hill warfare, it appears to me that incidents in the Gomal are likely to be repeated.' Despite further efforts by the Mountain Warfare School during 1917 and 1918 to improve training, however, by the end of the First World War the efficiency of the border garrisons had plummeted far below pre-war standards.

LESSONS OF THE 1919-20

The short-lived Afghan invasion of British India in May 1919 was quickly repulsed by the Army in India, but the ensuing tribal rising in Waziristan (where various militias raised to police tribal territory had mutinied) was a far more difficult proposition. Heavy casualties were inflicted on the raw, ill-trained Indian troops comprising the Derajat Column when punitive operations were carried out in the winter of 1919-20. In the heaviest fighting ever witnessed in tribal territory, imperial troops were nearly defeated at Palosina between 19th-21st December 1919 by well-armed and trained Mahsud and Wazir *lashkars,* whose ranks included a significant number of ex-servicemen. A skilful combination of fire and movement was employed with deadly effect against demoralised Indian troops by tribesmen who engaged in hand-to-hand combat whenever an opportunity offered.

The possession of large numbers of modern.303 Lee Enfield service rifles transformed the fighting effectiveness of Pathan *lashkars.* It altered the characteristics of frontier warfare by slowing down every phase of operations and dramatically increased imperial casualties. In response a slow, deliberate and heavily contested advance, only 2-4 miles a day, was adopted as the Derajat Column advanced deeper into Waziristan. This heavy fighting taught British officers that existing methods had to be adapted and new tactics developed to ensure victory. The latter included the widespread use of permanent piquets on all commanding positions within effective rifles range (1,000-1,500 yards) of a column, a fixed line of communications to service spiraling logistical requirements, and the widespread use of night operations to nullify the effect of tribal riflemen. Despite deploying large numbers of men, modern aircraft, 3.7" pack howitzers, and Lewis light machine guns, by the end of the hostilities Waziristan Force had lost 366 dead, 1,683 wounded and a further 237 men missing. This unprecedented 'butchers bill' indicated that a new era had begun in frontier warfare. Henceforth all operations in tribal territory clearly had to be deliberate, governed by a fixed line of communication and carried out by large numbers of troops except where very light opposition was encountered.

The near disasters in Waziristan and the fact that large numbers of regular troops were deployed on the frontier following the Third Afghan War as part of the newly-designated Covering Troops, convinced the Indian General Staff that it had to act quickly to restore the efficiency of the Army in India in mountain warfare. On 1st February 1920 the Mountain Warfare School was re-opened at Abbottabad to provide sufficient qualified trained instructors for imperial units. Under the command of Colonel William Villiers-Stuart, it ran a series of courses during the spring, summer and autumn of 1920 beginning with an explanation of the basic principles of war-a deliberate attempt to avoid over specialisation-before introducing the modifications required in their application to 'trans-border' warfare. Members of the Directing Staff emphasised the importance of individual skills-skill-at-arms, self-reliance, vigilance and personal judgment-to overcome 'trans-border loneliness'. Particular attention was directed towards the various modifications in tactics and the lessons derived about the employment of modern equipment in mountain warfare during the recent fighting in Waziristan as confusion existed in the minds of many officers. Although the Mountain Warfare School proved highly successful expedient it was not retained by Army in India as a permanent training establishment, when at the end of the year unit COs were responsible for training under the direction of the staff of the formations to which they belonged.

It was realised by the military authorities that it take some time before the efficiency of regular British and Indian units was restored to pre-war standards. Indeed, the intrinsic difficulties were such that the re-establishment of the PFF was briefly considered by the high command on several occasions during the early 1920s, as it was widely accepted that specialised troops would be more effective in tribal territory. Following the closure of the Mountain Warfare School the provision of an authoritative source of guidance to units periodically serving tours of duty in the Covering Troops was of considerable importance. It was clear that something more was needed than *FSR* as the 1920 provisional edition still referred to 'savage warfare' solely in terms of fighting against opponents reliant on shock tactics and its small section on mountain warfare lacked the detail required by inexperienced junior officers and NCOs.

As a temporary measure a small pamphlet was hurriedly prepared during 1920 for units garrisoned in the NWFP and Baluchistan. A revised edition was published in January 1921 and 15,000 copies were issued that laid down general rules to conduct the conduct of 'uncivilized' warfare, as well as the general principles governing military operations against the trans-border Pathan tribes for all three arms of service. It covered piqueting, protection on the march, protection of the lines of communication, camps and bivouacs and night operations and, moreover, provided tentative guidance regarding the use of new equipment such as Lewis guns. For units in action in Waziristan the HQ of Wazirforce also produced and distributed its own tactical notes tailored to conditions in that area. Several unofficial text books discussing frontier fighting also appeared during the early 1920s written by experienced Indian Army officers which complemented official sources.

The low-intensity fighting in Waziristan between 1920-24 allowed many British and Indian units to gain practical experience of mountain warfare which, when combined with specialised instruction, meant that by 1924 most had reached a semblance of their pre-war war standard of training. It also supplied further valuable practical experience about the capabilities and limitations of new equipment hitherto utilised only in small quantities on the North-West Frontier (aircraft, machine guns, motor transport and modern mountain artillery).

Many officers were eager to employ other military technology originally developed on the Western Front. For example, gas warfare was considered in 1919-20, and tanks were given trials in tribal territory with mixed success during the early 1920s. Due to the terrain most heavy weapons and equipment, however, could not be employed except on or near the growing network of roads built in accordance with government policy in Waziristan and the NWFP. Other factors militated against the use of more destructive types of military equipment. As Colonel Frederick Keen reminded readers of the *Journal of the United Service Institution of India* (*JUSII*) in 1923: 'We should realise, as we have perhaps not done in the past, that in fighting the Pathans we are engaging in civil war and that it is to our advantage that enemies of to-day should be turned into our friends of to-morrow In a word, our coercive measures should always be directed with a view to eventual pacification and control.'

The need for authoritative up-to-date guidance in frontier fighting for the large numbers of imperial troops deployed in close contact with the trans-border Pathan tribes had been clearly demonstrated between 1919-24. Although the revised 1924 edition of *FSR* incorporated a chapter dealing with warfare in 'undeveloped' and 'semi-civilized countries', it was clearly accepted by the military authorities in India that the general principles of war and small section on mountain warfare that it contained was an insufficient basis for training. In response the lessons learnt in Waziristan since 1919 were compiled at AHQ that year and incorporated in a new manual intended to complement *FSR* and the training manuals for the various arms of service.

The *Manual of Operations on the North-West Frontier of India*, published in 1925, reflected the important changes that had occurred in frontier warfare since the First World War. No fewer than 35,000 copies were printed and by October 1925 had been issued to units serving throughout India. Its pages reflected the Indian Army's extensive experience of frontier operations and brought up-to-date the existing doctrine and system of training caused by improved tribal tactics, leadership and equipment as well as changes in the organisation, training and equipment of imperial troops. It represented a significant improvement over solely relying on *FSR* as the basis of all training, although it still discussed the conduct of mountain warfare with close reference to the principles of war. This manual included chapters describing the trans-border Pathans and tribal territory; fighting troops and their characteristics; protection on the march and when halted; the organisation and protection of the lines of communication; the conduct of the attack and withdrawal for all three arms; foraging and demolitions as well as administrative routine in camp and on the line of march. It emphasised the importance of appropriate training for all three arms of service, especially with regard to the development of individual skills of self-reliance, vigilance and initiative to overcome the peculiar difficulties encountered when fighting in tribal territory. The use of the RAF in co-operation with troops was discussed and it even went on to cover the employment of tanks in hill warfare, although they were still unavailable in India. Finally, imperial troops on duty in tribal territory were specifically warned to stay alert despite prolonged periods without contact with hostile tribesmen and officers were encouraged to read histories of past campaigns to prevent the repetition of mistakes previously committed by imperial troops.

The Search for Mobility

The Army in India quickly settled down into the normal routine of peacetime service. Throughout the remainder of the inter-war period Indian regiments served a two year tour of duty out of every six in the Covering Troops' Districts, allowing them to steadily accumulate a cadre of trained and experienced officers and men. By comparison, British infantry battalions served only an infrequent one year tour of duty in the area. While stationed in the border cantonments, imperial units trained intensively in mountain warfare based on the *Manual of Operations on the North-West Frontier of* India, supervised by the staff and senior officers of the formations to which they belonged. Standing Orders periodically issued by the formations permanently stationed in the NWFP provided further source of guidance for both peacetime training and active service, amplifying points laid down in the official manual and taking into account local conditions and requirements at each station. Those British and Indian units serving in the Field Army concentrated on conventional 'open' warfare against a 'second class enemy', during individual and collective training into which each year was divided.

The priority attached by the Army in India to training in mountain and open warfare was a subject of considerable professional controversy between officers, whose attention focused on a likely conventional conflict, and those concerned with the day-to-day requirements of Indian defence. Many British service officers were highly critical of the specialised doctrine for 'savage warfare' employed on the frontier, believing that the lesser was by default contained in the greater. Most Indian Army officers for whom frontier service formed such a large part of normal military experience, however, more readily appreciated its importance.

The criticism leveled at the methods employed by British and Indian units on the North-West Frontier redoubled during the summer of 1930 when civil disturbances in the NWFP sparked widespread unrest in tribal territory. During the ensuing operations it appeared to many outside observers that army units had grown ponderous, over-cautious and their tactics too stereotyped, especially after large Afridi *lashkars* raided Peshawar District and then escaped largely unscathed. In comparison, the high mobility of the lightly equipped Scouts and Frontier Constabulary (elements of the Civil Armed Forces) enabled them to deal successfully with elusive tribal raiders, prompting accusations that the military was incapable of performing its allotted role in the watch and ward of tribal territory. The very fact that the garrison in Peshawar District had had to be reinforced with irregulars from elsewhere in the NWFP appeared to indicate that its effectiveness had declined, prompting several suggestions in the press for the re-establishment of a localised force organised, trained and equipped exclusively for operations against the trans-border Pathans.

Most of the lessons the Indian Army learnt from the 1930 operations were mixed and contradictory. The mobility conferred by the road network in Waziristan and within the NWFP, together with the provision of armoured cars and MT, had clearly altered the strategic, tactical and administrative conduct of frontier warfare, enabling reinforcements to be rushed to threatened points along the border. For example, two and a half infantry battalions and a company of sappers were transported 42 miles by lorry between 7th-9th July 1930 from Bannu to reinforce Razmak. The speed of MT convoys also eased piqueting and lightened the task of the road protection troops in areas where light opposition was encountered. Perhaps more significantly, MT greatly simplified the logistical and administrative problems encountered by troops operating in tribal territory. Indian columns utilising MT were tied, however, to advancing along predictable routes, enabling hostile tribesmen to anticipate their lines of approach, to concentrate and prepare defences.

The off-road mobility and tactical effectiveness of imperial columns in Waziristan, however, had sharply declined due to the large numbers of troops deployed and changes in their organisation, equipment and training. As a result the pace of an advance and the distance a column could march in a single day were lower than fifty years earlier as the number of mules on which they depended had dramatically increased due to the higher scales of arms, equipment, supplies and maintenance services now required in the field. This growing 'tail' of pack animals compounded the administrative and tactical problem faced by Indian commanders and acted as a brake on mobility, reducing the circuit of action of columns and slowing down every stage of operations, lengthening the line of march and exacerbating the already difficult problem of ensuring all-round protection.

To complicate matters a company of Vickers medium machine guns formed in each British and Indian infantry battalion in 1929 (in accordance with a new imperial establishment adopted throughout the Empire) meant additional mules were now needed to carry these heavy weapons. This considerably reduced the rifle strength of Indian battalions despite restrictions being initially placed on the number of weapons to maintain mobility in the hills. An infantry battalion could not provide the same number of piquets as before, lowering the distance it could protect from three to two miles which in turn effectively limited the distance a column could march in a single day. The extra firepower conferred by the additional machine guns dramatically increased the expenditure of ammunition, making *lashkars* wary of engaging Indian columns or following up rearguards, thereby limiting opportunities to inflict heavy casualties. Further problems were caused by an obsession with security which overrode other operational requirements, slowed movement to a crawl and tied Indian columns to cautious and unimaginative advances along the valley floors. It now took longer to piquet a route as periodic halts were necessary while covering machine gun and artillery fire was carefully arranged to support the placement and withdrawal of piquets. Fear of casualties, the recovery of dead and wounded and efforts to prevent the theft of arms and ammunition also stultified efforts to bring hostile *lashkars* to battle or to achieve surprise. An inability to differentiate between the tactical requirements of conventional warfare and those on the frontier compounded the problem. On many occasions Indian commanders mounted deliberate set-piece attacks backed with a full panoply of supporting arms, despite the fact that the *lashkars* seldom awaited the results.

During the spring of 1931 the Army in India's performance on the North-West Frontier was carefully examined by members of the Tribal Control and Defence Committee. Its final report echoed earlier press criticisms and suggested that the military authorities should consider various measures to lighten the arms and equipment of regular units and the merits of forming a new PFF. The latter view was dismissed out of hand by the General Staff in India, however, which strongly opposed the idea given the inherent organisational difficulties involved and the fact it ignored the other important roles the Covering Troops performed. Instead, senior officers argued that an organisation, equipment and training designed to fight Afghanistan, supported by foreign troops and the frontier tribes, was by default automatically suited to fighting the tribesmen alone. Moreover, as long as the North-West Frontier remained the most likely theatre of operations of the Indian Army, it strongly believed that all imperial troops required experience of the terrain and tactics similar to those required in Afghanistan. This view was also supported in the service press.

Rather than fundamentally changing current organisation, the General Staff directed particular thought towards increasing the circuit of action of mechanised Indian columns and the cross-country mobility of India soldiers in the hills.

The strategic mobility and circuit of action of columns in the Covering Troops Districts was comparatively easily increased by the General Staff during the 1930s by further road building in the NWFP. Most work was carried out in Waziristan but to pacify new areas construction began on a further series of roads elsewhere in tribal territory in 1934, although it proved an expensive, time-consuming process and frequently provoked opposition. Henceforth punitive operations in tribal territory were normally combined with road construction to allow small, lightly-equipped columns to be supplied and operate in the hills as well as extending political control. Hand-in-hand with road building went the slow introduction into service in India of MT, tractors, half-tracks and fully tracked vehicles-Carden Lloyd Mark VI Armoured Machine Gun Carriers and Mk 1A Light Tanks-with much improved cross-country performance.

It proved far more difficult to improve the off-road mobility of imperial troops in mountainous terrain, although this was addressed by reducing or lightening personal clothing, arms and equipment, decreasing the scale of supporting weapons and changes in training. Many Indian battalions replaced their heavy ammunition boots with *chaplis* and substituted light weight clothing in place of the normal issue. Amounts of ammunition and equipment carried by each soldier were also reduced and from 1934 a considerably lighter and more reliable replacement for the cumbersome Lewis Gun, with its attendant mule, began issue. Yet despite continued criticism of the new machine gun company the number of Vickers MMGs in each battalion was increased during 1931 by two weapons, to maintain a uniformity with the rest of the British Army.

Since it represented the main brake on the mobility of columns operating in tribal territory the reduction or complete replacement of the large quantity of pack transport was carefully considered. This administrative tail was successfully 'docked' by cutting down superfluous animals and the number of troops required for their care and protection. However, despite being regarded as anachronistic by many officers, pack mules and camels still remained essential in all operations mounted beyond a road head in tribal territory. Air supply was also carefully examined as an alternative means of maintaining troops and reinforcing isolated posts now that two Bomber Transport aircraft were in India. Despite the potential demonstrated by air supply on two occasions in 1930, the General Staff remained skeptical because of the limited number of aircraft available, the expense and their inability to evacuate casualties.

No radical changes were made by the General Staff in the system of periodic relief of units stationed in the NWFP or the training methods used by the Army in India apart from greater emphasis on light infantry training. By the mid 1930s Indian Army regiments were highly proficient in frontier warfare. Most now contained a large cadre of officers, NCOs and other ranks with both practical experience and training in frontier warfare enabling them to quickly achieve a high standard of efficiency when they returned to a border station. In comparison, British regiments were the 'natural prey' of the tribesmen as most of their training was predicated on conventional 'open warfare' or Internal Security duties. An intermittent one year tour of duty in the NWFP prevented them accumulating a cadre of 'frontier hands', placing even greater reliance on theoretical instruction and 'on the job' training. A combination of cap-badge rivalry between regiments, rapid changeovers in personnel, the comparative 'amateurism' of British officers, professional arrogance, and racism often militated against the assimilation of military skills required on the frontier from experienced Indian units.

Training of British officers, NCOs and men was facilitated by the publication of an unofficial textbook in 1932 written by General Sir Andrew Skeen specifically directed at junior British Army officers 'as he is less likely in his wider range of service to be trained for the local problem which all officer in India have to keep in mind.' *Passing it On: Short Talks on Tribal Fighting on the North-West Frontier of India* provided a detailed source of clear and comprehensive information in an easily readable form regarding the trans-border Pathan tribes, tactics and administration in hill warfare, based on the author's extensive experience. It assumed an authoritative position, running to three editions, and was widely read in Britain and India. Two copies were specially issued to British Army officers' and sergeants' messes and one copy to other British and Indian combatant units in India at the orders of the Commander-in-Chief, Sir Philip Chetwode, to allow British soldiers to benefit from the tactical and administrative guidance provided by perhaps the Indian Army's most experienced frontier soldier.

The tactical handling of frontier operations remained a subject of controversy in the service press during the early 1930s. For example, in the question set for the 1933 JUSII prize-essay competition the growing complexity of modern weapons, mechanisation and the increasing dependence of Indian columns on maintenance services in the field was explicitly linked to the declining effectiveness and relative mobility of the Indian Army. 'Borderer' argued in the winning essay that military organisation, equipment and training devised for 'civilised' European warfare were inappropriate for operations against lightly armed tribesmen. In a telling critique, he identified a fundamental conflict between the requirements of tribal control and European warfare that had been made explicit with the initial hesitant attempts of the Indian Army to modernise during the early 1930s. 'Borderer' believed that the growing divergence, in terms of training, organisation and equipment, between the military requirements of 'savage' and 'civilised' warfare could no longer be reconciled, and presented such an insuperable problem that he presented a controversial scheme for the formation of a localised frontier force for service on the North-West Frontier.

The Mohmand Campaign (Aug-Sep 1935)

The Mohmand operations provided a practical test of the various changes introduced during the early 1930s. A combination of lightened personal equipment and light infantry training speeded up piqueting and improved cross-country mobility, but the Vickers machine gun company in each battalion remained a serious brake on mobility. Perhaps the most striking feature of the campaign was the willingness of Indian commanders to undertake large operations at night, enabling them to seize the initiative, upset tribal plans, and avoid the delay inherent in mounting deliberate attacks. As a result columns penetrated deeper into tribal territory before they had to return to the security of a perimeter camp each night.

New equipment also made its debut. A single tractor-drawn battery of 18lb supplemented the mountain artillery, whose longer ranged and more powerful guns were able to support several widely separated Indian columns. Perhaps of greater significance was the successful deployment of a single company of Mk II light tanks. Their invulnerability to rifle fire and cross-country mobility quickened the pace of operations as tanks could easily advance through tribal positions. Although cavalry was needed to reconnoitre the ground and engineers had to construct tank crossings over nullahs and improve the track across the Nahakki Pass, the terrain in Mohmand country did not present an appreciable obstacle nor did an attempt by the tribesmen to impede movement by digging pits and strewing the roads with rocks and boulders.

'Mohforce' was heavily dependent on large quantities of ancillary units throughout the fighting which had both tactical and administrative implications for frontier warfare. A large number of non-combatant signallers, field ambulances, engineer parks, ordnance depots and motor vehicles accompanied 'Mohforce' and each day MT carried ammunition, supplies and water to a roadhead from where pack transport carried it to the forward troops. To encompass the large number of vulnerable vehicles and non-combatant troops, perimeter camps grew in size and complexity. It often proved difficult to find a flat space large enough for all troops and equipment and their construction was both time consuming and required considerable labour. The amount of manpower required for their defence, moreover, was considerable but as the proportion of infantry to other arms had fallen it was often difficult to provide sufficient troops. A heavy consumption of ammunition made it vital to maintain and protect a permanent line of communication along the Gandab Road to service growing logistical requirements, facilitate the movement of reinforcements and evacuate casualties. Armoured cars regularly patrolled the Gandab road, but the burden of protection, as always, fell on the infantry. Permanent piquets were constructed in the Karappa Pass, but the intricate and relatively low-lying land between Kialgai and Karappa lacked terrain features that afforded a field of vision and fire. Nowshera Brigade and 3rd (Jhelum) Brigade adopted a new system based on mobility and offensive defence employing lightly equipped fighting patrols who operated between strong posts constructed on either side of the road to deny tribal marksmen good positions.

Units throughout India were ordered by the Commander-in-Chief to follow guidelines laid down in this publication during the forthcoming training season which incorporated various lessons learnt regarding the employment of night operations, light tanks, armoured cars and the protection of the lines of communication. Sufficient practical experience of the impact of changes in the tactics, training, organisation and equipment on the conduct of hill warfare had now been gained to prompt the military authorities to begin preparation of a long awaited replacement for *The Manual of Operations on the North-West Frontier of India.*

The improving relations between the Air Staff and the General Staff, following the appointment of Air Marshal Edgar Ludlow-Hewitt as AOC in India, meant the RAF also took a greater interest in tactical co-operation with the army in mountain warfare during 1936. Under his command in April 1935 the Air Staff in India had already issued instructions that RAF training in the subcontinent should henceforth be directed solely towards efficiency in tribal warfare, although primarily employing independent bombing operations. This decision had strengthened Wing Commander John Slessor's-CO of No. 3 (Indian Wing)-growing conviction that a radical change should be made in the system of army co-operation used in India, as the existing 'Aldershot model'-devised for conventional European warfare-was largely ineffective in mountainous terrain.

During the summer 'Tactical Exercises Without Troops' were held near Rawalpindi to demonstrate the effectiveness of close air support and study the inherent problems from the viewpoint of ground troops, while the Vickers-Bomb-Lewis (VBL) ground attack method was developed at Peshawar. 2nd (Rawalpindi) Brigade and aircraft from No. 3 (Indian) Wing took part in a large combined exercise at Khanpur between 17th and 25th November 1936, to both develop and test close air support tactics in mountain warfare, based on a provisional close-support manual written by Slessor and a draft of the new frontier warfare manual. These manoeuvres, (simulating tribal opposition to an Indian column engaged in road construction) conclusively demonstrated the practicalities of close-support and indicated the importance of RAF liaison officers at column HQs to direct operations, as well as an effective means of inter-communication between the aircraft and forward troops and between columns and airfields.

LESSONS OF THE 1936-37

The Waziristan Military District provided the RAF and Army in India with an immediate opportunity to test the effectiveness of their new fighting methods when hostilities broke out in the Khaisora Valley in November 1936. This fighting, ultimately involving 61,056 regular and irregular troops, dragged on during 1937 as imperial forces endeavoured to bring to battle an estimated 4,000 hostile tribesmen. Most of the lessons learnt during the Mohmand operations were confirmed, indicating that there was no need for a major change in imperial tactics. It also provided further important practical experience regarding the use of light tanks, medium artillery and aircraft in frontier warfare, although infantry remained the predominant arm during frontier fighting now divided into two main categories: operations by columns operating in rugged, mountainous areas and those associated with road protection along Wazirforce's extended lines of communication.

The infantryman and the pack mule still remained the key to all operations in mountainous terrain impassable to wheeled transport and where limited scope existed for tracked vehicles. In November 1936 the Khaisora operations graphically demonstrated that the maximum distance a fully equipped Indian column could march, taking full precautions and allowing sufficient time to establish a perimeter camp before nightfall, was limited to 8-10 miles. Despite reductions in their number, the factor which above all dictated the speed of movement and circuit of action of a column remained the protection of the masses of pack transport still required to carry supplies. It was only possible to move further or faster by reducing piqueting below an acceptable margin of safety, or by neglecting to provide sufficient supporting artillery and machine gun fire.

To provide security all commanding features up to 1,500 yards with a full platoon, to protect Indian columns on the move or troops halted at night, from sniping. Perimeter camps were also justified when a massed assault was made on 2nd (Rawalpindi) Brigade on the night of 27th April 1937. Night operations were once again thoroughly vindicated, reducing tribal resistance and increasing mobility in the border hills, but they needed surprise and careful planning to prevent confusion. Two companies of Mk II and Mk IIb Light Tanks were employed when ground permitted in sections or sub-sections to carry out reconnaissance, protect flanks, cover withdrawals and directly attack *lashkars*, adding to the strength and quickening the pace of movement. Yet while the weight of firepower provided by machine guns, artillery, light tanks and aircraft proved highly effective against large concentrated *lashkars* in the opening phases of the operations, it conversely exacerbated the problem of bringing the elusive tribesmen to battle. Moreover, the unrestricted employment of superior firepower was now a thing of the past, as the political restrictions associated with the 'hearts and minds' campaign in Waziristan exerted a powerful influence on the fighting.

It was clear that the Army in India was now more than ever dependent on roads which increased the mobility of units in Waziristan and facilitated the supply of imperial columns. Lorries were employed on an unprecedented scale allowing a considerable reduction in the number of pack animals and non-combatants. The circular road allowed lightly equipped imperial troops to quickly concentrate and operate off a secure line of communication, greatly simplifying the whole problem of transport and supply as well as reducing the size and unwieldiness of columns. MT delivered troops, pack animals and supplies to the point where columns left the roads, refilled supply echelons and dumped stores at roadheads and were, to that extent, able to increase the radius of action of accordingly lightly equipped Indian troops. Roads also allowed heavy weapons to be deployed in Waziristan. Five batteries of mechanised field artillery, as well as a section of the 20/21st Medium Battery, equipped with a mixture of 18lb, 4.5" and 6" guns firing a heavier weight of shell than normally used in frontier warfare, supported columns within range and road protection troops.

Road protection was the main task carried out by imperial troops deployed in Waziristan as reliance on MT increased. A full infantry brigade was normally required to piquet 10-12 miles of road with mobile reserves held in each sector ready to respond to tribal raids. The stereotyped tactics most units employed for 'Road Open Days'-normally held three days a week-allowed little opportunity for personal initiative or any variation in minor tactics when positions of tactical importance had to be repeatedly occupied. Most road protection schemes employed in Waziristan also surrendered the initiative and provided hostile tribesmen with an idea of the time, direction, method and destination of each detachment as they piqueted a road each day making them vulnerable to attack. Armoured cars and on occasion Light Tanks proved an effective and economical means of patrolling roads, escorting convoys and providing fire support to road protection troops. A clear lesson of the campaign following the ambush of a convoy in the Shahur Tangi, however, was that MT was still highly vulnerable to sniping and ambushes in hilly areas outside the security provided by static protective piquets.

Perhaps the outstanding feature of the Waziristan operations was the close co-operation between the RAF and the Army in India at the tactical level, although independent bombing operations were also carried out. Six squadrons-equipped with Westland Wapiti, Hawker Audax and Hawker Hart aircraft-were used in the largest air operation ever undertaken in India operating under detailed restrictions imposed by the Government of India intended to prevent the death of non-combatants and attacks on friendly tribal sections. Daily reconnaissance sorties located hostile *lashkars* and enabled column commanders to, determine the number and location of piquets and perimeter camps in advance, and to direct long-range artillery fire. Bomber Transport Aircraft frequently dropped supplies to imperial columns, maintained isolated posts and evacuated casualties.

This increased the administrative and hence the tactical mobility of columns to the extent that following the Khaisora operations it was proposed that supply drops of food, fodder and ammunition should form a normal component of military operations in tribal territory to reduce the amount of pack transport required, remove the need for a permanent line of communication, extend the circuit of action of ground columns and to increase both their speed and mobility.

Throughout 1937 the close-support tactics developed at Khanpur formed an integral part of most operations in Waziristan with aircraft engaging hostile tribesmen in contact with imperial troops and those advancing or retiring in 'proscribed' areas in advance or along the flanks of columns. Writing in March 1937 General Sir John Coleridge, GOC Northern Command, acknowledged: 'These operations have definitely proved the great value which close support by aircraft in mountain warfare can afford. As had been anticipated, close communication between pilots and the forward troops was essential. R/T between aircraft and mule-pack sets accompanying column HQs formed the basis of communication, while a simple 'XVT' 'Close Support Intercommunication Code' enabled forward troops to indicate their position and targets to supporting aircraft.

The 1936-37 Waziristan campaign demonstrated once again the necessity of a high standard of specialised training in frontier warfare for units in the Covering Troops and elements of the Field Army detailed as immediate reinforcements. During 1937 the recent lessons learnt in tribal territory were included in reports issued by Northern Command and the annual report on collective training distributed throughout India. Training in frontier warfare was extended to form part of the individual and collective training period of every unit and brigade in India. Units of 1st (Rawalpindi) Division and those stationed in Lahore District were also temporarily attached to columns operating in tribal territory. The *Manual of Operations on the North-West Frontier's* planned replacement was not immediately available to these troops, however, despite agreement between the General Staff, Air Staff in India and the Foreign and Political Department regarding its contents.

Controversy over the politically sensitive sections dealing with aircraft, however, prevented publication when the Secretary of State for India decided they should be issued separately. This decision bitterly disappointed Major-General Claude Auchinleck, who had drafted the manual and secured agreement between the RAF, army and political authorities in India. General Sir Robert Cassels, the Commander-in-Chief in India, personally intervened in May 1937 to prevent the 'emasculation' of the manual, which he believed presented a comprehensive picture of frontier warfare under modern conditions. As a result the entire manual was finally reclassified as 'For Official Use Only', although further differences over air operations meant it was not until November 1938 that it was approved for publication. During this period a small section on frontier fighting was included in the *A.H.Q. India Training Memorandum* issued in July 1938, although the information it contained was deliberately kept limited pending the arrival of a new training manual. Perhaps the most important means of disseminating information regarding the recent fighting was the service press. Many officers were eager to record their experiences and discern lessons from the recent operations, although not all expressed satisfaction with the current tactics or system of training employed in India.

Frontier Warfare (Army and Royal Air Force) 1939 was issued to British and Indian units and RAF squadrons during March

1939, providing them with a detailed and up-to-date formal written doctrine of frontier warfare. 20,000 copies were printed which it formed the basis of training for companies and higher formations for the remainder of British rule. This manual was considerably larger than its predecessor and codified the existing doctrine of frontier warfare currently in use in India modernised to the extent of discussing the use of aircraft, light tanks, and heavy artillery in tribal territory.

Its contents reflected the greater understanding and co-operation between the Indian Army and the RAF that emphasised the need for co-operation of land and air forces and their dependence on each other. It described, in considerable detail, how aircraft could perform air blockades, proscriptive air action, destructive air action and ground/air co-operation in mountain warfare. Despite growing criticism, the manual still emphasised the continued importance of the established orthodox methods of frontier warfare, columns, protective piquets and perimeter camps, but did It warn officer against the dangers of operations becoming too stereotyped,. Officers were encouraged to read histories of military operations and it also included a bibliography of books dealing with both the frontier and frontier warfare. Other sources of unofficial guidance complemented the new manual during 1939.

CONCLUSION

The constant 'threat' posed by the trans-border Pathan tribes prompted perhaps the most detailed official military response to the demands of colonial warfare in the British Empire. As the General Staff in India faced a definite, long term military problem it adopted a far more pragmatic approach than the War Office (which directed military training elsewhere in the British Empire) that recognised the paramount importance of an officially sanctioned specialised doctrine and a system of training for frontier fighting.

Following the 1919-20 Waziristan Campaign the General Staff again acknowledged that the inherent difficulties of frontier fighting-exacerbated by improving tribal military effectiveness-meant imperial troops could not be left to 'make it up as they went along' or rely on 'on the job training' without running the risk of incurring significant casualties. As a result it devoted considerable time and effort to collating, analysing and disseminating lessons learnt by imperial troops fighting in tribal territory. These were passed on in new training manuals, annual training memoranda and Standing Orders that incorporated new developments. Outside official channels, the service press, textbooks written by serving or retired officers and a large cadre of experienced men within units also provided an important means of 'passing on' information. This was an important reflection of military professionalism directed towards colonial military requirements rather than in imitation of European practice. The recurrence of so-called 'regrettable incidents' in tribal territory underscored the need for training and this need was further emphasised by the fact that imperial troops never really enjoyed a decisive technological advantage in weaponry over their Pathan opponents.

The effectiveness of the Army in India on the North-West Frontier is open to question. Much criticism was directed by British officers at the so-called anachronistic methods employed in tribal warfare which has since been echoed by several historians. Yet Indian Army officers were not dyed-in-the-wool conservatives clinging to long outdated methods. The traditional approach to frontier warfare still remained remarkably effective as it was determined more by the unchanging factors of the mountainous terrain and tribal military characteristics than any other reasons.

It must also be remembered that frontier warfare was not the sole task performed by the Army in India and the training, organisation and equipment for its other roles directly affected both its tactical effectiveness during operations in tribal territory and its training approach. Both British and Indian units serving in India were always primarily organised, trained, and equipped for conventional military operations against a second class opponent, either in Asia or as part of an imperial expedition. Their Second function was frontier warfare and their final function was Internal Security duties. As a result of these disparate tasks it often proved difficult to achieve the correct balance between time devoted to training for conventional operations and that for frontier warfare or Internal Security duties, especially during peacetime when local day-to-day military requirements always loomed larger in the minds of Indian Army officers.

Following the First World War, the conflicting and often contradictory requirements of frontier fighting and conventional warfare became explicit as modern weapons and equipment, intended for 'civilised warfare', were adopted and dependence on supporting arms and services increased. As a result, the relative mobility of Indian columns operating in the hills progressively declined and they were tied to fixed lines of communication. While the construction of roads in tribal territory considerably eased supply and administrative difficulties, and allowed heavy weapons and higher scales of equipment to be used, they did not remove the essential problem encountered by imperial troops when they moved off-road. Apart from light tanks, the mountainous terrain afforded little scope for mechanisation or heavy weapons, and pack mules and infantry remained essential when columns operated in the hills. As it was simply impossible to reconcile the heavy scale of equipment carried by regular troops with rapid cross-country movement through tribal territory, the tactical flexibility and mobility evident in prior frontier campaigns progressively declined. The army's commitment to both frontier warfare and conventional military operations were largely mutually exclusive. While the commitment to frontier warfare reduced the army's effectiveness in conventional military operations, the army's pre-occupation with conventional war made it less fit for its frontier warfare. The various discussions regarding the relative merits of resuscitating the PFF in the 1920s and 1930s reflected widespread recognition that specially trained and lightly equipped localised troops would be much more efficient and mobile than regulars on periodic tours of duty.

However, such proposals were unacceptable to the military authorities as long as Afghanistan remained the most likely theatre of operations for the Army in India, as tribal territory provided invaluable practical experience of the terrain and tactics likely to be encountered across the Durand Line. In any event, the Scouts and various militias now performed the policing and, to a lesser degree, many of the military tasks previously carried out by the frontier force when it had been under civil control.

14

National Defence: Scientific Formula

INTRODUCTION

The past few years have seen an increase in intractable regional conflicts that the international community has been powerless to resolve. The global relief and freedom from fear that resulted from the "grand handshake" between the superpowers in 1988 has soon become meaningless, ending up in the Gulf Wars, Somalia, the Balkans as well as other hot spots. Many of these conflicts are so deeply rooted within the societies in which they manifest that only fundamental changes in the methods being employed to resolve conflicts have any hope of success. This article outlines an approach to conflict prevention and resolution, and social progress that has its roots in India's ancient Vedic tradition. Scientist and educator Maharishi Mahesh Yogi has recently brought this ancient knowledge to light. The programmes underlying this approach have been validated by almost fifty scientific studies, some of which are reviewed below. The positive effects of these programmes were demonstrated in Mozambique. Comments from Lt. Gen. Tobias Dai, (Ret.) now the Defence Minister of Mozambique, are also included below.

The basis for this approach to preventing and resolving conflict is the understanding that conflict, and other forms of social disorder, are manifestations of accumulated stress within society. Stress in the individual leads to a wide range of problems, from ulcers and heart disease to anxiety, hostility, and aggressive behaviour. In a similar way, Maharishi's Vedic Science suggests that stress in the collective consciousness of society creates a fertile ground for a wide range of social problems-including violent crime and socio-cultural conflict leading to the disintegration of society and ultimately war. The means proposed to reduce violence and social disorder is a coherence-creating group that reduces stress in the collective consciousness of society as a whole.

SCIENTIFIC RESEARCH

As early as 1960, Maharishi predicted that when 1% of a population practiced the Transcendental Meditation programme, a measurable increase in orderliness, coherence, and positive trends would be observed in society. On the basis of initial research in 1974 and the introduction of the more powerful TM-Sidhi programme in 1977, it was predicted that when the square root of 1% of a population practiced the TM and TM-Sidhi programme together as a group, a similar increase in orderliness would be observed in society. The formulae for the size of the group necessary to create a "phase transition" to a measurable higher quality of life in society were calculated. These calculations were based on analogous phase transitions from disorder to orderliness as studied in physics.

The earliest research documenting reduced violence throughout society examined the effects of the Transcendental Meditation programme on twenty-four U.S. cities that had 1% or more of their population individually practising this technique in their own homes. Research found that the total crime decreased 16% in the "1% cities" compared to matched control cities. The study also found that crime rate trends remained significantly reduced in the 1% cities compared to controls over the next five years.

A dramatic experiment testing the ability of the practice of the Transcendental Meditation programme to reduce armed conflict was conducted in the Lebanese village of Baskinta, population 10,000, situated at the centre of the Lebanese conflict. The number of shells coming into the village, the number of people killed and wounded, and property damage in Baskinta was compared with the same statistics from three control villages in the same area. The baseline period was from the autumn of 1978 to the spring of 1982, and the experimental period from the summer of 1982 through the winter of 1984. The TM programme was first introduced to Baskinta in May 1981 and the town reached the 1% threshold in June 1982.

The results sharply contrasted with the village's history, and to what was happening to control villages in the same area. As predicted, hostilities completely ceased in Baskinta from the time 1% of its population began to practice the TM programme. This cessation of violence in Baskinta was in sharp contrast to the worsening trends in all surrounding control villages.

More recently, research has evaluated the effects of the advanced technology-group practice of the TM-Sidhi programme. These studies report that when even a relatively small group of individuals (approximately the square root of 1% of a population) practiced the TM-Sidhi programme together in groups, crime and other indicators of social disorder decreased in the whole society. When these coherence-creating groups were dispersed, crime and other societal disorders returned to their former levels. The following is a brief review of some of the studies on coherence creating assemblies, showing reduced crime, violence, and warfare, and improved international relations.

In Britain, the ability of a coherence-creating group to reduce crime has been convincingly demonstrated in the Merseyside metropolitan area. The crime rate has shown a relative fall of 60% compared to national trends since a coherence-creating group was established in the area. In six years, the crime rate has fallen from the third highest of all metropolitan areas to the lowest in England. Over a two-year period, a week-by-week study showed that whenever attendance at a large coherence-creating group in Washington D.C. increased, violent crime decreased.

Another, more recent study in Washington, D.C. demonstrated that during a two-month coherence-creating assembly in the city from June to July 1993, violent crime in the city decreased by 20.1%. The public's decreasing confidence in the Clinton administration dramatically reversed. The Washington crime results were based on statistics received from the District of Columbia Metropolitan Police Department. Analysis of the results was approved by an independent Project Review Board of thirteen leading scientists in the field of social science.

An analysis of public statements of the U.S. president concerning the Soviet Union indicated a warming of U.S.-Soviet relations associated with periods of high participation in a coherence-creating group in the U.S. In another study, statistics provided by the Rand Corporation showed that during the three largest coherence-creating assemblies ever held (approaching or exceeding 7,000 participants), worldwide terrorism dropped by 72%. At the same time, all international conflict reduced by more than 30%.

A day-by-day study of a two-month-long coherence-creating assembly in Israel showed that, on days of high attendance, war deaths in neighbouring Lebanon decreased by 76%. On the same days, a composite quality-of-life index showed decreased crime, traffic accidents and fires in Jerusalem, and decreased crime accompanied by improvements in the stock market and national mood throughout Israel. Other possible causes (weekends, holidays, weather, etc.) were statistically controlled for and could not account for the results. A follow-up day-by-day study of more than two years showed that during seven different coherence-creating assemblies, war deaths in Lebanon decreased by an average of 71%.

The research results on the effects of coherence-creating assemblies on the Lebanese conflict are of particular significance to UN peacekeeping forces. One study covered the period from July to August 1983, and the other covered the two-year period from 1983-1985. During these periods, international peacekeeping forces were on duty with UNIFIL in South Lebanon. The research indicates that during the coherence-creating assemblies, decreased stress and increased coherence in regional collective consciousness may have diminished violent outbursts in Lebanon and facilitated more co-operative interaction among typically antagonistic factions. This research provides strong evidence for the reliability of coherence-creating groups even under extreme conditions of protracted political violence.

The Mechanics of Social Coherence

The idea that individuals in one place can influence individuals at a distance with no apparent behavioural interaction between them is counterintuitive to most people. The natural sciences, however, provide strong support for this sort of action-at-a-distance phenomenon.

Gravity and the transmission of radio and television signals are both examples of action-at-a-distance phenomena that have become familiar to us today. To understand these phenomena, physicists developed the concepts of "fields" to mediate these long-range effects. The basic understanding given to us by the quantum theory of physics is that the entire manifest creation is the fluctuations of underlying universal fields, and that all bodies and processes are connected at fundamental levels.

In recent years, the concept of fundamental force fields, and matter fields has been replaced with a single field-the unified field or "superstring" field. Thus modern science has identified a single, universal field of nature's intelligence at the basis of all forms and phenomena in the universe.

The Transcendental Meditation technique is a systematic procedure to refine human awareness to experience and explore deeper levels of intelligence of the mind. This systematic refinement of human awareness culminates in the experience of a level of intelligence that is completely unified and universal in its nature-the experience of the unified field itself.

The generation of social coherence through the group practice of the TM and TM-Sidhi programme takes place at this most fundamental level, where the influence is most powerful and pervasive in its effect.

Many countries have experience of how a small group of disciplined people can completely disrupt a nation, having an effect that is completely disproportionate to their size and resources. The opposite can also be true-national incoherence can be neutralised by small groups of experts functioning from the Unified Field of Natural Law.

INVINCIBLE NATIONAL DEFENCE

In view of the empirical research on the effectiveness of coherence-creating assemblies it is now possible to envision a new type of National Defence Strategy based on the establishment of permanent coherence-creating groups of experts in the military. Such a strategy, by ensuring the integrity of national consciousness, will create an invincible nation-one without internal incoherence and thus less susceptible to external threats to its well being. Thus, if there are no internal or external threats, there are no enemies. No enemies, no wars. The nation becomes invincible in the sense that it prevents enemies from arising. Victory before war.

A universal principle in nature is that internally coherent systems possess the ability to protect themselves against disruptive influences, while incoherent systems are easily penetrated by disorder from outside.

This principle is clearly illustrated in the quantum physics of superconductivity as the Meissner Effect. In an ordinary electrical conductor, incoherent, disorder electrons allow penetration by an external magnetic field.

However, in a superconductor, coherent collective functioning of the electrons spontaneously excludes an external magnetic field, and maintains its impenetrable status. This example of invincibility is not unique in nature; parallel phenomena of invincibility are found in many areas of the physical and biological sciences. In each case, the ability of the system to resist disorder is always based on coherent collective functioning.

Maharishi's Vedic Science suggests that such an effect can be created on the national level through the growth of harmony in society resulting from the practice of Transcendental Meditation and Yogic Flying by a small proportion of the population. When this influence-known as the Maharishi Effect, in honour of Maharishi, who predicted it-reaches a sufficient intensity, an integrated national consciousness is created.

The result is the development of self-sufficiency and an invincible armour for the nation, which automatically repels any negative influence coming from outside. Thus the integrated state of national consciousness created by the Maharishi Effect produces a "Meissner Effect" for the nation, rendering it impenetrable to external disorder.

Scientific studies have shown that the Maharishi Effect can be created by as little as the square root of one per cent of the population of a nation, region, or large city practising Transcendental Meditation and TM-Sidhi programme together in one place. One group comprising of the square root of one percent of the world's population (about 7,000 at that time of the study) was found to create the Maharishi Effect for the whole world. Ultimately the Global Maharishi Effect needs to be created because even if one nation does not enjoy invincibility, that nation will be a danger to the entire world.

In his book *Maharishi's Absolute Theory of Defence,* Maharishi has brought out a new approach to achieve the ultimate strategy of defence-create a Prevention Wing of the Military whose responsibility will be to maintain integrated national consciousness and make the nation invincible.

Maharishi proposed to train 3% of the military forces of every nation to be Yogic Flyers-experts in enlivening the underlying unity in nature. These experts will create a strong, integrated national consciousness that will disallow the rise of any destructive influence from inside or outside the country.

Such groups established in every nation will enjoy victory before war by preventing an enemy from arising, and fulfill the supreme goal of every military force. The other 97% of the military forces in each nation will continue their dynamic approach to the defence of the nation. Only 3% forming a Prevention Wing of the Military will be enough to prevent war, and avert the danger before it arises.

MILITARY PRACTICALLY DEMONSTRATED IN MOZAMBIQUE

Mozambique was the first country in the world to establish a Prevention Wing of the Military. This step was taken after the signing of a General Peace Agreement in Rome in 1992, which followed a disturbed period of war during the previous 16 years.

Shortly after the peace agreement, individuals at high levels in the country's government were informed about the research on the Maharishi Effect. After serious and critical study of the technologies that were being offered, the Joint Chiefs of Staff of the Armed Forces of Mozambique were charged with analysing the possibilities of its implementation in the Armed Forces. According to Lt. Gen. Tobias Dai, Chief of the Delegation for the creation of the new Armed Forces for the Defence of Mozambique and Former Commander of the Armed Forces.

After having completed a thorough evaluation of the proposal, the Joint Chiefs of Staff decided to implement the Transcendental Meditation and TM-Sidhi Programme, including Yogic Flying, in the Armed Forces of Mozambique with the aim to create the Maharishi Effect in the country. It was a matter of decision. Either to try it or leave it aside. Our decision was to try. This occurred before the arrival of the UNO forces in Mozambique.

The Transcendental Meditation programme was taught to the different military units of the country, involving Ground, Naval, and Air Forces. During 1993, about 15,000 people were taught, and in 1994 a further 1,000 were taught. Also, schools of police training, pertaining to the Ministry of Home Affairs, began the programme, and in all, more than 3,000 people were trained in the TM-Sidhi Programme.

Maharishi Effect predictions were made prior to the implementation of the training programme. According to these predictions, the increase of coherence in collective consciousness created by the Maharishi Effect was going to maintain the peace, bring reductions in crime, decrease the number of car accidents, and bring an improvement to the economy.

After thousands of people were trained in the Transcendental Meditation and TM-Sidhi programmes, it was possible to assess a decrease of 20% in the crime index in certain areas, and the number of car accidents reduced by 75%, on a pro-rata basis. During 1993, an economic growth of 6% was expected, but in fact growth was 19%.

According to Lt. Gen. Dai, it is clear is that once the positive effect is created, if group practice is stopped, the previous tendencies of higher collective stress, as determined from crime indexes, and the tense situations in the country, begin to rise again. He comments that,

In 1994, there was a remarkable decrease in coherence in the country as a result of decreased participation in the group practice of the Transcendental Meditation and TM-Sidhi Programme. This was due to the demobilisation of the troops practising the programme and the anticipated ending of police courses that included the programme, two months before the elections.

Finally, Lt. Gen. Dai noted that although with several difficulties, the maintenance of peace had been possible because during 1993/94, the free and just elections had been carried out-the only successful UNO mission in the world.

Conclusion

This article has outlined a new approach to conflict prevention and resolution based on the deployment of a Prevention Wing of the Military. This approach has age-old authenticity. However, it is also supported by extensive modern scientific research that validates the power of the TM and TM-Sidhi programme to bring peace even to the most troubled areas of the world.

Another consideration is the individual benefits of stress-reduction that military personnel could gain from the regular practice of the Transcendental Meditation and TM-Sidhi program. These programmes have been adopted to reduce stress and increase performance in military, governmental and other institutional settings. (*India Defence Consultants* has published a paper that summarizes research relating to military performance.)

The positive effects of these human resource-based technologies are well documented in over 600 scientific studies. For these benefits alone, military and civilian leaders would be wise to deploy a Prevention Wing of the Military.

Defence based on the accumulation of destructive military force has proven to be a failure over the course of human history. Great military powers have risen and fallen, at a huge expense to humanity.

Clearly, a new strategy of defence is the requirement of every military force. This strategy must enable them to fulfill the responsibility that every nation has given the military-to keep the nation safe and protected from any danger of destruction.

A group of retired Indian military leaders assert that the time has come for all militaries to adopt such a new strategy. It is based on the ancient Vedic tradition of Ayodhya, which created peace under the rulership of Sri Ram. This group includes Major General Kulwant Singh, Major General D.D. Ghoshal, Major General K.K. Ganguly, Major General G.K. Sahney, Major General G.H. Israni, and Colonel S.P. Bakshi.

They are the directors responsible for organizing an initiative to create a Prevention Wing of the Military in India. Today's militaries are increasingly required to fulfill a peacekeeping role, but are only armed with the technology of destruction rather than the technology of peace. This initiative hands military leaders another weapon: the weapon of peace. If civilian and defence leaders deploy the Prevention Wing of the Military, Ayodhya may no longer be an ancient Vedic legend, but a historic, achievable reality.

Bibliography

Alperovitz, Gar. *The Decision to Use the Atomic Bomb.* New York: Vintage Books, 1996.

Arend, A.: *International Law and the Use of Indian Military,* London, Routledge, 1993.

Bellamy, C.: *Knights in White Armour: The New Art of War and Peace,* London, Random House, 1997.

Chandra, R.: *Judicial System in India,* Lucknow, Print House (India), 1992.

Damrosch, L.F.: *Law and Force in the New International Order,* Boulder, Westview Press, 1991.

Davies .A.: *Telecommunications and Politics in Indian Defence. The Secentralised Alternative,* London, Pinter, 1994.

Heimanson, Rudolph: *Dictionary of Indian Military,* N.Y.: Oceana Publications, 1967.

Huntington, S.P.: *The China Modernisation Military and the State,* N.Y., Vintage Books, 1964.

Jones, W.H.: *Government and Politics of India Military,* London, Hutchinson, 1971.

Mary, W.: *Asian Power and Politics: the Cultural Dimensions of Authority,* Cambridge, Belknap Press, 1985.

Posen, B.R.: *The Sources of Indian Military Doctrine,* Ithaca, 1984, Cornell Univ. Press.

Rhodes, Richard, *The Making of the Atomic Bomb,* New York: Simon and Schuster, 1988.

Rosen, P.: *Societies and Military Power: India and its Armies,* Ithaca, Cornell University Press, 1996.

Simon, D. : *Public Administration and Policy of Indian Military,* New York, Knopf, 1950.

Simon, D. : *Public Administration,* New York, Knopf, 1950.

Index

A

Anti-ship Missile, 33, 40, 41.
Anti-submarine Warfare, 37, 41, 155, 156.

C

Central Industrial Security Force, 76, 87, 88, 90.
Central Reserve Police Force, 72, 75, 76, 84, 86, 90.
Civil War, 208, 214, 221, 273.

F

Frontier Warfare, 260, 281.

G

Global Air Traffic Management, 203.
Gorkha Regiments, 129, 131.

I

Indian Air force, 63, 66.
Indian Armed Forces, 1, 3, 34, 45, 71, 72, 74, 90.
Indian Cavalry Corps, 16, 17, 94.
Indian Naval Air Arm, 37, 157.
Indian Police Service, 71, 75, 76, 81, 89.
Indian Rifles, 121.
Indian Security Guards, 71.

M

Maratha Light Infantry, 11, 67, 122, 133, 134, 135, 136, 137, 190.
Maritime Patrol Aircraft, 43.
Military Aviation Unit, 197.

N

National Security Guards, 71, 73, 76, 80, 81, 186, 194.
Nuclear Weapon, 60, 223.

R

Rajputana Rifles, 11, 67, 122, 126, 127, 128.
Royal Gurkha Rifles, 131, 132.
Royal tank Regiment, 119.

S

Sikh Regiment, 11, 67, 122, 138, 139, 149, 150, 151.
Sonar, 31, 41.
Special Frontier Force, 76, 77.
Submarine Warfare, 37.

T

Tank Regiment, 12, 70, 101, 113, 114, 115, 116, 117, 118, 119, 120.
Traffic Management, 161, 163, 173, 174, 203, 246.

W

Weapon Systems, 32.
World Wars, 14, 129, 150, 223.

□□□